CLIMATE CHANGE AND BIODIVERSITY

CLIMATE CHANGE AND BIODIVERSITY

Edited by

Dr. Pawan Kumar 'Bharti'

Centre for Agro-Rural Technologies (CART-India)
20, Jamaalpur Maan, Raja Ka Tajpur
District- Bijnore (UP)-246 735 (India)

&

Dr. Avnish Chauhan

Department of Applied Science, College of Engineering
Teerthanker Mahaveer University, Bagarpur,
Moradabad (UP) – 244 001, (India)

Associate Editor

Dr. Kamal Kant Joshi

Department of Environmental Science,
Uttarakhand Graphic Era Hill University
Dehradun Uttarakhand
(India)

DISCOVERY PUBLISHING HOUSE PVT. LTD.
NEW DELHI-110 002

Published by:
Tilak Wasan
DISCOVERY PUBLISHING HOUSE PVT. LTD.
4383/4B, Ansari Road, Darya Ganj
New Delhi-110 002 (India)
Phone : +91-11-23279245, 43596064-65
Fax : +91-11-23253475
E-mail : discoverypublishinghouse@gmail.com
sales@discoverypublishinggroup.com
parul.wasan@gmail.com
web : www.discoverypublishinggroup.com

***First Edition:* 2013**

ISBN: 978-93-5056-360-1

Climate Change and Biodiversity

Printed at:
Aditi Fine Art Press
Delhi

Preface

The entire world is running fast on the track of development and creating many environmental problems behind. As development and pollution are the two faces of the same coin and nobody is thinking about global environment. Out of these environmental problems, many will come into the force after a long period of time and then we will not have time to do anything for environmental protection.

Climate change is one of the hottest issues at global level. Many research and studies are running currently in various parts of the entire world. Climate change is really one of the biggest problems of the worlds with few unrecoverable problems. Climate change will significantly shift many aspects of weather, such as wind patterns, the amount and type of precipitation, and the severity and frequency of extreme weather events. It is influencing our living, wearing, eating and choice of lifestyle. Changes could have far-reaching health, environmental, social and economic consequences.

'Biodiversity' is generally defined as the variety of all living things. Biodiversity can be measured on a number of levels ranging from genetic diversity within a species to the variety of ecosystems on Earth, but the term most commonly refers to the number of different species in a defined geographic region.

Habitats and species are often precisely adapted to their climatic environment and thus, climate change poses a major challenge for biodiversity. Changes in temperature, rainfall, sea levels and the magnitude and frequency of extreme weather events will have a direct impact, but indirect impacts will also arise from increased pressures on the natural environment as human society adapts to climate change. We need to help biodiversity adapt to these impacts, in order to conserve environmental assets and the social and economic benefits they provide.

Climate change and what it means for biodiversity is a complex issue, with understanding, policy and practice in this area continuously evolving.

This book is intended to give an overview of some of the key issues that are commonly used in relation to biodiversity and climate change adaptation.

This book provides comprehensive coverage of the fundamental principles and current practices and trends in the field of climate change, agriculture system, ozone depletion, global warming and biodiversity.

The approach to presenting this book is traditional covering of environmental pollution, climate change and biological diversity. We have carefully ingrate the subject matter in each area so readers can clearly understand the interrelationship between environmental pollution, climate change, ozone depletion and global warming. The extension use of illustrations is intended to increase the understanding the concepts and show modern facilities also.

Particularly thanks are due to all contributors from Egypt, Ethiopia, India; co-editor and publisher also for their contribution and assistance.

The present book mainly deals with environmental pollution, climate change, global warming and the changing climate pattern of the entire earth system, which gives a baseline data about the current research and status of climate change. I hope this book will be of benefit to both present and future colleagues, who teach, study and working in the field of environmental pollution, global warming and climate change.

Dr. Pawan Kumar 'Bharti'
(gurupawanbharti@rediffmail.com)

Contents

List of Contributors

1. **Animesh Dey,** Department of Zoology, Tripura University, Suryamaninagar, West Tripura – 799022, India
2. **A. K. Upadhyay,** Professor and Head, Department of Fish Processing Technlogy, College of Fisheries, G. B. Pant University of Agriculture and Technology, Pantnagar, Uttarakhand, India
3. **Bhasker Joshi,** Department of Basic Science, Surajmal Agarwal Girls P.G. College (Kumaun University, Nainital), Kichha, Uttarakhand, India
4. **Bhupendra Singh Jina,** Department of Botany, DSB Campus Kumaun University Nainital, Uttarakhand, India
5. **B. C. Joshi,** Assistant Professor, Department of Science, Surajmal Agrawal Girls P.G. College, Kichha, Kumaun University, Nainital, Uttarakhand, India
6. **Chandrapal Singh Bohra,** Department of Forestry, SSJ Campus Almora, Kumaun University Nainital, Uttarakhand, India
7. **Dinesh Bhatt,** Department of Zoology and Environmental Science, Gurukula Kangri University, Haridwar Uttarakhand, India
8. **Emeka Daniel Oruonye,** Department of Geography, Taraba State University, P.M.B.1167, Jalingo, Taraba State, Nigeria
9. **E.D. Oruonye,** Department of Geography, Taraba State University, Jalingo, Nigeria
10. **H. Singh,** Department of Zoology, S. S. J. Campus Almora, Kumaun University, Nainital, Uttarakhand, India
11. **Ila Bisht,** Department of Zoology, S. S. J. Campus Almora, Kumaun University, Nainital, Uttarakhand, India
12. **Kala Jina,** Department of Geography, DSB Campus Kumaun University Nainital, Uttarakhand State (India)
13. **Kamal Kishor Gangwar,** Centre for Agro-rural Technology (CART-India), Regional Office, Roorkee, Uttarakhand, India

14. **Kamal Kant Joshi,** Department of Environmental Science, Uttarakhand Graphic Era Hill University, Dehradun Uttarakhand, India
15. **M.K. Mustapha,** Dept. of Zoology, University of Ilorin, Ilorin, Nigeria
16. **Neelam Mewari,** Department of Basic Science, Surajmal Agarwal Girls P.G. College (Kumaun University, Nainital), Kichha, Uttarakhand, India
17. **Neelam Garg,** Department of Microbiology Kurukshetra University Kurukshetra, Haryana, India
18. **Pankaj Sah,** Department of Applied Sciences (Applied Biology Section), Higher College of Technology, Al-Khuwair, PO Box 74, PC 133 Muscat (Sultanate of Oman)
19. **Pawan K. Attri,** Institute of Integrated Himalayan Studies, (UGC-Centre of Excellence) H. P. University, Shimla-5 (H.P.), India
20. **P. S. Chaudhuri,** Department of Zoology, Tripura University, Suryamaninagar, West Tripura – 799022, India
21. **Radhey Shyam Gangwar,** Centre for Agro-rural Technology (CART-India), Regional Office, Roorkee, Uttarakhand, India
22. **Stuti Sah,** Department of Microbial Biotechnology, Amity Institute of Biotechnology, Amity University Noida, Uttar Pradesh (India)
23. **S.S. Sanusi,** Department of Biological Sciences, University of Maiduguri, Maiduguri, Nigeria
24. **S. C. Joshi,** Assistant Professor, Department of Science, Surajmal Agrawal Girls P.G. College, Kichha, Kumaun University, Nainital, Uttarakhand, India
25. **S. K. Agarwal,** Department of Zoology, S. S. J. Campus Almora, Kumaun University, Nainital, Uttarakhand, India
26. **Tribhuwan Chandra,** Department of Biotechnology, Graphic Era University, Dehradun Uttarakhand, India
27. **Vibha Bhardwaj,** Department of Microbiology Kurukshetra University Kurukshetra, Haryana, India
28. **V.K. Santvan,** Institute of Integrated Himalayan Studies, (UGC-Centre of Excellence) H. P. University, Shimla-5 (H.P.), India

The Impact of Climate Change on Fishing Activities in the Lake Chad Region of Nigeria

—S.S. Sanusi, *Nigeria*
—E.D. Oruonye, *Nigeria*

ABSTRACT

Fish contributes about half of the animal protein intake in Africa and inland artisanal fisheries provide about 40 per cent of this. For most landlocked states, inland fishery is the main source of dietary protein and, in some coastal states, freshwater fish are more important than marine fish; the former contributing up to 90 per cent of the total landings. In Nigeria, inland artisanal fisheries, chiefly on Lake Chad and Kainji Lake, contribute about 33 per cent of the fish production and support the livelihood of millions of people, particularly rural dwellers for whom national government is remote. Although fishing is a very important human activity in the Lake Chad region, the area is fragile with high climate variability and extremes of weather as well as unsustainable human activities. As this inland water is also used for domestic and agricultural purposes, salt mining as well as for transportation, it is an area of transboundary water conflicts.

This paper examines the part played by climate change in the decline of fishery resources and activities in the Lake Chad region of Nigeria. Data from field studies, structured interview and secondary sources show that fish catches and fishing activities have declined tremendously in recent times due to several factors including overexploitation and increasing demands on the aquatic resources. Findings from the study show that droughty periods have resulted in the reduction of open lake water surface from about 25,000 km^2 in 1973 to less than 2,000 km^2 in the 1990s

This has led to the diminishing aquatic and other resources in the region as well as potentially major challenge to social and economic development of the region. Although the importance of fisheries is known, mechanisms for mitigating and/or responding to climate change are not in place. A call is made in this paper to support the earlier advocate by scholars for inter-basin water transfer from the Congo Basin to the Lake Chad Basin and the construction of canals on the Lake Chad to boost fishing.

Keywords: Climate Change, Fishing Activities, Lake Chad.

Introduction

Hitherto, equity was significant in the negotiations of the United Nations Framework Convention on Climate Change (UNFCCC). Today, poverty, sustainable development (SD) and 'co-management' have risen to prominence. This is largely attributable to the 2001 Report of the Inter-Government Panel on Climate Change (IPCC) which identified the vulnerability of the poor to climate change impacts, and to the growing donor attention to poverty reduction through the Millenium Development Goals (MDGs) as an example (Richards, 2003). Understanding climate is thus central to building policy in the area of natural resources management especially common resources like aquatic resources, both in yearly weather forecasting, and prediction over a longer time-scale in order to mitigate impacts.

Weather is the day-to-day state of the atmosphere and is a chaotic non-linear dynamical system. On the other hand, climate—the average state of weather—is fairly stable and predictable and it includes the average temperature, amount of precipitation, days of sunlight and other variables that might be measured at any given site. However, there are also changes within the Earth's environment that can affect the climate. Thus, climate change is any long-term significant change in the "average weather" that a given region experiences. Average weather may include average temperature, precipitation and wind patterns. It involves changes in the variability or average state of the atmosphere over durations ranging from decades to millions of years. These changes can be caused by dynamic process on Earth, external forces including variations in sunlight intensity, and more recently by human activities (IPCC, 2007; Ruddiman, 2005). In recent usage, especially in the context of environmental policy, the term "climate change" often refers to changes in modern climate. These changes reflect variations within the Earth's atmosphere, processes in other parts of the Earth such as oceans and ice caps, and the effects of human activity (Fig. 1.1). The external factors that can shape climate are often called climate forcings and include such processes as variations in solar radiation, the Earth's orbit, and greenhouse gas concentrations.

Although climate change is real, there are uncertainties how it will affect food security in the different economies of the globe. The consensus of scientific opinion suggests that agricultural land may be gained in higher latitudes that are presently too cold for cultivation, if relatively small temperatures are experienced. Thus, overall world food production may even increase because of global warming (Devereux and Edwards, 2004). However, this increase is likely to most benefit only the large surplus producers in North America and northern Europe. In others, including Africa, it will intensify food insecurity where already crop production per capita is declining and population growth is doubling the demand for food. However, climate change is not only about global warming but also changes in the frequency and magnitude of extreme weather events like pressure and wind systems and temperatures causing floods, droughts and other weather-related famines.

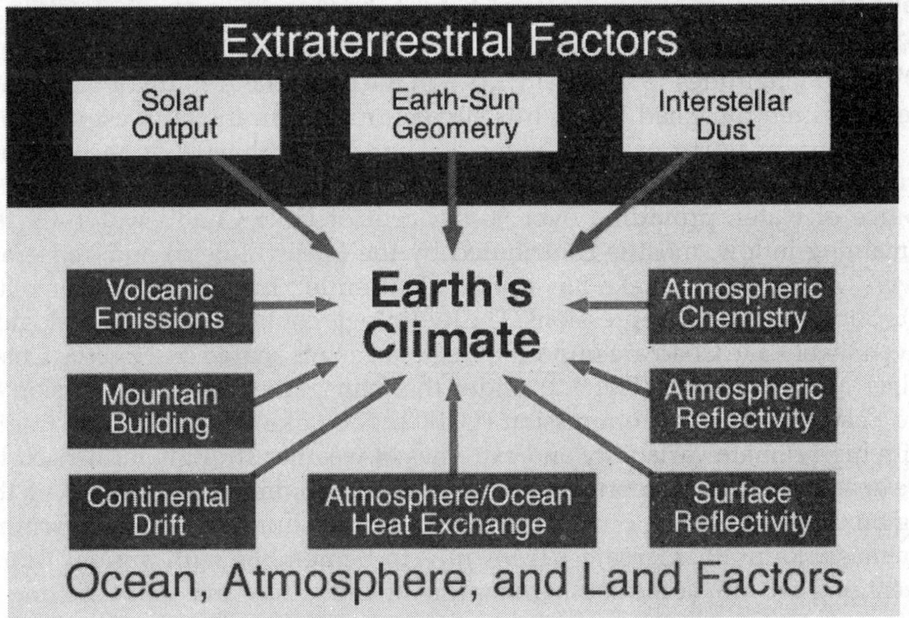

Fig. 1.1 : Factors Influencing the Earth's Climate

Fisheries contribute to the food security of over 200 million Africans and provide income for over 10 million people (Chimatiro, 2006). They support economic growth through exports and provide environmental services, such as increasing the value of water. In order to reap the full potentials of aquaculture, inland fisheries and coastal/marine fisheries, the New Partnership for Africa's Development (NEPAD) launched a Fisheries and Aquaculture Programme in August 2005. Today, several African governments, including Nigeria, Senegal and Malawi, have declared Presidential Initiatives on Fisheries and Aquacultural Development.

Nigeria is blessed with extensive inland water mass estimated at about 12.5 million hectares as natural lakes, reservoirs and ponds as well rivers and wetlands with their flood plains. Capable of producing over 500,000 metric tons of fish under adequate management, the catch is dominated by Lestes spp., Gymnarchus spp., Synodontis spp. Claris spp. and Chrisychthys spp. The demand for fish in Nigeria is currently estimated at about 1.2 million metric tons per annum, but current fish production is only over 25 per cent of the estimated annual potential yield. Thus, there is a huge supply-demand gap for fish and fishery products in Nigeria. The inland artisanal fisheries are contributing about 48 per cent of the total production (Ayeni, 1992). Of this, about 33 per cent is from Lake Chad and Kainji Lake and, supporting the livelihood of millions of people, particularly rural dwellers for whom national government is remote.

Lake Chad

Lake Chad is a transboundary lake located between latitudes 12° 20′___14° 20′ N and longitudes 13° 00′__–15° 20′ E in the borderland south of the Sahara Desert within the Chad Basin. It is situated mainly in the far west of Chad, bordering on north eastern Nigeria. The Chari (Shari)-Logone system, originating in the mountains of the Central African Republic, is its largest source of water, providing over 90 per cent of Lake Chad's water. Of the remaining inflow, most is contributed by the Ebeji (El-Beid) and Yedseram rivers. However, the Lake has no apparent outlet, but its waters percolate into Soro and Bodele Depressions. The hydrologic contributions and biological diversity of Lake Chad are important regional assets shared by Nigeria, Chad, Niger and Cameroon (Fig. 1.2) under the management and supervision of the Lake Chad Basin Commission (LCBC). The Lake Chad region is fragile with high climate variability and extremes of weather strongly influenced by the seasonal migration and interaction of the dominant air masses of the region: a dry, subsiding continental air mass and a humid, unstable maritime air mass. Rainfall is greatest from July to September with annual figure averaging 560 mm at the southern margin of Lake Chad and about 250 mm at

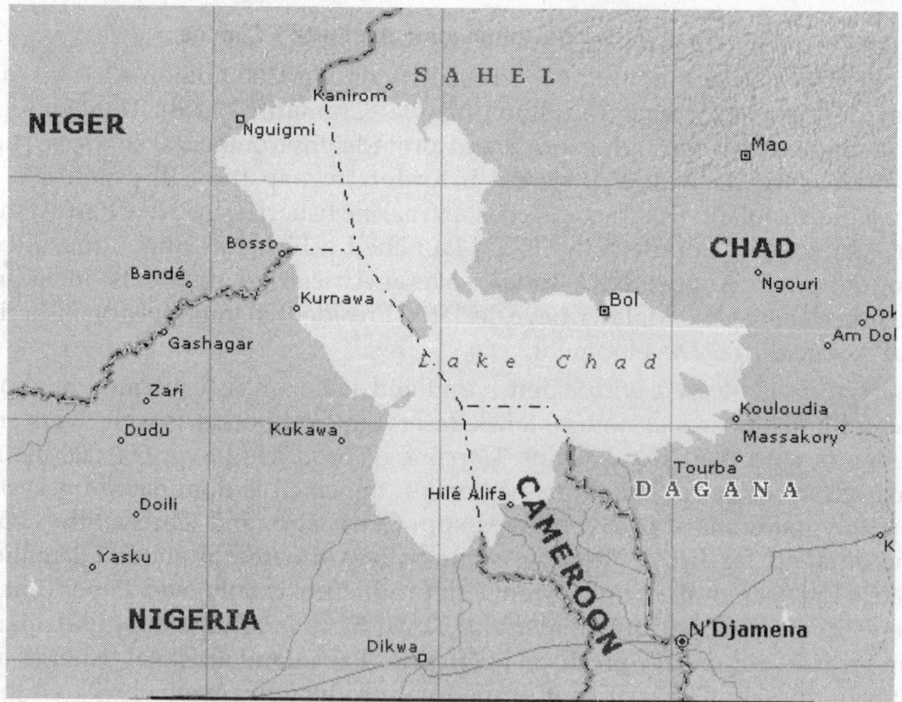

Fig. 1.2 : Political Boundaries of Lake Chad

the northern margin. Its annual variability is high and this increases from south to north. Whereas temperatures during the rainy season are moderate with highs of about 32° C, the dry season (March-June) is the hottest, occasionally exceeding 43° C. It is semi-arid, characterised by patchy resources and dispersed human populations. The Lake is thus economically very important, providing water and other resources to more than 20 million people living in the four countries which surround it; attracting a multiplicity of users including pastoralists, fishers, cultivators, salt miners, etc.

Lake Chad, first explored by Europeans in 1823, gave its name to the country of Chad (Chad is a local word meaning "large expanse of water" or simply "lake"). Travellers reported high water levels and overflow into the El-Ghazal, a link to the Bodele Depression, during the 18th and 19th centuries. The account by explorer Barth (1857) refers to a "vast expanse of water inundating the entire settlement of Ngorno during 1854-1855". Similarly, another explorer's sketches showed a high level Lake Chad with elephants and hippopotami on the shores (Natchtigal, 1889). The Lake was formerly larger, attaining a depth of about 285 metres in the 19th century; 60,000 years ago, it covered 388,500 km^2, roughly the size of the Caspian Sea (Room, 1994). The history of the inland sea is documented in the stratigraphic record, which includes thick layers of diatomaceous earth, lacustrine sands, terraced shorelines and the remains of modern fish and mollusks in now-arid tracts of the basin. It is a 'relict' of previous paleo-lakes (Mega-chad) dating back about 10,000-8,000 years B.P. (Carmouze *et al.*, 1983, Thambyapillay, 1983).

As the people are land resource-poor, they tend to rely most on common resources, such as fish for market and trade opportunities and employment (working in small-scale, household-based or artisanal fishing enterprises) and nutrition (important source of nutrients, protein, fatty acids and minerals). As a main source of dietary protein, fish provides many benefits such as contributing to low blood cholesterol and as a source of omega-3 fatty acids that reduce cholesterol levels and the incidence of heart disease, stroke and pre-term delivery (Anderson and Wiener, 1995). These fisheries contribute to economic growth and human welfare.

Fish landing sites, like Baga town in Borno State, are often the focus for local growth and centres for markets and cash economies. However, several attempts made in the past in projects to improve fishing on Lake Chad have been unsuccessful. These included National Accelerated Fish Production Programme (NAFPP) of the Federal Department of Fisheries; Fisheries Extension and development Programme of the Borno State Ministry of Agriculture and Natural Resources, Fisheries Section; Improvement of Fish Processing and Transport on Lake Chad by FAO and Extension and Training Activities of the Lake Chad Research Institute (LCRI). Several ambitious projects have also been tried including the South Chad Irrigation Project (SCIP) in 1980 and the Baga Polder Project (BPP) in 1982; both for abstracting water from the Lake. This paper reports the potential effects of climate change on the fishery resources and activities in the Lake Chad region of Nigeria.

Materials and Methods

This study focuses on the use of the water resources in shrinking Lake Chad. The data used was generated from field observations, use of structured interview schedule and focus group discussion method. Secondary materials were also gathered and used to generate additional information to advance our understanding of the effects of climate change on activities, particularly fishing, in the Lake Chad region.

Results and Discusson

Lake Chad today is the largest shallow water lake in Africa. Historical accounts suggest that the Lake is probably at least 20,000 years old and has shrunk and expanded over thousands of years but, the recent decline is by far the greatest. According to Ahmed (2007) and Bababe (2007), once one of the African continent's largest bodies of fresh water sixth largest in the world, Lake Chad has dramatically decreased in size to as little as 1,425 km^2 in 2003 as compared to the about 10, 000 and 25, 900 km^2 (during dry and rainy season respectively) in the 1960s (Fig. 1.3). The Lake has shrunk to one twentieth its original size and presently has an average depth of only 1.5 metres (Mayell, 2001). Whereas the northern part is completely dry, the southern section is densely vegetated area with scattered swamps and pools.

Much of the harvest of the fish is taken by subsistence fishers and thus, it is often not included in national catch statistics. The most common species caught are various types of catfish (Clarias lazera, Bagrus spp. Synodontis spp.) and tilapias (Sarotherodon galilaeus, Hemichromis spp. and Tilapia zillii). However, residents complain of decreasing or less fish due to shrinking Lake Chad. For example, large predatory fish, like Lates, Heterotis Gymnarchus, are now rare. Ahmed (2007), Ajepe (1983) and Hopson (1967) have reported the decline and loss of some fish types in the Lake. Some said that when they started fishing about three decades back, they used to catch 20-30 basins of fish daily, each as large as a man but today, the fish are smaller in size and very hard to get five basins (fewer in quantity). Bego (2007) reports of catch decline from about 100, 000 to 60, 000 tonnes annually. Some fishermen claim that their daily incomes have also declined from about N10, 000 to less than N1, 000.

Farmers and herders around Lake Chad are also feeling the effects of the shrinking waters. As the Lake recedes and water resources become scarce, permanent and floating islands emerge, with the latter clogging up the waterways. The influx of fishermen, herders and farmers puts pressure on the resources (water, fish stocks, vegetation, and land). The region's biodiversity also suffers. In the competition for scarce resources, trans-boundary

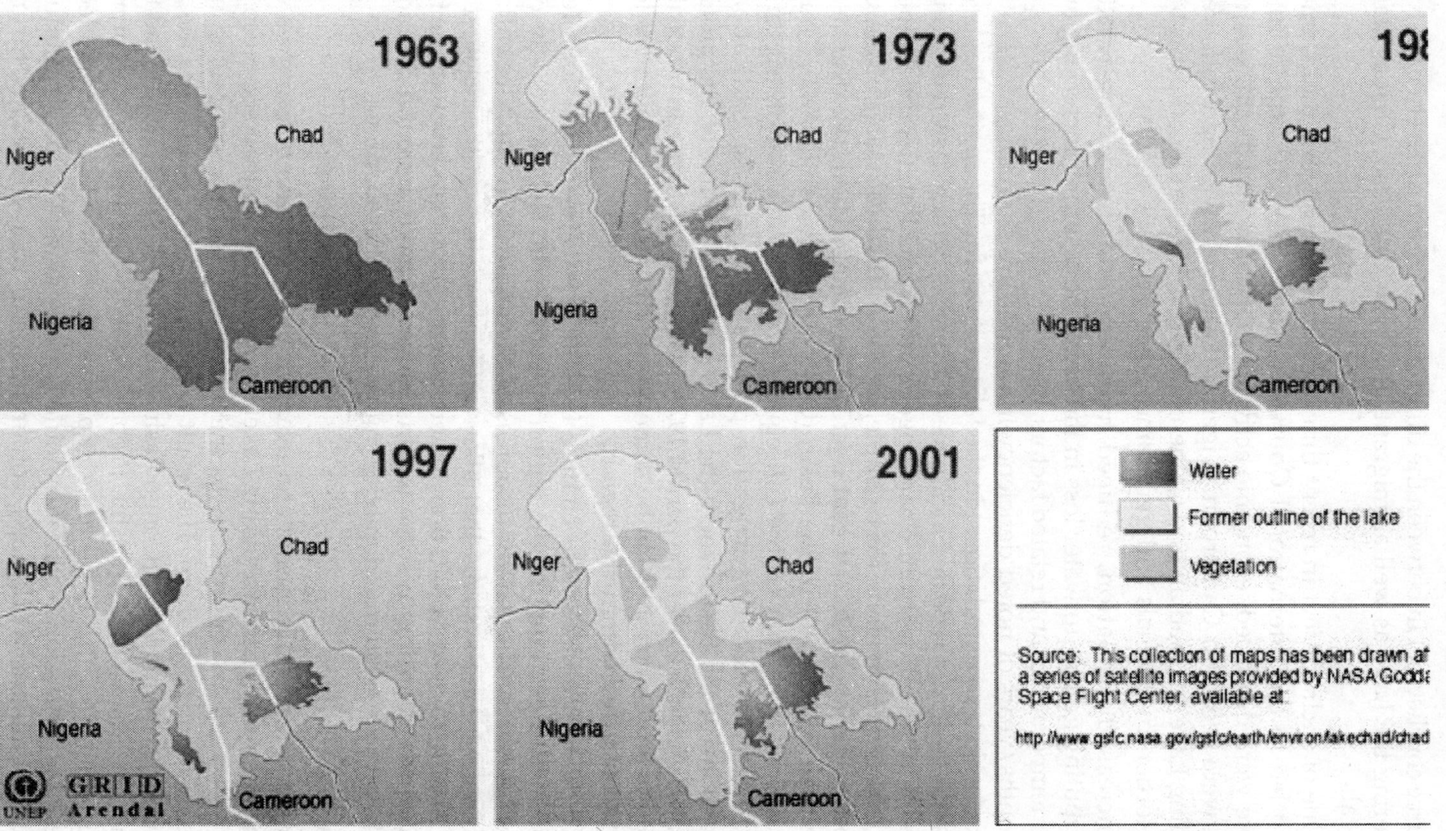

Fig. 1.3 : Disappearance of Lake Chad

resource conflicts set in between the different users from different nationalities bordering the Lake as well as migrants from Burkina Faso, Ghana, Mali and Senegal.

One of such conflict in recent times was between Nigeria and Cameroon which led to the International Court of Justice (ICJ) intervention in 2002. People were displaced, economic activities stagnated and 33 villages on the Lake were ceded to Cameroon. Nigerian fishermen who had followed the receding Lake to Chadian and Cameroonian territories still complain bitterly of extortion by officials and gerndames (their security agents).

Increased insolation, reduced humidity, and desiccating winds are contributing greatly to water loss in the lake. The resulting increasing air and water temperatures and related factors, including droughts or extended period of months/years of noted deficiency in rainfall, are shrinking water and fish stocks (and algae populations) in the lake ecosystem. The region has over the years suffered from repeated incidence of droughts, which has led to significant decrease in the inflow from Chari-Logone and Komadougu-Yobe. In the 1963 and 1984 droughts alone for example, although the headwater of the Chari-Logone experienced 20 per cent decrease in precipitation, the decrease was more than 50 per cent in the Basin (Oteze and Tomajong, 1987). Thus, the poor rainfall itself may be the consequence of climate variation triggered by human actions including irrigation projects as well as desertification and overgrazing of the Basin where the Lake is located. Similarly, the prolonged rainfall deficiencies over the period 1971-1980 in West Africa can be attributed to a reduction in evaporation by some 40 per cent associated with the loss of vegetation cover within the region.

This continued climate change is having severe implications for the nutrition and economy of the region's people, who depend heavily on the lake's resources. The patchy resources of the region also imply intentionally ambiguous tenure systems that allow multiple claims on the resources and thus leading to overexploitation and environmental degradation of the fragile ecosystem. According to some experts however, environmental degradation is solely due to resource depletion rather than global warning.

Recommendations

Although the resource users are aware of the diminishing resources of the region as a result of the shrinking Lake and the impact on their socio-economic activities, they are optimistic. As they are helpless, they are calling on the Commission to assist them. The result was the proposed plan, since the 1960s, to divert the Ubanji River (Congo Basin) into Chari-Logone (Lake Chad Basin) in an Inter-Basin Water Transfer. Probably due to cost and the environmental implications, the plan is yet to be implemented. It is thus recommended that stakeholders on global climate should partner with the local communities through seminars, workshops, conferences and train-the-trainer forums on the water resource management in this fragile ecosystem. .

REFERENCES

Ahmed, M.I., 2007. Studies on Freshwater fishes, their habitats and parasites in Lake Chad of Nigeria. An Unpublished Ph.D. Thesis submitted to the Department of Veterinary Medicine, University of Maiduguri.

Ajepe, G.R., 1983. Preliminary survey of fishes in Lake Chad. A Final Year Project, Federal Fisheries School, Baga, Borno State.

Anderson, P.D. and Wiener, J.B., 1995. Eating fish, In: Graham, J.D. and J.D. Wiener, (eds.), Risk versus Risk: Tradeoffs in protecting health and the environment. Harvard University Press, Cambridge, MA., USA.

Ayeni, J.S.O., 1992. The Director's Address. In: Proceedings of the National Conference on two decades of research on Lake Kainji (eds. Dr. J.S.O. Ayeni and Prof. A.A. Olatunde), pp. 2-10., Organised and Published by National Institute for Freshwater Fisheries Research, P.M.B. 6006, 29th Nov.- 1st Dec. 1989. New Bussa, Niger State, Nigeria.

Bababe, B., 2007. Towards water balance of the Lake Chad. A paper delivered at the Regional Roundable on Sustainable Development of the Lake Chad Basin. University of Maiduguri, Maiduguri, 20th - 22nd February, 2007.

Barth, H., 1857/1965. Travels and Discoveries in North and Central Africa: 1849-1855. Centenary Edition, 3 vols. London, Frank Cass.

Bego, A., 2007. UNESCO and others hold Regional Roundtable on Lake Chad. Daily Trust (Lagos), 14th Feb., p. 31.

Carmouze, J.-P., Durand, J.-R and Leveque, C. (eds.), 1983. Lake Chad. Dr. W. Junk Publishers, The Haque.

Chimatiro, S.K., December 2006. Investing in Africa's fisheries. id21 insights No. 65: 2.

Devereux, S. and Edwards, J., December 2004. Responding to drought and food insecurity. id21 insights, No. 53:4.

Hopson, A.J., 1967. Federal Fisheries of Lake Chad, In: Fish and Fisheries of Northern Nigeria. Gaskiya Corporation, Zaria, Nigeria.

IPCC. 2007. Climate Change 2007: the physical science basis (summary for policy makers), International Panel on Climate Change.

Mayell, H., 2001. Shrinking African Lake Offers Lesson on Finite Resources. National Geographic News, April 26th 2001.

Nachtigal, G., 1889. Sahara and Sudan: Ergebnisse sechsjahriger Reissen in Africa, 3 vols., Berkin, Leipsig.

Oteze, G. E. and Tomajong, S. C., 1987. Drought and Lake Chad Basin. In: N.M. Gadzama, G.E. Oteze, T. Erdimi and O.C. Irivboje (eds.). Water Resources of the Lake Chad Basin: Management and Conservation. N'djamena, Lake Chad Basin Commission (LCBC).

Richards, M., 2003. Poverty reduction, equity and climate change: Challenges for global governance. Natural Resources Perspectives, Number 83, April 2003. ODI.

Room, A., 1994. African Placenames, McFarland and Company, USA.

Ruddiman, W. F., 2005. Plows, Plagues and Petroleum: How Humans Took Control of Climate, Princeton University Press

Thambyahpillay, G.G.R., 1983. Hydrogeography of Lake Chad and Environs: Contemporary, historical and paleoclimatic. Annals of Borno, 1: 105-145.

The Significance of Forest Councils for Carbon Trading in Indian Central Himalaya

—Bhupendra Singh Jina, *India*
—Pankaj Sah, *Muscat (Sultanate of Oman)*
—Kala Jina, *India*
—Chandrapal Singh Bohra, *India*
—Stuti Sah, *India*

ABSTRACT

The greatest fear scientific community is facing is that the augmented human domination is steadily degrading the environmental quality of biosphere. Increased level of CO_2 emissions through industries and automobiles are significantly responsible for these besmirched conditions. There is an urgent need to find out the worldwide potential sinks for augmented atmospheric CO_2. In this paper the importance of forest councils from Indian Central Himalayas of Uttaranchal in absorbing superfluous amounts of atmospheric CO_2 has been critically analyzed. The Indian Central Himalayan state, Uttaranchal has about 66 per cent forest cover and presently more than 12064 Van Panchayats (VPs) are occupying nearly 5,23,289 ha of the total forest area. A detailed study was conducted on three VPs (*viz.* Dhaili, Toli and Guna) in Lamgarha development block in Almora district. Out of which, Toli has the highest forest area (103 ha) followed by Dhaili and Guna (60 and 40 ha respectively). At the moment carbon is being traded internationally at the rate of US$ 13 t^{-1} C. The studied VP forests sequester carbon at the rate of 4-5 t ha^{-1} yr^{-1}. The need of the hour is to link biodiversity conservation and ecosystem services with economic benefits for the betterment of rural people. From the present study it can be concluded that Toli VP sequesters a total of 412 t carbon ha^{-1} yr^{-1} (worth US $ 5356), followed by Dhaili (US $ 3120) and Guna (US $ 2080), annually at the rate of US $ 13 ton^{-1}. So, the study recommends "carbon credit" for poor villagers of Uttaranchal Himalayas *in lieu* of conserving forests and biodiversity as an effective tool against the menace of global warming.

Introduction

The international community is seeking commitment to reduce the emissions of CO_2 and other greenhouse gases globally. The Kyoto Protocol is an attempt to set-up an international process to address the problem of increase in the atmospheric CO_2. It provides an economic process that puts a value on not emitting CO_2 and enables countries to trade carbon emission. Under the Kyoto Protocol, there is a provision (under the Clean Development Mechanism, CDM) to derive monitory benefits from developed countries to support certain forestry operations in developing countries, such as carbon sequestration through afforestation and reforestation techniques. In a way, this is a mechanism to get payment for providing a life supporting ecosystem service. Such a concept can be applied on a regional or country-scale, to compensate the regions sequestering carbon.

Deleterious Effects of Global Warming

If the global warming process is not stopped then the world will witness a mass extinction. Global warming will cause biotic impoverishment; species will be lost, specific ecotype-specific combinations of genes accumulated for each location by selection through many generations will also be lost. Forests will be replaced by savannah shrub land or grassland *(IPCC, Climate change, 2001).*

The Central Himalayan Region

In Central Himalaya forest is the potential vegetation up to 3500-4000 m elevations *(Singh & Singh, 1987).* However, as data collected from satellite imageries indicate, right now about 40 per cent of the reported area (51,000 km^2) is forested, and good forests (with more than 60 per cent crown cover) occur in much smaller area *(Singh et al., 2006).* The carrying capacities of fodder and firewood production systems have far exceeded in most areas *(Singh et al., 1988).* Consequently, the Himalayan region has become a net releaser of carbon. Next to combustion of fossil fuels, forest harvesting is regarded as the biggest source of net release of CO_2 to the atmosphere *(Hoghton et al., 1983).*

Poor Conditions of Himalayan Villagers

In Himalayan mountain regions people are among the poorest. The communities in Uttaranchal consist of small holders (generally < 1 ha per household of 5-6 persons) who depend critically on community forests for subsistence living. Around 90 per cent of their crop fields are rain fed with food grain yield sufficient only to fulfil their need for 6-7 months in a year. Almost nothing has been done to provide training on silvicultural practices to manage community forests on sustainable basis. Though the forest cover of Uttaranchal, India is about 40 per cent, the threat of degrading forces continues to be high largely because of poverty of the people and lack of any alternative strategies for development. Forest stands in general have a lower biomass and productivity than their potentials *(Singh and Singh 1992)* Some species, like *Querçus semecarpifolia,* are failing to regenerate because of excessive lopping, livestock grazing, frequent fires, poaching and the spread of invasive/exotic plant species *(Phartiyal and Tewari, 2006).*

Kyoto Protocol and Eligibility for Carbon Credits

Though in Kyoto protocol, afforestation and reforestation are eligible for carbon credits, in the present context of immediate threat of climate change they are important mainly because they can prevent deforestation of natural forests, such as those managed by VP's. It may be pointed out that what matters is Carbon pool size, not the rate at which carbon cycles through this pool *(Steffer et al. 1998)*. The slow refilling (through raising plantations) of carbon gap created by previous logging is a small counter-weight to the release of carbon by ongoing logging. With regard to efficiency, a dollars '$ value' per unit of preventing forest clearing would be far greater than the gains from a dollar invested in raising a plantations *(Körner, 2001)*. Activities which lead to the maintenance of existing mature forests need to be given priority for carbon saving. They may include: assisting natural regeneration in existing forests; preventing forest fires; cultivating trees next to crop fields and homesteads so that pressure on VP forests remains within the sustainable limits, and restoring forest sites still with adequate remains of old stands.

Uttaranchal's Van Panchayat (*aka*. Forest Council or Forest Committee) and its Governance

Van Panchayat (Forest Council or Forest Committee) were introduced to Kumaun region of Uttaranchal (erstwhile United Provinces, UP in British India) in 1920's following agitation against British expansion of control over forest areas. The landmark Van Panchayat Act 1931 handed over control of designated community forests to elected Van Panchayat (VP) members in place of the State Forest Department. The Van Panchayat probably represents one of the largest experiments in common property management in collaboration with the state (both State Forest Department and State Revenue Department). It has a legal backing and has an elected body, called forest committee or forest council which holds responsibility of using and managing village forest resources. However, the various activities are undertaken under the control and supervision of the rules of the Revenue Department, and the State Forest Department is supposed to provide technical inputs. In a way, the village forest is a kind of natural resources, used by a definite user group (the village people) and is liable to degradation due to over use. Though called village property, the land in legally belongs to the state. The village people however, consider it as their property and resent government interferences. Most community forests were initiated on degraded sites, officially on a kind of Civil/Soyam forests (forests managed by the Gram Panchayat on behalf of the revenue department) falling under administration of the Revenue Department. But unlike Civil Soyam forests the community forests are not open-access forests.

Depending on the number of households in a village, there are generally 5-9 elected members in a Van Panchayat, who elect a 'Sar Panch' from among themselves. The Sar Panch is the elected head of the village forest committee or VP and has the following responsibilities:

(*a*) To convene and preside over all meetings of VP

(*b*) Keep watch over the finances and bring any irregularity in finance in notice of VP

(*c*) Look after the legal matters

(*d*) Supervise and control the staff and establishments maintained by VPs. Elections are held after 5 years. At least one schedule caste and/ or woman member should be elected to the committee *(Singh et. al., 2003)*. Recently the government of the new state, Uttaranchal (Now Uttarakhand) has taken initiatives to include more villages under VPs.

Current State of Van Panchayats in Uttaranchal

The total geographical area of Uttaranchal (UA) is 5,563,174 ha, of this agricultural land is 792,000 ha (about 13% of the total area) and forest area 3,671,695 ha (about 66%) and others about 21%. At present there are more than 12064 Van Panchayats (VPs) in UA occupying nearly 5, 23,289 ha of the total forest area. The Van Panchayats are located only in the hill districts of UA. The average forest area under the control of one VP is close to 44 ha. Variations are common in size of VP forest, for example, the Makku VP in Garhwal region has about 2500 ha forest area. The total population of UA is 8,879,562 of which 4,316,401 are males and 4,163,161 females as per 2001 census. The literacy level in UA is 72.28 per cent in which the male % being higher (84.01%) than females (60.26%). The female ratio in UA is 964 per 1000 male.

Responsibilities of Van Panchayats (VPs)

The responsibilities are laid out in the law as following:

1. To ensure that only those trees that have been considered silviculturally fit for cutting by the State Forest Department (SFD) would be cut.
2. To ensure that the village forest land is not diverted to any other use.
3. To erect and maintain boundary pillars.
4. To carry out the directions and execute the orders given to it by the state Revenue Department (on the advice of SFD) to maintain, improve and utilize the trees.
5. To utilise the forest produce to the best advantage of village community and of the right holders (A right holder is a person who owns land in the village where a Panchayati Forest has been constituted or a person who has been given rights to graze cattle,

collect fodder, fuel and timber in a Panchayati Forest under law or any order of the court) recognised by established customs or permitted by the State Revenue Department.

6. To close generally at least 1/5 of the grazing area to promote conservation.
7. To protect the forest from fire, illicit felling and damage to trees due to lopping.

Functioning of Van Panchayats

A watchman is appointed to guard the forest, and his salary is paid by the community. The watchman's services can also be taken on voluntary basis. He is authorised to take action against offenders. In some villages, households watch the forest on a rotational basis. The VP may grant permission for cutting grass, grazing and collection of fallen wood, and may charge fees for these provisions with the permission of the government. The other rights include extraction of pine resin for domestic and medicinal purpose and disposing of trees with the permission of State Revenue Department (on advice of State Forest Department). The trespassers can be fined up to Rs. 50 and up to Rs. 500 with the permission of State Revenue Department. If rules for grazing are violated cattle can be detained up to 48 hours, and the Van Panchayat has the right to disallow the use of privilege of any person found guilty. The Van Panchayat rules are framed by the State Government in consultation with the local people. However, within a certain framework, each Van Panchayat makes its own local rules and regulations i.e. imposition of fines, making micro plans etc. as per needs and wisdom. The technical support to the VP is provided by the State Forest Department (DFO at the Division level) and the State Revenue Department has the responsibility for the creation of VP.

Motives for forest management are founded upon expectations of immediate product returns as well as to make sacrifices for forest conservation (e.g. foregoing community forest use). Desire to prevent outsiders from using forest and to become self-sufficient in firewood, leaf litter (for manuring) and fodder is said to be the driving force for the development of community forests in some villages with a high level of success.

Biomass Extraction and Conservation

The VP forests are used to sustain the subsistence living, involving biomass extraction almost each day. The biomass extraction involves collection of firewood, fodder and ground floor litter, grazing/browsing by domestic animals and occasional cutting of "whole trees" for timber. Rotational grazing and collection of biomass are followed to allow a forest stand to get time to recover. Another effective way then to save these VP forests is to find alternatives. Some NGOs have been popularising biogas as a means to save fuel wood and also improve lives of the hill women who spend several hours every day collecting wood. Biogas generation is a biochemical process where organic mater such as cow dung is digested anaerobically by microbes (in the absence of oxygen) to yield a mixture of Methane (65%) and carbon dioxide (about 35%). Methane is a highly combustible gas and can be used for cooking heating and lighting applications.

Role of Non Government Organisations (NGOs)

NGOs in certain cases have made useful contributions. For example, CHIRAG, of Almora district while working in Kilmora and Katural Van Panchayats of Nainital districts redefined the forest guards as "forest maintainer" and were trained to improve the growth conditions of tree seedlings and saplings, repair boundary walls and protect trees from excessive lopping.

At Makku Van Panchayat, the NGO AT-India, Rudraprayag has made an attempt to establish NTFP's based enterprise by involving village individuals as shareholders. The NGO is also undertaking activities relating to sustainable harvest of resources and monitoring of bodies.

Gender Issues in Van Panchayats

At least one woman representative is required to be in every Van Panchayat; however, her forced inclusion has not lead to genuine representation at least in above mentioned Van Panchayats of Nainital district. The female representatives either send their son or husband; they are reluctant to attend the Van Panchayat meetings themselves. The most obvious constraint is the heavy workload mostly involving childcare, collection of fuel wood, litter for mulch, fodder for animals, water, cooking and other household and agricultural activities. Also it is felt by women that they are not encouraged by men to attend the meetings. In the VPs of Lamgarha block in Almora district the women position have been lying vacant in 3 of the 4 VPs studied while in the remaining one VP the women members have never attended the meetings. In recent years this issue has been raised repeatedly and men in some cases welcome women participation, but not much progress has yet been made.

Success and Failure of Van Panchayats

At present there are more then 12064 Van Panchayats in Uttaranchal occupying nearly a quarter of the forest area. The district-wise number of Van Panchayats and the area covered is as following table (Table 2.1).

Typically, the Van Panchayats become dysfunctional where the village forest area is inadequate to meet the community needs (at least 1 ha of forest is required per household) or the community is very large (over 100 households) or where out-migration is high or where the government official are insensitive or where members are busy along with other occupations like maintaining shops and jobs in nearby areas. The fact that in many areas Van Panchayats have been successful in conserving forests clearly indicates their importance. Apart from this, village forest in a way represents (*i*) a kind of empowerment to the people, and (*ii*) people's participatory role in the functioning of the nation. It represents an important social institution in which more creative activities can be initiated.

Table 2.1 : District-wise Distribution of VPs in Uttaranchal Covering More than 0.5 Million ha Area

S.No.	District	No. of Van Panchayats	Area covered by VP forests (ha)
1.	Almora	2,199	69,854
2.	Nainital	496	28,068
3.	Pithoragarh	1,661	87,054
4.	Champawat	629	31,233
5.	Udham Singh Nagar	0	0
6.	Bageshwar	822	38,783
7.	Pauri Garhwal	2,430	52,184
8.	Haridwar	0	0
9.	Chamoli	1,073	1,67,310
10.	Rudraprayag	574	20,702
11.	Uttarkashi	643	5,510
12	Dehradun	205	7,659
13.	Tehri Garhwal	1,332	14,932
	Total	**12,064**	**5,23,289**

Source: Uttaranchal Forests Department, July, 2005

Inventory of Existing Community Forestry Policies

As far as the rules and regulations concerning the management of the Van Panchayat forests, they remained almost unchanged until recently, when forest administrators gave some attention to their plight. In recent years an attempt has been made to improve the gender equity in the constitution of Van Panchayat, utilisation of money generated through Van Panchayat forests, and in attitude of the forest official towards community. Environment based NGOs have taken active part in activities of community forest management.

Some of the steps indicating the above policy changes are as following:

- The Forest Policy of 1988 facilitated involvement of local communities and voluntary agencies in the development of degraded lands.

- The Van Panchayats evolved because of protests by the locals. Communities against centralised tendencies of State Governments, which looked at the forests as an economic resource.
- Till date, it is the only JFM mechanism, which has full and legal backing of the Forest Act 1925 *(Tolia, 1996).*
- For the creation of new Van Panchayats no permission is required under the Forest Conservation Act, 1980, as creation of Van Panchayat is a 100 per cent "forestry activity" *(Tolia, 1996).*
- The Forestry Training Institute, at Haldwani was re-named as Forestry and Van Panchayat Training Institute by an order of Forest Department of the new state of Uttaranchal.
- **Training to VP officials:** A budget-head for the training of Van Panchayat office bearers was opened in the Uttaranchal Development Department.
- **The Government took some initiatives to develop cooperation between the corporate sector and Van Panchayat:** For example, Century Paper and Pulp Mills, Lalkuan helped a few Van Panchayats in establishing bamboo nurseries with 50% subsidy in saplings purchased by Van Panchayat in addition to local employment.
- **More freedom for Van Panchayat to use money generated from the forest:** The cumbersome process of taking out money from the state exchequer which existed in previous policies has been mitigated to some extent by the Van Panchayat Rules 2001.
- **Enhanced coordination between Van Panchayat inspectors and Van Panchayat functioning:** In Van Panchayat rules of 1976, Forest Panchayat Inspector (FPI) was responsible for various activities in Van Panchayat but in new rules of 2001 the role of FPI is negligible.
- **Women representation:** Representation has been provided to women in Van Panchayat rules 2001.

As per 2001 census the total population of Almora district is 630,446, of which male and female numbers are 293,576 and 336,870, respectively. The total literacy rate in Almora district is 74.53 per cent, with male and female literacy percent being 90.15 and 61.43 per cent, respectively. There are 1147 females per 1000 males in Almora district. Almora district has 2199 Van Panchayats covering about 69,854 ha (that is approximately 31.78 ha per Van Panchayat).

We studied three Van Panchayats in Lamgarha Development block of Almora district; these are in the villages of Dhaili, Toli and Guna. These Van Panchayats are situated between 79°41.44′-79°41.2′ E longitudes and 29°32.98′-29°34.32′ latitudes.

Table 2.2 : Brief socio-economic and ecological information about the studied Van Panchayats in Lamgarha block of Almora district

Van Panchayat	Dhaili	Toli	Guna
Block	Lamgarha	Lamgarha	Lamgarha
District	Almora	Almora	Almora
Physical Information			
Area of Van Panchayat	60 ha	103 ha	40 ha
Total village Population	956	1030	240
Total number of Families	116	132	22
Number of Males	503	540	122
Number of Females	453	490	118
Literacy % in Males	70%	80%	80%
Literacy % in Females	30%	49%	56%
Year of formation of Van Panchayat	1999	1955	1937
Member number in Van Panchayat	07	09	07
Number of Males in Van Panchayat	07	07	06
Number of Females in Van Panchayat	0	02	01
Frequency of meeting	Every month	Once in two months	Once in two months
Do Female members attend meetings	NA	No	Yes
Source of Income of Van Panchayat			
• Govt. Grants	No Grant	Rs. 4 lac have been given under JFM by Govt. in 2000	No grant
• Sale of NTFP's	Rs.-10 family^{-1} for dry leaf collection Rs.30 family^{-1} for green leaf collection Dry wood 10 Rs per annUAl head load	Rs.10 family^{-1} for grass collection (yearly collection Rs.1000-2000) Rs. 2 lakhs are present in Van Panchayat account from sale of resin.	Rs. 5 family^{-1} for grass collection (yearly collection Rs.1000-2000) Dry wood Rs. 6-8 per annual head load
• Any other Source	No	No	No

Silviculture/ Ecological information			
Dominant tree species of Van Panchayat Forests	-Banj (*Q. leucotricho-phora*) **60%** -Burans (*R. arboreum*) **15%** - Kaphal (*M. nagi*) **10%** -Chir (*P. roxburghii*) **15%**	-Chir **50%** -Banj approx **30%** -Kaphal **10%** -Burans **10%**	-Chir **55%** -Banj approx **35%** -Kaphal **5%** -Burans **5%**
Condition of trees	Healthy trees with moderate lopping	oak trees severely lopped but chir pine, burans, kaphal growing well.	oak trees moderate lopping but chir pine, burans, kaphal growing well.
Regeneration of species	Forest is regenerating saplings of all dominant species present	saplings of chir pine, rhododen-dron and kaphal present. banj oak absent	saplings of chir pine, rhododen-dron and kaphal present. banj oak absent
Van Panchayat	**Dhaili**	**Toli**	**Guna**
Afforestation/ reforestation in Van Panchayat (last 5 years)	Done in 6 ha by community	Yes, done in 2 ha of pine, cedar and acacia	No
Fire Protection done	Yes	Yes	Yes
Frequency of fire in Forest	No fire since last 5 years	Fire had occurred in May 2002	Fire had occurred in June 2003
Fire lines made	Yes	Yes	Yes
Fire line cleared regularly	Yes	Yes	Yes
Canopy/crown cover	58%	30%	42%
Ground litter cover	40%	57%	50%

Growth even/uneven	Even-aged banj oak forest with under canopy to kaphal and rhododendron	Uneven aged forest of chirpine	Uneven aged forest of chirpine
Grazing control	None	Yes	Yes
Other information			
Is extraction of fuel wood, fodder rotational	Green leaf fodder extraction-seasonally periodic (Spring)	Fodder extraction in seasonally periodic (Spring)	Fodder extraction in seasonally periodic (Spring)
Other NTFP's Extracted			
Resin	No	No (Extraction closed for last 13 years)	No
Medicinal Plant	No	No	No
Lichens etc.	No	Yes (2% of sale money given to village)	No
Salary of Forest Guard if appointed	Rs. 600 month^{-1} appointed for 12 months	Rs.1000 month^{-1} (From JFM fund) appoint-ment for 12 months.	Rs. 800 month^{-1} appointed for 12 months
Source of salary			
Horticulture	12445.50	10500.0	7850.0
Floriculture	2500.0	1000.0	800.0
Milk production	4500.0	5200.0	3800.0
As Labour @ 65 Rs/day	2575.0	2000.0	2520.0
other NTFP's extracted as Resin, Medicinal plant, Lichens, Mushrooms	No	No	no
Total annual income	**22020.50**	**18700.0**	**14970.0**
Number of people using LPG/ Biogas	3-4	4-6	3-4
Number of people fined	Rigorously followed	Mildly followed	Mildly followed
• 2000-2001	12	05	08
• 2001-2002	16	09	05
• 2002-2003	30	04	08
• 2003-2004	20	11	14

Van Panchayat	Dhaili	Toli	Guna
Amount generated from fines in last 5	Approx. Rs. 10,700	Approx. Rs. 2600	Approx. Rs. 2000
Perceptible change in Panchayat Van after the creation of Van Panchayat	Condition has improved	Condition of forest has improved	Condition of forest has improved
Has there been any change in distance travelled for fuel wood, fooder and drinking water collection before and after the creation of Van Panchayat	No	Distance travelled for drinking water has reduced, moderately	Distance travelled for drinking water has reduced, moderately
Water source Protection	Yes, they are cleaned regularly and have been covered	Yes, regularly and base covered with concrete	Yes, regularly cleaned and base covered with concrete
Check dams made and their number	Stone check dams 06 Temporary ponds 150	Stone check dams 02 Temporary water ponds 50	Stone check dams 02 Temporary water ponds 20

(**Source:** Data collected from Lamgarha block office)

DHAILI VAN PANCHAYAT (VP)

Social Aspects

The Dhaili VPs are situated between 29°32.98′ N latitude and 79°-44.2′ E longitude, located at an altitude of about 1830 m. The area under VP forest is about 60 ha, of which 48 ha is good forest (58% crown cover) (Fig 2.1). Of the 956 villagers in Dhaili, 503 are males and 453 females, which form 116 families. The average literacy per cent of Dhaili Village is 50.0 per cent, with male and female literacy being 70.0 and 30.0 per cent, respectively. The female ratio at Dhaili VP is 1044 per 1000 male (Table 2.2). The VP has 7 members. All the members are males. The VP meetings are generally held once a month. Women folk also attend these meetings.

In Dhaili Village all the families are using fuel wood for cooking and heating purposes. Though LPG is available in the area only 3-4 families are using LPG and that also occasionally. The daily requirement of fuel wood is about 6-7 kg of dry fuel wood (by field checks) per family. Pattern of collection of fuel wood shows that about 75 per cent is from VP forest, 10 per cent from trees on private areas and 15 per cent from government or reserved forest. Other non-timber product, for example, resin, medicinal plants, and lichens are rarely extracted from VP forest.

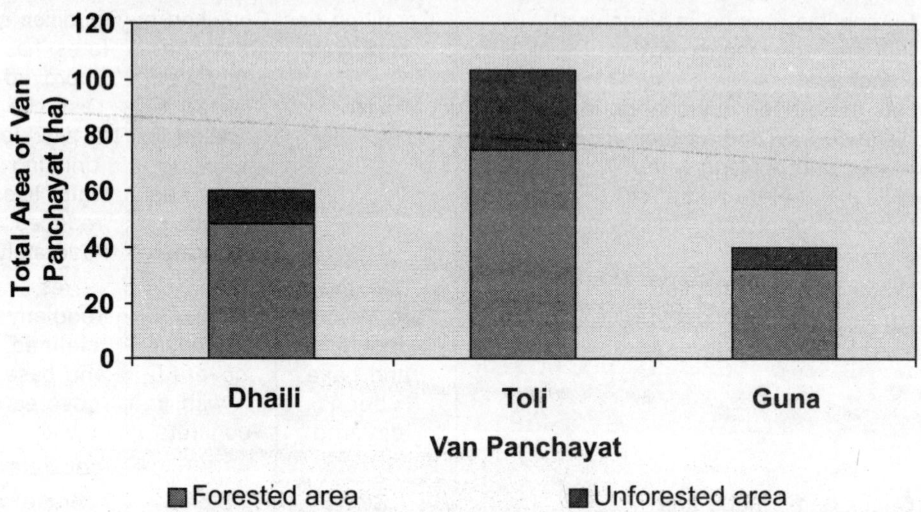

Fig. 2.1 : Forested and unforested area (ha) of Dhaili, Toli and Guna Van Panchayats.

Forest Condition in VPs

The year of the formation of VP is 1999. The VP forest comprises of even-aged banj oak (*Q. leucotrichophora*) forest with under canopy of *M. nagi* and *R. arboreum* (Fig 2.2). The condition of the VP forest is good; trees are in

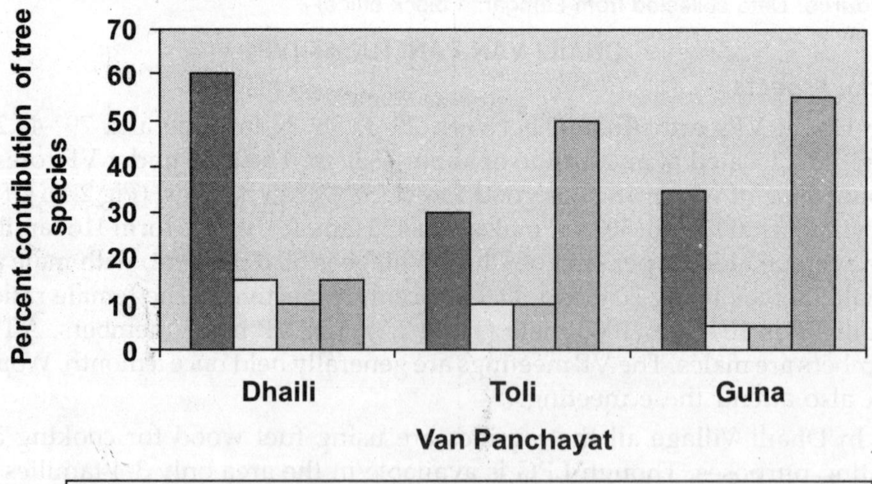

Fig. 2.2 : Percent contribution of different tree species in VP forest of Dhaili, Toli and Guna.

healthy condition with moderate lopping. Regeneration is also good as saplings of all species are present in the forest. The average canopy cover of Dhaili VP forest is close to 60 per cent and the ground litter cover about 40 per cent. After the creation of VP the people of Dhaili accepted that the condition of their forest has improved, as indicated by the reduction of distance travelled for collection of fuel wood, fodder and drinking water. About 150 small earthen ponds dug during 2003-2004 in the catchments of 4 major springs have increased water in them during the lean summer month. The VP of Dhaili also arranges a forest guard every year and pays his salary of about Rs. 600/month from the income generated. In Dhaili VP many people have been fined in last 5 years. In the VP plantation of bamboo, bhimal (*Grewia optiva*), utis (*Alnus nepalensis*) species was done in 2004-2005 in about 6 ha with the help of villagers. The villagers also clear fire lines for the protection of forest during the dry summer season. The livestock numbers in Dhaili VP were: 180 buffalos, 50 cows, 445 goats and 200 oxen (Fig 2.3). However, there was no control of grazing in Dhaili VP (Table 2.2).

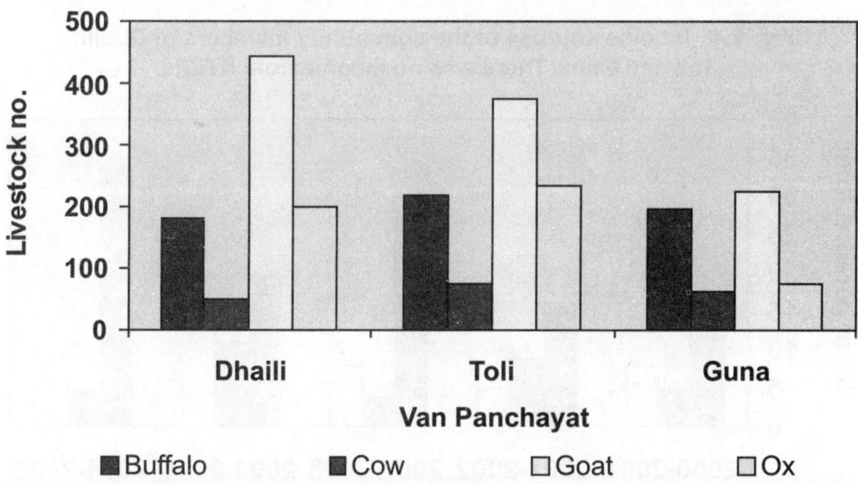

Fig. 2.3 : Livestock population in the VPs of Dhaili, Toli and Guna.

Income Sources

The total income of Dhaili Village is Rs. 22,020 yr^{-1} $family^{-1}$ (Fig 2.4). The cropping pattern in Dhaili village is mainly rice, maduaa, millet and wheat. Annually agriculture income in Dhaili village is Rs. 12,445.50, which is 56.52 per cent of the total income. Floriculture, milk production and as daily labour (@Rs.65 day^{-1}) contribution is Rs. 9575 of which 41.48 per cent of the total income.

The main source of the income of VP is from the sale dry fodder @ Rs. 10 per family, green fodder @ Rs.30 per family or Rs. 10 per head load, besides these the imposition of fines also generates some income for the VP (Table

2.2). Thus, the total income generated by the Van Panchayat was Rs 9,500 from the sale of permits and fines in year 2005 (Fig. 2.5).

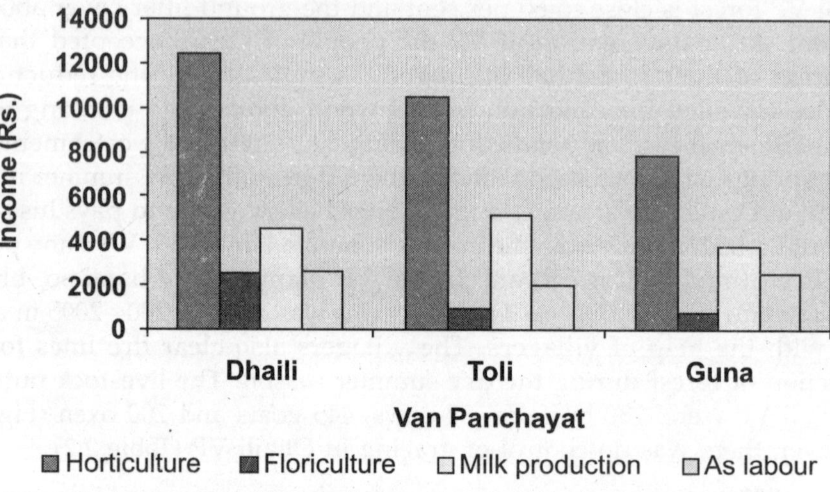

Fig. 2.4 : Income sources of the community members of Dhaili, Toli and Guna. There was no income from NTFPs.

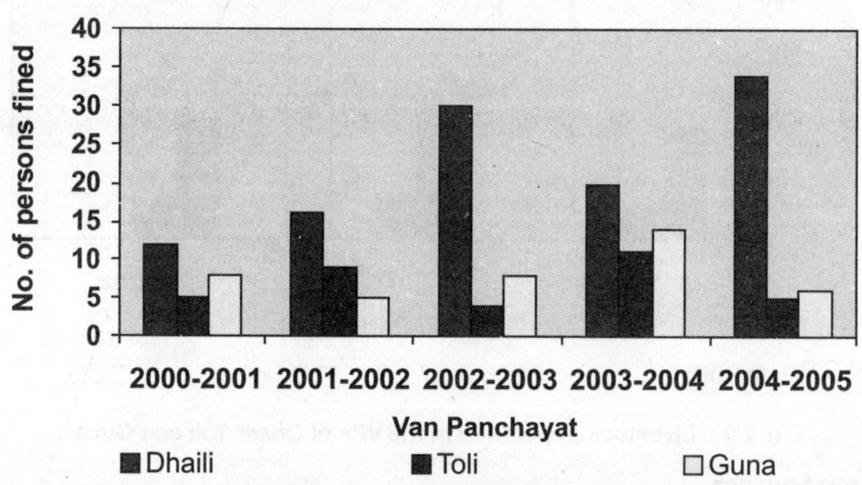

Fig. 2.5 : Fines imposed on individuals for committing forest crimes in Dhaili, Toli and Guna Van Panchayats.

TOLI VAN PANCHAYAT (VP)

Social Aspects

The Toli VPs are situated are between 29° 33.04′ N latitude and 79°-41.19′ E longitude, located at an altitude of about 1839 m. The area under VP forest is about 103 ha, of which 75 ha is good forest (Fig 2.1). The total number of families is 132 while the population of Toli is 1030 comprising of 540 males and 490 females. The total literacy rate of Toli VP is about 65.0 per cent, with male and female literacy at 80.0 and 49.0 per cent, respectively. The female ratio at Toli is 1120 per 1000 males. The present number of VP members is 9 and is composed of 7 males and 2 females (Table 2.2). The VP meetings are generally held once in about two months. These meetings are attending sometimes by women folk also.

In Toli VP all the families are using fuel wood for cooking and heating purposes. Though LPG is available in the area only 4-6 families (shop keepers in Lamgarha market) were found to use LPG. The daily requirement of fuel wood is about 5-8 kg. Pattern of collection of fuel wood is about 60 per cent from Van Panchayat forest, 15 per cent from Private forest and 25 per cent from government or reserved forest. Any other non timber product, for example, resin, medicinal plants, lichens was some times extracted from Toli VP (Table 2.2).

Forest Condition in VP

The year of the formation of VP was 1955. The VP forest is uneven-aged forest of chir pine mixed with banj, burans and kaphal (Fig. 2.2). The condition of the Toli VP forest is averaged, banj trees severely lopped but chir, burans and kaphal growing well. Regeneration is also good as saplings of all species (except banj) are present in the forest. The canopy cover of Toli VP forest is estimated at 30 per cent and the ground litter cover 57 per cent.

After the creation of Van Panchayat the peoples of Toli Van Panchayat accepted that the condition of the Van Panchayat become better, as indicated by the reduction of distance travelled for collection of fuel wood, fodder and drinking water. The water source of Toli village is about 50 temporary small ponds (naulas) and 2 stone check-dams have increased water in them during summer months, which are cleaned regularly by the community people and have been covered to protect from dust. The VP of Toli arranges the forest guard for every year and pays his salary of about Rs. 1000 month^{-1} from VP income. In Toli VP many people were fined in last 5 years and VP generated fines about Rs. 2600. In Toli VP plantation of pine, cedar, bamboo and acacia species was done in 2004-2005 about in 3 ha by the help of community members. Community members also made the fire lines and clear them regularly for protection of forest in summer season. The livestock numbers in Toli VP were: 220 buffalos, 75 cows, 375 goats and 235 oxen (Fig 2.3). However, there was no control of grazing in Toli VP (Table 2.2).

Income Sources

The total income of Toli Villager is Rs. 18700.0 yr^{-1} family^{-1}. The cropping pattern in Toli Village related that the rice, maduaa, millet, wheat, and potato are the main sources of agricultural income. The dependency on agricultural sources in Toli VP is about 65 per cent. Annually agriculture income in Toli village is Rs. 10500.0 yr^{-1} family^{-1}, which is about 56.15 per cent of the total income per family. The other main source of the village is milk production which is about 27.81 per cent (Rs. 5200.0). As daily labour basis and floriculture income are Rs. 2000.0 (10.69%) and Rs. 1000.0 (5.35%) family^{-1} yr^{-1}, respectively (Fig 1.4).

The source of the income of VP is from the sale of NTFPs which is Rs. 10 per family for dry fodder collection, Rs.30 per family for green fodder collection and Rs.10 per head load, besides these the imposition of fines also generates by the VP (Table 2.2). Thus, the total income generated by the VP was Rs. 4500 from the sale of permits and fines in the year 2005 (Fig 2.5).

GUNA VAN PANCHAYAT (VP)

Social Aspects

The Guna VP is located at about 1843 m. The area under VP forest is about 40 ha, of which 32 ha is good forest (Fig 2.1). The total number of families is 22 while the population of Guna is 240 comprising of 122 males and 118 females. The total literacy rate of Guna VP is 68 per cent, with male and female literacy at 80.0 and 56.0 per cent, respectively. The male female ratio at Guna VP is 1000:1180 (Table 2.2).

The present number of VP members is 7 and is composed of 6 males and 1 female. The VP meetings are generally held once in about two months. These meetings are attended from time to time by women folk also.

In Guna VP all the families are using fuel wood for cooking and heating purposes. Though LPG is available in the area only 3-4 families (shop keepers in Lamgarha market) were found to use LPG. The daily requirement of fuel wood is about 5-9 kg. Pattern of collection of fuel wood is about 65 per cent from Van Panchayat forest, 15 per cent from Private forest and 20 per cent from government or reserved forest. Any other non timber product, for example, resin, medicinal plants, and lichens were rarely extracted from Guna VP. In Guna VP the extraction of fodder is done on rotational basis. After 3 days interval the members of the family visit the forest for collection of fuel wood and fodder. The weight of one fuel wood head load is approx. 25-30 kg (by field checks) and green leaves (fodder/grass) head load is 18-22 kg (by field checks).

Forest Condition

The year of the formation of Van Panchayat was 1937. The VP forest is even-aged banj-oak forest with under canopy tree species of kaphal (*M. nagi*) and burans (*R. arboreum*) (Fig. 1.2). The dominant tree species of Guna VP are banj (*Q. leucotrichophora*) 60 per cent, burans 15 per cent, kaphal 15 per cent and chir 10 per cent (*P. roxburghii*). The condition of the Guna VP forest is good, oak trees are in healthy condition with moderate lopping. The trees of chir, burans and kaphal are growing well in this forest. Regeneration is also good as saplings of all species are present in the forest except banj oak species.

The canopy cover of Guna VP forest is estimated at 42 per cent and the ground litter cover 50 per cent.

After the creation of VP the peoples of Guna VP accepted that the condition of the VP has improved, as indicated by the reduction of distance travelled for collection of fuel wood, fodder and drinking water. The water source of Guna village is about 20 temporary small ponds (naulas) dug during 2001-2002 in the catchment of two major springs have increased water in them during lean summer months. Ponds are cleaned regularly after 3 months and have been covered to protect from dust. The VP of Guna arranged the forest guard for every year and arranged their salary about Rs. 800 per month from Van Panchayats income. In Guna VP many peoples were fined in last 5 years and VP generated from fines about Rs. 2000. In Guna VP plantation was not done in past two years (Table 2.2). Community members also made fire lines for protection of forest in summer season, and regularly cleared these lines every six months. The livestock numbers in Guna VP were: 195 buffalos, 64 cows, 225 goats and 75 oxen (Fig. 2.3). However, there was no control of grazing in Guna VP.

Income Sources

The total income of Guna Village is Rs. 14970.0 family^{-1} yr^{-1} (Table 2.2). The cropping pattern in Guna village is similar with that of Toli VP (wheat, rice, millet, maduaa, and potato). Annually agriculture income in Guna village is Rs. 7850.0, which is 52.44 per cent of the total income. Floriculture, milk production and as daily labour (@Rs. 65 day^{-1}) contribution is Rs. 7120.0 which is 47.56 per cent of the total income (Fig. 2.4).

The main source of VP income is from the sale of NTFPs which is Rs.5 per family for dry wood collection, Rs. 10 per family for green fodder collection besides these the imposition of fines also generate money by the VP. Thus the total income generated by the VP was Rs. 6500 from the sale of permits and fines in the year 2005 (Fig 2.5).

Conclusion

The local communities VPs of Uttaranchal (UA) are extremely poor and depend critically on the forests for their fodder and fuel wood requirements. These communities have been conserving their forests for many years (without external financial support on a regular basis), and thus play an important role in promoting ecosystem services like carbon sink, without any financial motivation *(Singh, 2004)*. In contrast, in another area of about 2865 ha in UA where communities were not involved in forest management, *Rathore et al. (1997)* found depletion in carbon stock biomass at the rate of about 5 t yr^{-1} over a period of 16 years, though there was only a small reduction in forest areas. This is a good example of the amount of carbon that can be saved by local people by managing their forests effectively. However, the general size of a VP forest should be close to 150 ha, as smaller VP forests (< 50 ha) are not able to sustain the dependent pressure.

Carbon is now being traded internationally at the rate of US$ 13 t^{-1} C. Van Panchayats (VPs) of Uttaranchal are conserving these forests, their biodiversity and ecosystem services for a long time. It is important to link conservation with economic benefits for sustainable development. The studied VPs forests sequester carbon at the rate of 4-5 t ha^{-1} yr^{-1}. From the present study it is observed that Toli Van Panchayat forest sequesters a total of 412 t of carbon ha^{-1} yr^{-1} (worth US $ 5356), followed by Dhaili (US $ 3120) and Guna (US $ 2080), annually at the trading rate of US $ 13 ton^{-1}. Once the people start realizing that the carbon of their forests is profitable, they will be motivated to conserve them.

Acknowledgements

The authors are extremely grateful to Prof. S. P. Singh, *FNA* (former Head, Department of Botany, DSB Campus) Kumaun University Nainital and CHEA India for helping in the running this project.

REFERENCES

1. Houghton, R.A. J.E. Hobbie, J.M. Melillo, G.R. Shaver and G.M. woodwell (1983). Changes in the carbon content of terrestrial biota and soil between 1860 and 1980: a net release of CO_2 to the atmosphere. *Ecological monographs.* 53(3): 235-262.
2. IPCC, Climate change (2001). The Scientific Basis. Contributions of working group I to the III assessment report of the intergovernmental Panel on Climate change (Eds. Houghton, J. et al.), Cambridge University press, Cambridge, U.K.
3. Körner, Ch. (2001). Experimental plant ecology: some lessons from global change research, 227-247p.
4. Phartiyal, P. and A. Tewari (2006). Challenges before marginalized hill communities for managing community forests, status of the village forest councils in Uttaranchal, India. 11th Biennial conference of International association for the study of common property, Bali, Indonesia.
5. Rathore, S.K.S., S.P. Singh, J.S. Singh and A.K. Tewari (1997). Changes in forest cover in central Himalayan catchment: Indequacy of assessment based on forest areas alone. Journal of environment management. 49:265-276.
6. Singh, J. S. and S.P. Singh (1987). Forest vegetation of the Himalayan. *Bot. Rev.*53 (1): 82-192.
7. Singh S. P., G. S. Mer and P. K. Ralhan (1988). Carbon balance for a central Himalayan crop field soil. *Pedobiologia* 32:187-191p.
8. Singh, J. S. and S. P. Singh (1992). Forests of Himalaya-structure, functioning and input of man. Gyanodaya Prakashan, Nainital, India.
9. Singh, S.P., R. Thandani and M. Kumaiyan (2003). Eds. National Biodiversity Strategy and Action plan for Western Himalayas India Final report.

10. Singh, S.P. (2004). A case for incorporating values of ecosystems services of Uttaranchal and other Himalayan states in National accounting systems submitted as supplementary memorandum to 12th Finance commission, Govt. of India by the Govt. of Uttaranchal.
11. Singh, V., A. Tewari, M. Gupta and J. Ram (2006). The prelogged stocks of carbon in *Shorea robusta* and *Q. semecarpifolia* forests of Uttaranchal and their C sequestration rates-A Tradable NTFP. *Int. J.For. Usnf. Mngt.*, 7(1):1-5.
12. Steffer, W., I. Nobel, and J. Canadell (1998). The terrestrial carbon cycle: implications for the Kyoto Protocol. *Science* 280:1393-1394.
13. Tolia, R.S. (1996). British Kumaun Garhwal: An Administrative History of a Non-Regulation Hill Province 1836-1856 (Vol. 2), Indus International, New Delhi.

Climate Change and Livelihood Sustainability in the Lake Chad Region of Nigeria

—Emeka Daniel Oruonye, *Nigeria*

ABSTRACT

The unique location of Lake Chad in the Sudan-Sahel region of Africa made it more vulnerable to climate change and environmental externalities resulting from both natural and anthropogenic driving factors. Climate variability dominates rural food production and strongly influences hunger, health, access to water and hence poverty in the rural areas. Although climate change is real, there are uncertainties about how it will affect food security. The Lake Chad region is a very critical flash point of climate change induced human insecurity in Africa. Although the Lake Chad is a rich environment which attract multiplicity of users, with over 20 million people depending on it for various means of livelihood such as fishing, pastoralism, crop cultivation, transportation and mining, the area is fragile with high climate variability and extremes of weather as well as unsustainable human activities.

This paper examines the impact of climate change on livelihood activities and sustainability in the Lake Chad region of Nigeria. The findings of the study show that livelihood activities have been adversely affected in recent times due to several factors including high water abstraction for irrigation, increasing population, overgrazing, overexploitation and increasing demands on the aquatic resources. Findings from the study show that droughty periods have resulted in the reduction of open lake water surface from about 25,000 km^2 in 1973 to less than 2000 km^2 in the 1990s. This has led to the diminishing of aquatic and other resources in the region as well as potentially major challenge to social and economic development of the region. Although, the importance of Lake Chad to the economy and social well being of the people is well known, mechanisms for mitigating and/or responding to climate change are not in place. A call is made in this paper to support the earlier advocate by scholars for inter-basin water transfer from the Congo Basin to the Lake Chad Basin and the construction of canals on the Lake Chad to boost fishing and transportation.

Keywords: Climate Change, Livelihood Sustainabilty, Lake Chad

Introduction

The Millennium Development Goals (MDGs) cannot be achieved in Africa without good management of climate variability: too many livelihoods are over dependent on the weather. Climate variability dominates rural food production and strongly influences hunger, health, access to water and hence poverty in the rural areas. The Sahelian Drought of 1968-73 and the continuing drought 'episode' of the 1980s in the Sahelo – Sudanian region has made the issue of climate change to become of real concern. Climate and environmental change processes lead to changes in the biophysical life support systems including land (surface vegetation), water resources, soil and atmosphere which constitute the elements that support the long term sustainability of life on earth. It also affect the social and economic structure and framework, and by implication survival of the people. The global chain-effects of microclimate change affects human livelihood and security at communal levels and even family levels.

Although climate change is real, there are uncertainties about how it will affect food security. However, climate change is not only about global warming but also changes in the frequency and magnitude of extreme weather events like pressure and wind systems and temperatures causing floods, droughts and other weather related famines (Sanusi and Oruonye, 2008). Thus understanding climate is central to building policy in the area of natural resources, especially common resources like aquatic resources, both in yearly weather forecasting and prediction over a longer time-scale, in which conceptual models of climate are constructed on the assumption of some consistency in weather patterns (Sanusi and Oruonye, 2008). The struggle for diminishing resources (farmlands and fishing grounds) has increased as a result of climate variability (Mayowa and Omojola, 2005). Communal and International clashes over who owns the land and the struggle for control of exploitation of fishing resources has indeed increased in the Lake Chad region. The inhabitants of the region are land resource poor, with marginal climates and consequently their livelihoods are extremely vulnerable to climatic fluctuations.

The Lake Chad region is a very critical flash point of climate change induced human insecurity in Africa. The region has over the years suffered from repeated incidence of droughts, which has led to the significant decrease in the inflow from the major tributary rivers such as the Chari-Logone and Yobe. The Sudano-Sahelian drought of the decade 1971-1980 spells great consequences for the people and their livelihoods in the Savanna region of Nigeria (Ojo, 1987). The natural result is ecological migration towards the south, which translates to pressure on land and land resources of the wetter Guinea savanna region. This in turn accelerates poverty and tension (amongst farmers, grazers, refugees and fishermen).

The shrinking of the Lake Chad following the drought led to an outbreak of war between Nigeria and Chad over emerging islands in 1983. Thus, in effect, socio-economic activities are greatly reduced in the Lake Chad region during drought regime. The Lake Chad due to its receding waters has adversely affected the lives of several people. People were displaced, economic activities stagnated and 33 Lake Chad villages of Nigeria was ceded to Cameroon following the International Court of Justice verdict on the Land and Maritime border dispute between the two countries. This has greatly reduced fishing and other livelihood activities around the Lake Chad and most fishermen abandoned their age-long profession and converted to other trades.

The Lake Chad Scenario

Lake Chad is a large, shallow lake in Africa. The Lakes drainage basin holds one of the largest areas of wetlands in the Sahelian region, with more than 10 million ha in Chad alone (Odada *et al*, 2004). The wetlands include Sategui-Deressia in Chad, the Yaeres in Cameroon and Chad and the Hadejia – Nguru in Nigeria. It is economically very important and is seen as the life blood of the region, providing water to more than 20 million people living in the four countries which surround it – Chad, Cameroon, Niger and Nigeria (Fig. 3.1).

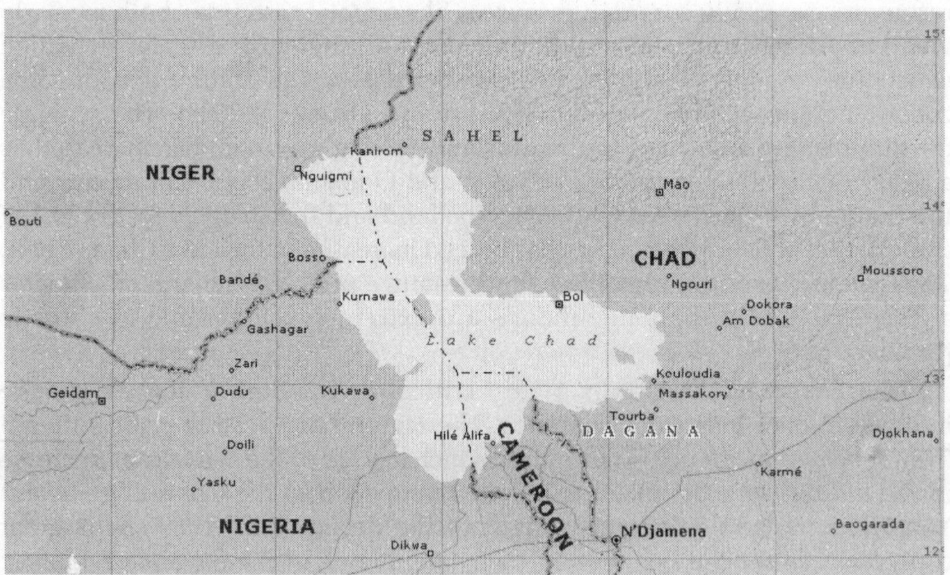

Fig. 3.1 : Lake Chad Basin

The Chari River is its largest source of water, providing over 90% of Lake Chad's water. The Lake possesses many small islands and mud banks, and its shorelines are largely composed of marshes. Because it is very shallow

– only 10.5 metres at its deepest – its area is particularly sensitive to small changes in average depth, and it consequently also shows seasonal fluctuations in size. The fringes of Lake Chad consist of large floodplains that are affected by alternating recession and flooding annually. Lake Chad has no apparent outlet, but its waters percolate into the Soro and Bodele depressions.

The commencement of the 20th century was marked by a most noteworthy decrease of precipitation not only in the Sahelo – Sudanian zone but almost everywhere in the Tropics (Thambyaphillay, 1980). The Lake Chad water level dropped drastically side by side, with a decrease in precipitation in all the adjacent zones. By the 1920s, Lake Chad's level has reached a respectable position and even the Grand Barrier had become submerged below the Lake waters. By the 1930s – 1940s, a wetter phase prevailed and Lake Chad's mean level of 282 m. was restored. The contemporary recurrent 4 year drought of the 1980s has caused much concern (Thambyaphillay, 1991). The Lake Chad level dropped, leading to the Lake drying up. Climatic data has shown a great decrease in rainfall since the early 1960's largely due to a decrease in the number of large rainfall events (Mayowa and Omojola, 2005). Lake Chad's primary source of water comes from the Monsoon rains that typically fall in June, July and August. Meanwhile, the use of water for irrigation in the basin has equally increased in response to the drier climate. Over the last 40 years, the discharge from Chari – Logone river system at the city of N'djamena in Chad has decreased by almost 75 percent, drastically reducing the input into the Lake (Odada *et'al* 2004). Between the increase in agricultural water use and the drier climate, there has been a massive decline in the amount of water in the Lake Chad. With a drier climate and less rainfall, agricultural areas became desperate for water to irrigate their crops, and will continue draining what is left of Lake Chad. Beginning in 1983 the amount of water used for irrigation quadrupled from the amount used in the previous 25 years. The red color in Fig. 2. denotes vegetation on the Lake bed and the ripples on the western edge of the Lake denote sand dunes formed by the wind. In the Lake Chad area, climate change is not just a future threat, but also a present danger that confronts the communities living around the lake (Akor, 2012).

The Lake Chad region is a fragile environment with high climate variability and extremes of weather strongly influenced by the seasonal migration and interaction of the dominant air masses of the region: a dry, subsiding continental air mass and a humid, unstable Maritime air mass. Rainfall is greatest from July to September with annual figure averaging 560 mm at the southern margin of Lake Chad and about 250 mm at the northern margin. Its annual variability is high and this increases from South to North. Whereas temperatures during the rainy season are moderate with highs of about 32^{0}C, the dry season (March - June) is the hottest, occasionally exceeding 43^{0}C. It is semi-arid, characterized by patch resources and dispersed human populations. The increasing temperature and decreasing rainfall have led to frequent drought and desertification (Akor, 2012). The Sahara desert is believed to be expanding to all direction at the rate of 10km per annum (Odjugo and Ikhuoria, 2003; Yakub 2007). The northern region of the Lake Chad is under severe threat of desert encroachment and sand dune migration. The migrating sand dune has buried large areas of arable lands, thus reducing viable agricultural lands and crops production.

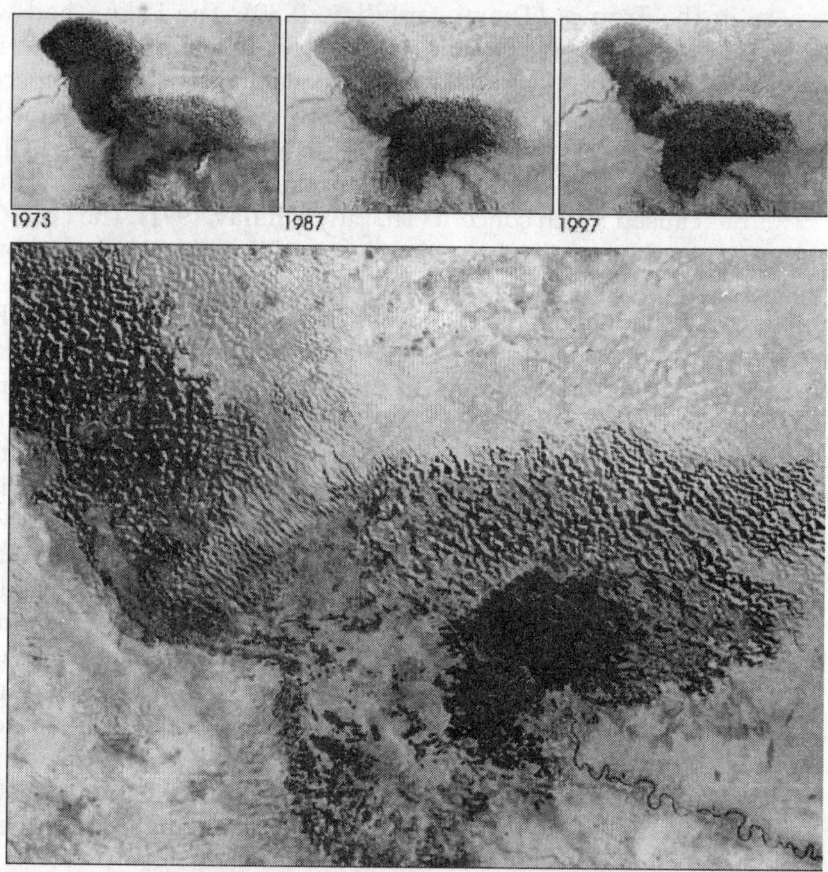

Fig. 3.2. The Lake Chad Floor Showing the receding Lake Water (2001)

Livelihood Opportunities in the Lake Chad Region

Lake Chad is a rich environment, which attract multiplicity of users for livelihoods. According to Odada *et al* (2004), the 1991 population census in the Lake Chad drainage basin shows that the region has a population of 22 million people with an average density of 22 persons per/km^2, but ranging from 1.5 to 37 persons/km^2 in the riparian countries. The population of the drainage basin has grown rapidly (between 2.4 to 2.6% per annum) and is presently estimated at 37 million people (UNEP, 2004).

The major contribution of the Lake to the well-being of the rural population in the remote area of the lake is the fishing activities on the open lake and in surrounding fishing areas and ponds Odada *et al* (2004). The annual fish catch in the Lake Chad was 130,000 to 141,000 tons up to the early 1970s. Presently the fish catch is about 60,000 to 80,000 tons/year. There are many important fish species in the Lake Chad and its numerous wetlands, including charachin *(Alestes baremoze)*, A. dentex, and Nile perch *(Lates niloticus)* Odada *et al* (2004).

Apart from fisheries, the Lake produce silt-covered swampy lands that are used for irrigable crops and rich pastures as water recede. Thus, agriculture provides livelihood opportunity to approximately 60% of Lake Chad basin population. Most of the farming in the drainage basin is rain-fed, harvested by hand and cultivated without the use of fertilizers and other agro-chemicals (Odada *et al*, 2004). The most common crops include cotton, groundnuts, sorghum, cassava, millet, rice and onions. Mixed cropping is widely practiced and rice is grown using both traditional and modern methods. Lake Chad provides the water and the agricultural springboard for the production of this and other commodities. The Lake Chad basin has an irrigation potential of over 1.16 million hectares but only less than 115,000 hectares are actually irrigated. The tributaries of the Lake Chad houses large irrigation projects in the region which include the Yaguou – Tekele dyke (on Chari - Logone) and the Maga dam in Cameroon. Others include the South Chad Irrigation Project, the Tiga dam, the Challawa gorge dam and Alau dam (in Nigeria) and the Mamdi Polder Project in the Republic of Chad.

The Lake Chad basin is also well known for soda ash mining which scholars believed contributes to keeping the lake water fresh. The mining of soda ash employs the services of hundreds of children and young people in the region, particularly girls who easily dig it out in areas severely affected by dry season floods, as in the Hadejia – Nguru Wetlands in Nigeria (Odada *et al*, 2004). Residents of the Lake Chad mine soda ash which is used to make soap, glass, paper and medicines.

Factors Responsible for the Drying up of the Lake Chad

There have been so many arguement and propositions put forward to explain the factors responsible for the drying up of the Lake Chad, Africa's largest inland lake. Some of these factors include human factors such increased population and high water abstraction for irrigation, as well as natural factor such as climate change. Although the Lake Chad area is a rich environment which attract multiplicity of users, with over 20 million people depending on it for various means of livelihood such as fishing, pastoralism, crop cultivation, transportation and mining, the area is fragile with high climate variability and extremes of weather as well as unsustainable human activities. Lake Chad was once the sixth-largest lake in the world, but constant drought since the 1960s has shrunk it to 1/10 its original size. The Shari River, at the southeast, which provides 90% of Lake Chad's water, now averages only about half of its original 40 billion cubic meters per year in the 1930-60s. The recent low levels are a concern, and have been monitored through satellite and other means by the Lake Chad Basin Commission and others. In addition, the region has suffered from an increasingly dry climate, experiencing a significant decline in rainfall since the early 1960s. The most dramatic decrease in the size of the lake is shown in the fifteen years between January 1973 and January 1987 (Fig. 3). Beginning in 1983 the amount of water used for irrigation began to increase. Lake Chad has been the source of water for massive irrigation projects in the region. Ultimately, between 1983 and 1994, the amount of water diverted for purposes of irrigation quadrupled from the amount used in the previous 25 years. This is further exercabated by increase in the number of dams constructed on the headwater of the tributary rivers of the Lake Chad. For example, river Yobe in Nigeria contributes about 3 per cent to the up keep of the Lake Chad and several dams have been constructed on its tributary rivers. This include the Challawa gorge dam, the Tiga dam and recently the Karfin Zaki dam which is still under construction (Oruonye, 2011). A profound example of the impact of human diversion of water from Lake Chad is illustrated in the (UNEP report), where it is pointed out that "Since the 1960's human demands for water near Lake Chad have grown rapidly.

Between 1960 and 1990, the number of people living in the lake's catchment area has doubled from 13 million to 37 million." This growing need for water has resulted in huge irrigation projects and dams along the rivers that feed Lake Chad. Of the Komadugu-Yobe river system the report states "The upper basin used to contribute approximately 7 km^3/yr to Lake Chad. Today, the bulk of this water is impounded in reservoirs within Kano province in northern Nigeria, and the system provides just 0.45 km3/yr." By this calculation that is enough impounded water each year to double the current volume of the Lake. The greatest inflow to Lake Chad comes from the south via the Chari-Logone River. However, since the 1970s the Chari-Logone stream flow has been drastically modified. The construction of the 30 kilometer wide Maga Dam for the creation of Maga Lake, and 80 kilometers of dykes along the Logone downstream from the dam have had a profound impact on Lake Chad. This construction was part of the well intentioned SEMRY irrigation project to open up more agricultural land (mostly rice) and fish farming. This diversion of water from the Chari River for agricultural purposes has contributed greatly to the decreasing stream flows and the discharges into, and extent of the Lake Chad. According to expert opinion the most significant immediate cause for low stream flow into Lake Chad is the increased diversion of rivers and the associated unsustainable use of water resources.

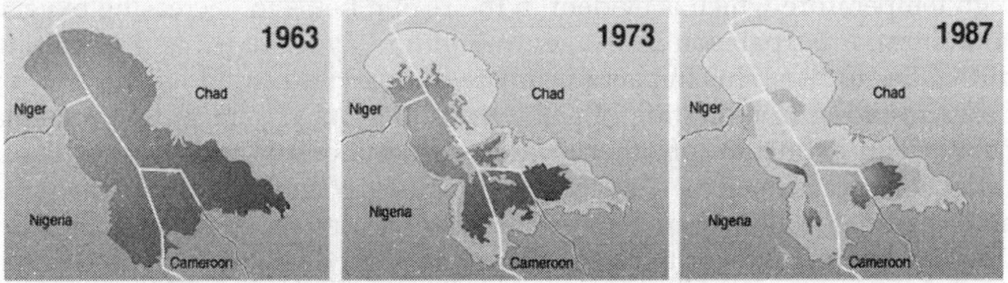

Fig. 3.3 (A-B): The Shrinking Lake Chad

The Impact of the Drying Lake Chad on Livelihood Activities in the Region

The Lake Chad, which provided a means of livelihood directly and indirectly to over 30 million people (including fishery, animal grazing, irrigation farming, flood retreat cultivation, natron mining, trading etc) has shrunk to a wetland one twentieth its original size and presently has an average depth of 1.5 metres only (Mayell, 2001). This has placed the livelihood of the people of the region at stake because of the high vulnerability of water resources to the effect of climate change. Because of the limited amount and uneven distribution of rainfall in time and geographic space in the study area, rainfall represents the most limiting factor for the resources of the Lake Chad (Ziervogel *et al*, 2006). With drought episode, water quantity became a limiting factor for the people to practice any alternative livelihood activities such as growing crops, fishing, pastoralism, harvesting forest products and so on. The lack of water, in association with high temperatures (up to 45^0C at certain periods of the year), is the most limiting factor for livelihood activities in the Lake Chad area.

The rearing of livestock is a very important aspect of life in the Lake Chad region, as it represents livelihood, income and employment. Recurrent droughts have forced some pastoralists to dispose of their cattle, lose their livelihood systems, and ultimately increase their vulnerability. Already pastoralists have been forced out of the Lake Chad area to move their herds to the wetter South. The southward movement of the isohyets has also resulted in the southward migration of pastoralists into lands formerly occupied by sedentary farmers. This has been one of the major sources of conflicts in the Lake Chad region leading to widespread destruction of farmlands and cattle, with adverse implications for food security (Oruonye, 2008).

The impact of climate change on fishing in the Lake Chad is enormous. The greatest impacts of climate change to fishing in Lake Chad region is the occurrence of droughts resulting in the drastic reduction in the Lake water level. This has greatly affected and reduced the carrying capacity for fish production in the Lake Chad. The increasing temperature of the Lake Chad region result in the heating up of the surface of the lake water which has a physiological effect to the fishes adapted to narrow temperature range. The high temperature which is evident in the region helps in decreasing oxygen concentration, expansion in oxygen minimum layer (OML) and breathing difficulties to fish. This impact of climate change has caused habitat lost for fishes resulting in migration of some fishes that may want to find suitable habitat and extinction of other swamp associated fish and species. Local extinctions occasioned by elevated temperatures, changes in current patterns and destruction of swamps and other habitat alteration, will lead to fish scarcity and fish insecurity as a component of food insecurity (Odada et al 2004). Thus, the shrinking of the Lake Chad has led to the decline in fishing activities, which is the major means of livelihood in the Lake Chad region. For example, Bego (2007) reports of catch decline from about 100,000 to 60,000 tonnes annually. Some fishermen claimed that their daily incomes have also decline from about N10,000 ($100 USD) to less than N1,000 ($10 USD). Some fishermen said that when they started fishing about three decades back, they use to catch 20 – 30 basins of fish daily, each as large as a man but today, the fish are smaller in size and very hard to get five basins (fewer in quantity). Also Ahmed (2007), Ajepe (1983) and Hopson (1967) have reported the decline and loss of some fish types in the Lake Chad.

Rainfed agriculture is very difficult to practice in the Lake Chad region because of the unpredictable and low amount of rainfall in the Sahelian region. Hence, most farmers engaged in irrigation farming and flood retreat cultivation on the receded lakebed. Many irrigation schemes have been adversely affected and some abandoned because of the shrinking of the Lake Chad especially the South Chad irrigation project (SCIP) in Nigeria, SEMRY in Cameroon and SODELAC in Chad (Oruonye, 2008). Many flood retreat cultivators (lakebed) have followed the receding Lake for several kilometers.

As the Lake recedes and water resources become scarce, permanent and floating islands emerged, with the latter clogging up the waterways. The influx of fishermen, herders and farmers puts pressure on the resources (water, fish stocks, vegetation and land). Most struggling fishermen resort to the selling of firewood as alternative sources of livelihood, thereby further degrading the environment. The fact that the seasonal ponds and receding channels are, in aggregate, the most common type of water-bodies fished across the basin indicates that a large part of the fishing activity has developed as a temporary activity to adapt to the seasonal dynamics of the environment and, in particular, to make the most of the seasonal flooding. However, the seasonality that characterizes the hydrological environment of the Lake area does not affect only fishing activity but the households' activity portfolio as a whole. The analysis by Neiland *et'al* (2005) reveals indeed that the households' livelihood relies on a strongly seasonal matrix of diversified activities the pattern of which is largely influenced by the local water-flood regime. These multiple activities are closely integrated and all households in the Basin irrespective of their wealth level are still heavily involved in a subsistence-based economy, where fishing, farming and cattle holding represent the three pillars of the system.

Petroleum has been discovered in the Lake Chad region by republics of Chad and Niger. Already, exploration activities have started in the Lake Chad region. Petroleum exploration activities involves deforestation, seismic and radioactive activities, sounding of rocks with gamma rays, all affects biodiversity and humans in the region and contribute to the global climate change. Seismic activities cause cancer and emit radiations which are hazardous to plant, animals and humans.

Although many people argued that the shrinking of the Lake Chad is mainly as a result of human factors such as increased population and high water abstraction for irrigation, the writer of this paper believes that climate change is also a major factor responsible for the shrinking of Lake Chad and decline in livelihood activities in the region. But as livelihoods are destroyed and the deserts heads over southwards, time is of essence for planners in the riparian nations and Lake Chad Basin Commission.

Coping Strategies to the Effects of the Drying Lake Chad

The people around Lake Chad are among Africa's most chronically vulnerable to food insecurity. They have dealt with variability through mobility and through diversity of food sources. People who raise livestock typically moved closer to the lake for grasses in the dry season, then move up to 100 km away in the rainy, mosquito season. After the 1970s droughts, herders shifted from grazing animals (cattle and camels) to browsing animals (sheep and goats), which affected the area's vegetation by incessant consumption of the woody plants. Cattle herders have also been burning the sparse, coarse vegetation that is left in the hope that new plant life will sprout and provide a more palatable diet for their livestock, but there is no evidence that this works. Instead, the process seems to loosen the dry soil and make it more susceptible to erosion. As areas dry up, farmers and cattle herders have had to move southward towards greener areas, where they end up competing for land resources with host communities. This has led to some of the conflicts between herders and farming communities reported in recent years in northeastern Nigeria. Government policy on land which does not make provision for grazing land for the nomadic cattle rearers further compound this problem.

Coping strategies have included farming the lake bottom and on "recessional lands", where the lake water recedes every year, in the "polder" depressions between dunes. In a traditional polder, one crop a year is grown as the lake water recedes. If dams and pumps are used, up to three crops a year can be grown. The potential impacts of increasing droughts in the Lake

Chad region would lead to further land degradation from browsing animals and the shorter shoreline from receding lake implies fewer polders to grow crops. Furthermore a low lake also means fewer fish, which may lead to an increase in other lake-related activities such as soda ash mining.

Conclusion

This paper has examined the impact of climate change on livelihood sustainability in the Lake Chad region of Nigeria. The study has shown that the surface water of Lake Chad has shrunk greatly as a result of climate change and human related factors. The study revealed also that the drying of the Lake Chad has drastically affected the sustainability of livelihood activities such as fishing, rainfed agriculture, irrigation, livestock rearing and mining among others. The study also shows that although the importance of the Lake Chad to the rural population is well known, the mechanism for mitigating or responding to climate change effects in the basin are not in place. Thus, understanding the present and future climate change impacts in the basin is important for policy decisions now, because it is a major threat to sustainable development in the region, and has the potential to undo hard worn development gains.

Recommendation

Improved predictability and understanding of climate variability could help in deriving optimal operating policies for water and infrastructure management in the Lake Chad area. Policies can be put in place to help the farmers with less water-intensive crops, or even alternative livelihood strategies to reduce pressure on the fishery. There is need to provide climate change effect mitigation measures such as storing surplus foodstuff in good years (safety net). Stakeholders on global climate change at the global level should partner with the local communities through organizing seminars, workshops, conferences and the train the trainer forums.

The local people should be involved in policy decisions so as to get their own view of how to solve the problem of this menace because they have been in the environment for long and have more knowledge and ideas about their physical environment. The UN should also help in facilitating and funding the Inter-Basin Water Transfer project in the Lake Chad region. The transfer of water from River Congo to the Shari River is believed to be the only practicable means of reviving the Lake Chad. By far, cooperation rather than competition among the riparian nations is very important in ensuring a lasting peace in the region.

REFERENCES

Ahmed, M.I., 2007. Studies on Freshwater Fishes, their Habitats and Parasites in Lake Chad Basin of Nigeria. An unpublished Ph.D. Thesis submitted to the Department of Veterinary Medicine, University of Maiduguri.

Ajepe, G.R., 1983. Preliminary Survey of Fishes in Lake Chad. *Final year Project*, Federal Fisheries School, Baga, Borno State.

Akor, G. 2012. Exploring the link between climate change and its impact on the livelihoods of farmers and agricultural workers in Nigeria. A paper presented at the conference on climate change impact on the livelihoods of farmers and agricultural workers Organized by Friedrich Ebert Stiftung (FES) Accra, Ghana, 10th – 12th April, 2012.

Bego. A., 2007. UNESCO, Others hold regional roundtable on Lake Chad. Daily Trust (Lagos). 14th February 2007. p. 31.

Hopson, A.J., 1967. Federal Fisheries of Lake Chad. *In Fish and Fisheries of Northern Nigeria,* Gaskiya Corpoiration, Zaria.

Mayell, H., 2001. Shrinking African Lake Offers Lessons on Finite Resources. National Geographic News, April 26th 2001.

Mayowa, J.F. and Omojola, A.S., Climate Change, Human Security and Communal Clashes in Nigeria. *An International workshop*, Holmen Fjord, Asker near Oslo, 21 – 23 June, 2005.

Neiland, A. E., Madakan S. P. and Bene C. (2005). Traditional Management Systems, Poverty and Change in the arid zone Fisheries of Northern Nigeria. Journal of Agrarian Change. Volume 5. No. 1 pp. 117-148.

Odada, E., Oyebande, L. & Oguntola, J. 2004. Lake Chad Brief. <http://www.worldlakes.org/uploads/ELLB%20ChadDraftûnal.14Nov2004.pdf>. as accessed on 18 November 2006.

Odjugo, P.A.O. and Ikhuoria 2003. The impact of climate change and anthropogenic factors on desertification in the semi arid region of Nigeria. *Global Journal of Environmental Science,* 2(2): 118 – 126.

Ojo, S.O., 1987. The Climatic Drama. *Inaugural Lecture Series.* University of Lagos Press.

Onuoha, F.C. 2008. Saving Africa's Shrinking Lakes through Inter-Basin Water Transfer: Reûections on the Proposed Lake Chad Replenishment Project. Nigerian Journal of International Affairs 34 (2), in press.

Oruonye E. D. (2011). The Impact of Dam Construction on Irrigation Aactivities Downstream of River Yobe, Yobe State, Nigeria. *Jalingo Journal of African Studies.* Vol. 1 (1).

Oruonye, E.D. 2008. *Impact of Climate Change on Livelihood Sustainability in the Lake Chad Region of Nigeria.* Proceedings of the 32nd Annual Conference of the Forestry Association of Nigeria (FAN) held at Umuahia, Abia State 20th – 25th October 2008.

Sanusi, S.S. and **E. D. Oruonye** (2008). The Impact of Climate Change on Fishing Activities in the Lake Chad Region of Nigeria. A paper presented at the 17th Annual Conference of the Botanical Society of Nigeria (BOSON), Ebonyi State University (EBSU), Abakaliki, 16th-19th March 2008.

Thambyaphillay, G.G.R., Precipitation trends within the ITCZ, *Proceedings on International Symposium on climatic change and food production.* Tokyo (Sept. 1980)

Thambyaphillay, G. G. R., 1991, Climate Change, Drought and Desertification. In Gadzama, N.M., *et al* (eds.) Arid Zone Hydrology and Water Resources. University of Maiduguri, Press, pp. 33-55.

UNEP. 2004. Fortnam, M.P. and Oguntola, J.A. (eds). Lake Chad Basin, GIWA Regional Assessment 43. University of Kalmar: Kalmar, Sweden.

Yakub C. N. 2007. Desert Encroachmɉent in Africa: Extent Causes and Impacts. *Journal of Arid Environment*, 4(1): 14 – 20.

Ziervogel, G., Nyong, A., Osman, B., Conde, C., Cortes, S., and Downing, T., 2006. Climate Variability and Change: Implications for Household Food Security. *AIACC Working paper* No. 20.

Forest Fire

A Major Threat for Conservation of Indian Forests

—**Bhasker Joshi,** ***India***
—**Neelam Mewari,** ***India***

ABSTRACT

The event of something burning is called as fire. A forest fire also known as wild fire, vegetation fire, grass fire, brush or bush fire is a natural disaster consisting of a fire which destroys a forested area and can be a great danger to people who live in forests as well as wild life. It is mostly common in Australia, South Africa, United States, India and Canada. Forest fires are generally started by lighting. It is caused by drying out of branches, leaves and therefore highly flammable. Fires are a widespread phenomenon in Indian forests. Most fires today are thought to be human-caused and are commonly considered to be a major cause of forest degradation. However, our knowledge of the causes of fire, about their extent, their effect on forest ecosystems, and their link to the goods and services that people derive from forests is extremely limited. So, in this chapter a detail discussion on forest fire, its types, significance of forest fire and preventation measures are described to create awareness among human beings.

Key words: Forest fire, vegetatation, Himalaya, ecosystem, environment.

Introduction

Earth is a magical planet of our universe, because there is life exist. Earth has three parts i.e. water, land and atmosphere which support life. Diversity of flora and fauna, forest, wild life, desert, mountains, river, lakes, plateau are important features of Earth. But this planet also suffering from various kinds of natural disaster and forest fire is one of them. India, with a forest cover of 20.55 per cent of geographical area, contains a variety of climate zones; from the tropical south, north-western hot deserts to Himalayan cold deserts (P.S. Roy) and possesses a distinct identity due to its vegetation which varies from tropical wet evergreen forests in Andaman and Nicobar islands in the

South to dry alpine forests high up in the Himalaya. In between the two extremes, the country has semi-evergreen forests, sub-tropical pine forests, mountain temperate forests and alpine forests. There are 16 major and 22 minor forest types have been recognized in India. Tropical moist deciduous forests occupy 37 per cent of the total forest cover, tropical dry deciduous forests forms 29.6 per cent of the total forest cover and the tropical wet evergreen forests occupy 8 per cent of the total forest cover.

Tropical and subtropical deciduous forests occur between 23° north and south latitudes, are characterized by a 4-7 month dry period, and receive up to 2500 mm of precipitation during 5-8 wet months (Murphy and Lugo 1986; Saha and Hiremath 2003). Deciduous forest plants show a variety of adaptations to rainfall seasonality and dry-season drought. Seed dispersal and germination are cued to rainfall, leaves are shed during the dry season, and percentage of biomass allocated to roots is greater than in less seasonal forests (Holbrook et al.1995; Reich 1995), presumably to maximize uptake of soil moisture. In most such forests, anthropogenic fires were set to clear land for agriculture or silviculture and promote fodder for livestock grazing; however, systematic fires to facilitate collection of non-timber products are of relatively recent origin (Gadgil and Meher-Homji 1985; Bowman 1998).

Table 4.1 : Land Area, Forest Area, Population and Per Capita Forest Area in Some Countries (State of the world's Forest 2009 (from Internet) and other documents)

S. No.	Country	Geographical Area (Crore Ha.)	Forest Area (Crore Ha.)	% of Forest Area to Geographic Area	Population (Crore)	Per Capita Forest Area (Ha.)
1.	United States	91.62	30.31	33.08	30.28	1.00
2.	Russian Federation	163.81	80.88	49.37	14.32	5.65
3.	Canada	90.93	31.01	34.10	3.26	9.51
4.	China	93.27	19.73	21.15	132.84	0.15
5.	United Kingdom	2.42	0.28	11.57	6.05	0.05
6.	Italy	2.94	1.00	34.01	5.88	0.17
7.	Australia	76.82	16.37	21.31	2.05	7.99
8.	Indonesia	18.12	8.85	48.84	22.89	0.39
9.	Brazil	84.59	47.77	56.47	18.93	2.52
10.	Nigeria	9.11	1.11	12.18	14.47	0.08
11.	India	32.87	7.69	23.40	102.70	0.07
12.	World	1301.39	395.20	30.37	659.30	0.60

The world's greatest forest fires disaster in terms of people affected are presented in Table 4.2.

Table 4.2 : Ten most catastrophic forest fires 1900-2007. (Source: EMDAT and South Asia Disaster Report 2007)

S. No	Country	Date	Total Affected
1.	Indonesia, Forest fire	October, 1994	3000000
2.	Macedonia FRY, Forest fire	July, 2007	1000000
3.	United States, Scrub/grassland fire	21 October, 2007	640064
4.	Argentina, Forest fire	22 January,1987	152752
5.	Portugal, Forest fire	January, 2003	150000
6.	Paraguay, Forest fire	September, 2007	125000
7.	Russia, Forest fire	20 July, 1998	100683
8.	China P Rep, Forest fire	May, 1987	56313
9.	Nepal, Forest fire	March, 1992	50000
10.	Myanmar, Forest fire	11 April, 1981	48588

Forest fire is a major cause of degradation of Indian forests. It is estimated that the proportion of forest areas prone to forest fires annually ranges from 33 per cent in some states to over 90 per cent in others. About 90 per cent of the forest fires in India are started by humans. According to Forest Survey of India, about 50 per cent of the forests in India are prone to fires. The fires cause huge losses in terms of timber and biodiversity. Official reports of losses often show low estimates, as they do not take into account the loss of lesser fauna and plants lacking in commercial value. According to one estimate, the annual losses from forest fires in the country would come to about Rs. 440 crores. Humans cause most of the fires deliberately or by accident. Fires ignited by natural causes such as lighting are rare.

Fire is one of the major reasons for degradation of forests in India. Repeated fires can reduce forests to grasslands. Though several measures such as controlled fires, cutting of fire line etc are used to check fires, they are not fully effective. Besides, the preventive measures themselves cause loss of biodiversity. Considering the availability of human resources, posting of firewatchers appears to be the best option for India.

Forest fires cause wide ranging adverse ecological, economic and social impacts. Fires cause indirect effect on agricultural production and loss of livelihood for the tribals, because tribals directly and indirectly depend upon collection of non-timber forest products. Forests fires posses a threat not only to the forest wealth but also to the entire regime to fauna and flora, disturbing the bio-diversity and the ecology and environment of a region. During summer, when there is no rain for months, the forests become littered with dry senescent leaves and twinges, which could burst into flames ignited by the slightest spark.

The Himalayan forests, particularly, Kumaun and Garhwal have been burning regularly during the last few summers, with colossal loss of

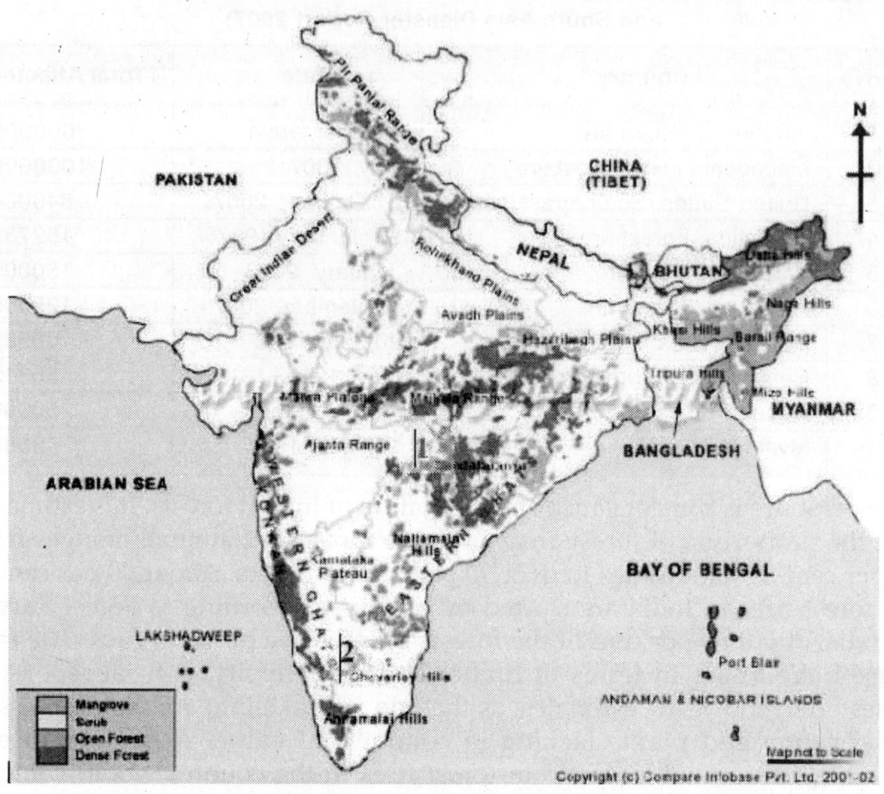

Fig. 4.1 : Vegetation map of India showing total forest cover (Saha and Hiremath 2003)

vegetation cover of that region. The production, provision and maintenance of grazing land are since long well known to be done also with the help of fire (Goldammer 1993, Government of India 1999, Bahuguna and Upadhyay 2002) and this is not a new phenomenon. Man has used fire as a tool for hunting and to create pasture land worldwide for nearly 50 000 years (Bowmann et al. 2009) and for India it is assumed that fire was used in the same way in prehistoric times (Pyne 1994). Fire removes the remaining negromass of the past season shoots, provides easily available nutrients and leads therefore to the production of fresh new shots uniformly on big areas. At the same time the establishments of unwanted plant species that limit the supply of the fodder plants are mitigated. Traditional methods of fire prevention are not proving effective and it is now essential to raise public awareness on the matter, particularly among those people who live close to or in forest areas.

Classification of Forest Fire

Forest fire can broadly be classified into three categories;

1. Natural or controlled forest fire.
2. Forest fires caused by heat generated in the litter and other biomes in summer through carelessness of people (human neglect).
3. Forest fires purposely caused by local inhabitants.

Types of Forest Fire

There are four types of forest fire

1. Ground Fire
2. Sub-surface fire
3. Surface Fire
4. Crown Fire

1. Ground fire: Ground fires occur in the humus and peaty layers beneath the litter of unrecompensed portion of forest floor i.e. the carpet of herbaceous plants and low shrubs, which cover the soil, with intense heat but practically no flame. Such fires are relatively rare and have been recorded occasionally at high altitudes in Himalayan fir and spruce forests.

2. Sub-Surface Fire: Sub-surface fires occur below the surface, e.g. where there is deep accumulation of raw humus or peat.

3. Surface Fire: Surface fire spreading along the ground as the surface litter i.e. senescent leaves and twigs and dry grasses etc, on the forest floor and is engulfed by the spreading flames. It is fire which not merely burns the ground cover but also the under growth. Such fires are relatively occurred in plains.

4. Crown Fire: A forest fire, which spreads through the crowns of the trees and consumes all or part of the upper branches and foliage. This type of forest fire common in coniferous forests and it is very devastating.

(a) Ground Fires

(b) Surface Fires

(c) Crown Fires

Fig. 4.2 (A,B & C): Types of forest fires (Sahin 2007)

Causes of Forest fire

There are two major causes of forest fires.

1. Environmental causes (Natural causes)
2. Human related causes (Man made causes)

1. Environmental causes: These are largely related to climatic conditions such as temperature, speed and direction of wind, amount of soil moisture and amount of dryness of atmosphere. Friction of bamboos sticks due to high wind velocity and rolling stones that result in sparks setting off fires in highly inflammable leaf litter on the forest floor also a major cause of forest fire.

Lightning is an important source of natural fires which have influenced savanna-type vegetation in pre-settlement periods. The role of natural fires in the "lightning-fire bioclimatic regions" of Africa was recognized early (Phillips 1965; Komarek 1968). Lightning fires have been observed and reported in the deciduous and semi-deciduous forest biomes as well as occasionally in the rain forest. However, rain extinguishes such fires without causing much damage. High atmospheric temperatures and dryness (low humidity) offer favorable circumstance for a fire to start.

2. Human related causes: These are result from human activity as well as methods of forest management. When a source of fire like naked flame, cigarette or bidi, electric spark or any source of ignition comes into contact with inflammable material cause forest fire, which quite damaging for the ground flora and young natural regeneration. Also honey gatherers and cattle grazers create forest fire. The problem of forest fire has been accentuated by the growing human and cattle population. The tribes of forest area light fires, during the collection of non-timber forest products, to make way within the densely grown patches of grasses and shrubs. They enter forests ever more frequently to graze cattle, collect fuel wood, timber and other minor forest produce. It has been estimated that 90% of forest fires in India are man-made, also fires started accidentally by careless visitors to forests who discard cigarette butts. On the other hand the tribals of certain areas set fire to the ground litter so that the ground below the Mahuda trees becomes clear and it becomes easy for them to collect Mahuda fruits and flowers at Balaram sanctuary of North Gujarat (Dabgar et al. 2012). The rural poor, as approximately 300 million people are directly dependent upon collection of non-timber forest products from forest areas for their livelihood.

Various causes of human related forest fire as follows:

1. Grazers and gatherers of various forest products starting small fires to obtain good grazing grass as well as to facilitate gathering of minor forest produce like flowers of *Madhuca indica* and leaves of *Diospyros melanoxylon*.
2. The use of fires by villagers to ward off wild animals.
3. Fires lit intentionally by people living around forests for recreation.

Forest fires are mostly anthropogenic in nature in India and may occur due to the following reasons (Bahuguna and Upadhyay 2002):

- Forest floor is often burnt by villagers to get a good growth of grass in the following season or for a good growth of mushrooms.
- Wild grass or undergrowth is burnt to search for animals.
- Firing by miscreants.
- Attempt to destroy stumps of illicit fallings.

Effect of Forest Fire

Forest fires reported regularly in many parts of India along the Himalayan foothills and also in the deciduous forests. The pine forests of the Himalaya are highly susceptible to fire. In the deciduous forest of southern India, leaf shedding begins early in the year and by April the forest floor is covered with large amounts of litter. This pattern in leaf shedding is common in the various forest types of India. According to Narendran, (2001) the biomass generated by many grasses such as *Themeda cymbaria* and *T. triandra* also contributes significantly to the combustible material of these forests. According to P.S. Roy, most pronounced consequence of forest fires causes their potential effects on climate change. Only in the past decade researchers have realized the important contribution of biomass burning to the global budgets of many radioactively and chemically active gases such as carbon dioxide, carbon monoxide, methane, nitric oxide, tropospheric ozone, methyl chloride and elemental carbon particulate. Biomass burning is recognized as a significant global source of emission contributing as much as 40% of gross CO_2 and 30% of tropospheric ozone. Fires are a major cause of forest degradation and have wide ranging adverse ecological, economic and social impacts, including:

- Loss of valuable timber.
- Degradation of catchment areas.
- Loss of biodiversity and extinction of plants and animals.
- Loss of natural regeneration and reduction in forest cover.
- Increasing global warming.
- Loss of carbon sinks resource and increase in percentage of CO_2 in atmosphere.
- Change in the microclimate of the area with unhealthy living conditions.
- Loss of productivity of soils and primary production due to soil erosion.
- Ozone layer depletion.
- Health problems leading to diseases.
- Loss of livelihood for tribal people.
- Species, which have thick corky bark, are comparatively less affected by forest fires than the species with thin bark. The broad-leaved trees are less affected by forest fires than the conifers as compare to niddle leaved tree. Tree, which is very old, dry and hollow, then it becomes more susceptible to fire, but if the tree is very green it is less susceptible to fire than the dry tree.
- Season also affects the damage by fire. Fires generally do not occur during rainy season. During the cold season fire does not occur in

snow-covered areas. Fires in summers are common as well as destructive because of high temperature, strong wind, dry undergrowth and ground cover and thick layer of dry fallen leaves support forest fire.

- Forest fires leaves the soils bare to the action of natural elements i.e. sun, wind and rain; consequently soil erosion starts, resulting in loss of top fertile soil. Destruction of soil organic matter affects the soil structure adversely. Nitrogen reserves of the soil are depleted. Fire also destroys humus and soil micro-flora, which in turn affects the forest growth.
- Forest fires causes serious health hazards by producing smoke and noxious gases, as the events in Indonesia after the forest fires on the islands of Sumatra and Borneo in 1977 have shown. The burning of vegetation gives off not only carbon dioxide but also a host of other, noxious gases (Green house gases) such as carbon monoxide, methane, hydrocarbons, nitric oxide and nitrous oxide, that lead to global warming and ozone layer depletion. Consequently, thousands of people suffered from serious respiratory problems due to these toxic gases. Burning forests and grasslands also add to already serious threat of global warming. Recent measurement suggest that biomass burning may be a significant global source of methyl bromide, which is an ozone depleting chemical.
- Repeated fires degenerate a valuable evergreen forests in to an inferior deciduous forest or even grassland. Valuable species disappear and their place is taken by other fire hardy species.
- Forest fire results in to enormous loss to wildlife and birds. Not only eggs and young ones, but sometimes bigger animals are also burnt to death. Forest fires cause loss of habitat for the wild fauna making them susceptible to death due to poaching, adverse weather conditions or killing by predator species. As destruction of wild animals destroys a valuable component of environment, natural equilibrium is seriously affected with consequent adverse effect on vegetation itself.
- As fire destroys the greenery of the forest, it destroys its recreational and aesthetic value. Forest no longer remains a fit place for recreation, as the ground is littered with ash and blackened stems of shrubs and poles of trees making the entire place desolate. Fire reduces the moisture level and leads to ecological degradation of the site.

Forest Fire in Uttarakhand

The Uttarakhand state has 64.79 per cent of its total geographical area declared as forest area with forest against all Indian state only 45.65 per cent, forest area is leagally under forest department. The per capita forest area of

Uttarakhand is 0.41 ha (Verma 2009). Uttarakhand has three major ecological zones as subtropical, temperate and alpine (Joshi 2011). In summer seasons (March to May) subtropical and temperate zone mostly suffered by forest fire. In temperate zone pine forests are responsible for forest fire. It leads destructions of forest flora and fauna. In submontane forest, wild fire is a major problem during spring and summer season. Fire affects flora and fauna of forest directly or indirectly, it leads removal of ground vegetation, reduces competition for moisture, nutrients and light (Joshi and Kumar 2011). The status of forest fire in last 15 years is shows in table 4.3.

Table 4.3. Status of Forest Fire in Uttarakhand in last 15 Years (Information received from CCF, Intelligence, Forest Department of Uttarakhand and Legal Cell)

S. No.	Year	Fire Affected Area Ha.	Estimated Loss in Lakh
1.	1996-97	4679.00	9.700
2.	1997-98	1381.00	1.750
3.	1998-99	6367.0	14.100
4.	1999-00	21305.00	52.760
5.	2000-01	925.00	2.990
6.	2001-02	1393.00	1.170
7.	2002-03	3231.00	5.190
8.	2003-04	4983.00	10.120
9.	2004-05	4850.00	13.14
10.	2005-06	3652.00	10.82
11.	2006-07	562.44	1.62
12.	2007-08	1595.35	3.67
13.	2008-09	2369.00	2.68
14.	2009-10	4115.50	4.79
15.	2010-11	1842.57	1.178

Measures for Preventation of Forest Fire

The followings measures should be taken in to consideration for preventation of forest fire:

1. To keep the source of fire or source of ignition separated from combustible and inflammable material from forest area.
2. To keep the source of fire under watch and control.
3. Not allow combustible or inflammable material to pile up unnecessarily and to stock the same as per procedure recommended for safe storage of such combustible or inflammable material.
4. To adopt safe practices in areas near forests viz. factories, coalmines, oil stores, chemical plants and even in household kitchens.

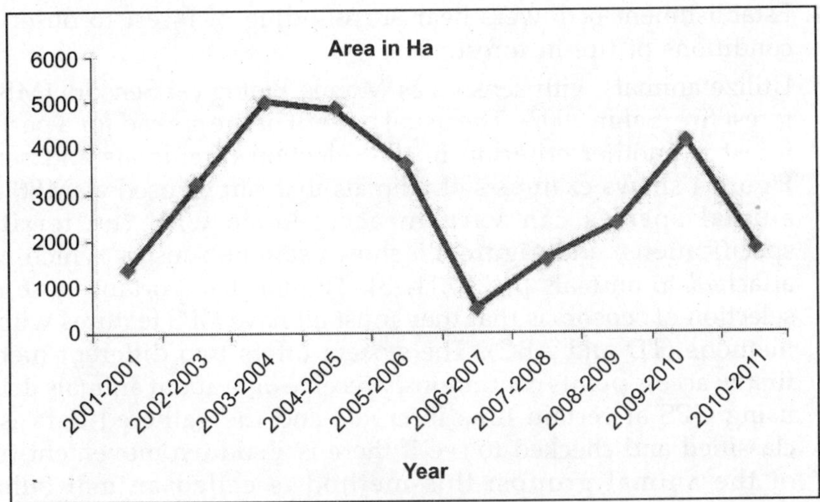

Fig. 4.3. Forest Fire (in hectare) in last 10 Years in Uttarakhand (Information received from CCF, Intelligence, Forest Department of Uttarakhand and Legal Cell)

5. To incorporate fire reducing and fire fighting techniques and equipment while planning a building or coal mining operation.
6. In case of forest fires, the volunteer teams are essential not only for fire fighting but also to keep watch on the start of forest and sound an alert.
7. To arrange fire fighting drills frequently.
8. Creating public awareness through press, radio, television, posters and films shows about the causes of fire and their effect will go a long way in preventing the fire.
9. Entry of common public in the forest restricted during fire season.
10. Collection of honey, seeds etc. should be restricted during the summer to reduce the chances of accidental fire.
11. Before the fire season begins, posters about fire hazards, prohibition of kindling and carrying of fire through the forest can be put up in prominent places to remind people about fire risk and preventing chances of fire.
12. A large no of accidental fires start from camping sites where people stay for short periods of time. Inflammable material around such sites should be cleared before the onset of dry season. Fires starting from Bidi or Cigarette stumps thrown carelessly by the roadside can be prevented by controlled burning all grass and leaves.
13. Reduce fire risk through awareness like signs, posters, advertisement, exhibits etc., through radio, still pictures, motion pictures and television etc., through personal contacts with individuals and groups and prevention through education to children.

14. Establishment of towers near surrounding of forest to observe the conditions of fire in forest.
15. Utilize animals with sensors as Mobile Biological Sensors (MBS) for forest fire (Sahin 2007). The usual pattern of fire spread for a particular forest is another criterion in the selection of animals and sensors. Figure 4 shows examples of animals that can be used as MBS (these animal species can vary in accordance with the territory's specifications) and Figure 4.5 shows sample sensors which can be attached to animals [6,7,10,11,23]. The most important issue in the selection of sensors is that they must all have GPS features with both methods (TD and ABC). The system offers two different methods, firstly: access points continuously receive data about animals' location using GPS at certain time intervals and the gathered data is then classified and checked to see if there is a sudden movement (panic) of the animal groups: this method is called animal behavior classification (ABC). The second method can be defined as thermal detection (TD): the access points get the temperature values from the MBS devices and send the data to a central computer to check for instant changes in the temperatures. This system may be used for many purposes other than fire detection, namely animal tracking, poaching prevention and detecting instantaneous animal death (Sahin 2007).

Fig. 4.4 : Some animals that can be used as MBS (Mobile Biological Sensors) in the system (Sahin 2007).

Figure 4.6 (*a*) and (*b*) show Loria Forest Snake which is a secretive, ground-dwelling species of forests and adjacent grasslands. Sightings are infrequent due to its secretive habits: the species lives amongst the confusing tangle of leaf litter, moss growth and rotting logs of the forest floor [9]. The figure (*c*) shows an Egyptian tortoise (*Testudo kleinmanni*), it is a ground-dwelling specie too and it lives amongst the grass [5]. The selection of these animals is very suitable for TD method because of their daily life habits, five of them have, therefore, been selected for simulation (Sahin 2007).

Significance of Forest Fire under prescribed conditions

Forest fire in most of cases is harmful for forest, wild life, flora and environment. But every fact has two aspects, so forest fire also essential for nature under prescribed conditions like:

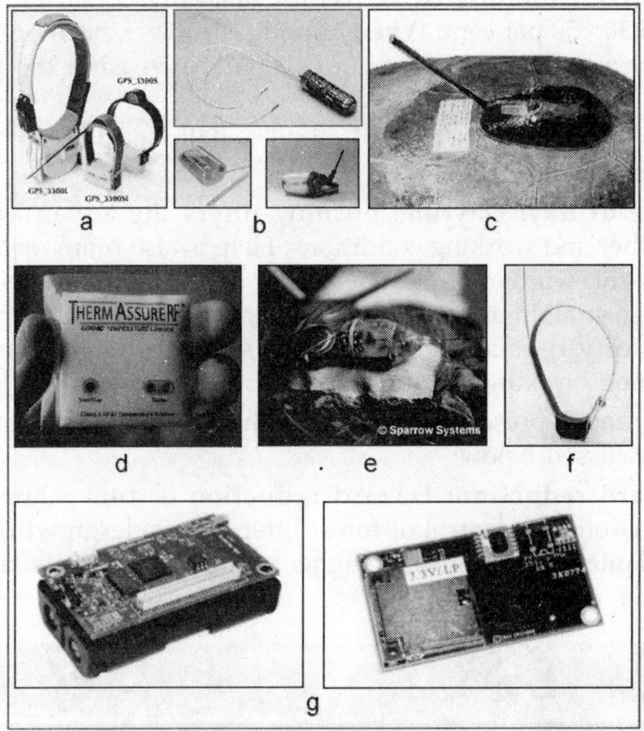

Fig. 4.5 : Sample sensors that can be used in the system [6,7,10,11,23]

Fig. 4.6 : Suitable animals for TD (thermal detection) method [5, 9].

- **Fuel Conditions:** Humidity is around 50 per cent and lower litter fuel moisture is at a relatively high level (20%) are favorable for prescribed burning.
- **Temperature:** Air temperatures 10 -15 °C are recommended for winter burring in young stands. Burning to control undesirable species or site preparation are often best accomplished with summer burns & air temperatures above 25 °C.
- **Wind:** Wind is also necessary to supply oxygen to the fire and dissipate the heat. Wind speeds from 2 to 10 km/hr on the site are best for most fuel and stand conditions.

- **Relative Humidity (RH):** RH for most prescribed burns should be from 30 - 50 per cent. When humidity is lower, burning is dangerous. A spark will burn longer in drier air, increasing the possibility of spot fires outside the area.
- **Rainfall:** About 2 – 4 cm of rain is usually needed, 5 -10 days before a prescribed burn.
- **Time of day:** Daytime burning offers the advantages of better weather and working conditions. Help is also more readily available. At night, winds normally lessen or die down. Thus heat and flames will go straight up and may cause serious injury to the timber. Relative humidity rises sharply when the sun goes down, causing patchy burning or extinguishing the fire.

Burning under prescribed conditions has various significance to forest as briefly discussed below:

1. **Hazard reduction:** Hazard reduction or fuel management (the reduction and control of forest litter and undergrowth) is important in plantations because of higher establishment costs and increasing timber values.

Fig. 4.7: General appearance of Ground Vegetation

Fig. 4.8: Loss of Ground vegetation due to forest fire.

Fig. 4.9: A prescribed burn in a Pine forest

Fig. 4.10: Reduction of forest fire

2. **Removal of Pathogens:** Various harmful bacteria, viruses, fungi and microorganisms which are harmful for flora and fauna are removed by forest fire.
3. **Establishment of New Community:** Some time forest fire cause nudation in forests. It is helpful for development of new community due to ecological succession.
4. **Enrichment of Nutrients:** Due to forest fire lot of vegetation has burned and release lot of ash in forest floor. This ash is rich in nutrients, which is helpful for development of plants.
5. **Site preparation:** Pines need bare soil and full sun to regenerate and grow. Fire is an economical tool that can be used to help provide these conditions. For natural regeneration, a programme of several prescribed burns may be needed before harvest, which reduce hardwood shade and competition and provide a suitable seedbed.
6. **Wildlife habitat Improvement:** Prescribed burns for other purposes often benefit wildlife as well. Fuel reduction burns can reduce predator cover, expose hidden seeds, and increase herbs and legumes. Control burns produce fresh low browse. Prescribed burning can help in controlling the spread of unwanted species and provide chance to other species to grow as a fodder for the wild animals.
7. **Disease Control:** Prescribed burning is a very practical method of controlling many diseases. When more than 25 percent of seedlings two years old or older are infected, a late winter burn is recommended.

A fire at this time will burn away the infected needles in case of pine and leaves of deciduous forests without killing the well-protected bud.

8. **Improve Accessibility:** Removal of excess underbrush improves accessibility and visibility. This cleaning is an aid in marking and cruising timber, harvesting operations, and other management and marketing activities. Prescribed burning can help to create and maintain a diversity of vegetation types and openings or park-like stands. Such diversity can improve recreational and aesthetic values in addition to providing access for bird watchers.

Acknowledgement

Author (BJ) is thankful to department of Tarai West Forest Division, Ramnagar and Forest Department of Uttarakhand for providing valueful informations regarding this chapter.

REFERENCES

Bahuguna V.K. and Upadhyay, A. (2002): Forest fires in India: policy initiatives for community participation. *International Forestry Review* 4: 122-127.

Bahuguna, V.K. and Singh, S. (2002): Fire situation in India. Int. Forest Fire News No. 26, 23-27.

Bowman D.M.J.S., Balch J.K., Artaxo P., Bond W.J., Carlson M.J., Cochrane M.A., D'Antonio C.M., DeFries R.S., Doyle J.C., Harrison S.P., Johnston F.H., Keeley J.E., Krawchuk M.A., Kull C.A., Marston J.B., Moritz M.A., Prentice I.C., Roos C.I., Scott A.C., Swetnam T.W., van der Werf G. R., Pyne S.J. (2009): Fire in the Earth System, *Science* 324, 24:481-484.

Bowman, D.M.J.S. (1998): Tansley Review No. 101: The impact of Aboriginal landscape burning on the Australian biota. *New Phytologist* 140: 385-410.

California Turtle and Tortoise Club, Egyptian tortoise, Testudo kleinmanni, Retrieved from: http://www.tortoise.org/gallery/picklein.html, available Nov, 15th 2007.

Caribbean Conservation Corporation & Sea Turtle Survival League, How Tracking Sea Turtles by Satellite Works, Retrieved from *http://www.cccturtle.org/satellitetracking.php?* page=satintro, available Nov, 13th 2007.

Cochran, J. Sparrow Systems, Automated radio telemetry system initiative, Retrieved from:http://www.princeton.edu/~wikelski/research/physiology.htm, available Oct, 20th 2007.

Dabgar, P.J., Jain, B.K. and Dabgar, Y.B. (2012): The Study of Anthropogenic Pressure on the Biodiversity of Balaram Sanctuary (North Gujarat). *Life Sciences Leaflets* 2: 64.

Ecology Asia, Loria Forest Snake, Retrieved from: http://ecologyasia.com/verts/snakespng/loria-forest-snake.htm, available Nov, 14th 2007. 9

Evidencia, ThermAssureRF, Retrieved from: *http://www.evidencia.biz/products/* prototemp_pr.htm/ThermAssureRF.htm, available Oct, 20th 2007.

Fornaro, R., Coblentz, D., Hawkins, D., Lewis J., Noffsinger, B. (2005): NEAT-Networks for Endangered Animal Tracking, Computer Society International Design Competition 2005 Final Report. pp. 7.

Gadgil, M. and Meher-Homji, V.M. (1985): Land use and productive potential of Indian savannas. In Ecology and management of world's savannas, ed. J.C. Tothill and J.C. Mott, 107-113. Canberra: Australian Academy of Science.

Goldammer J.G. (1993): Feuer in Waldökosystemen der Tropen und Subtropen. Birkhäuser, Basel, Boston, Berlin.

Government of India (1999): Ministry of Environment & Forests, National Forestry Action Programme-India, Vol. 1, New Delhi.

Holbrook, N.M., Whitebeck, J.L. and Mooney, H.A. (1995): Drought responses of neotropical dry forest trees. In: Seasonally dry tropical forests, ed. S. H. Bullock, H. A. Mooney, and E. Medina, 243-276. Cambridge: Cambridge University Press.

http://www.encyclopedia.com

http://www.fao.org/forestry/docrep/wfcxi/PUBLI/V5/T30E/2-2.HTM.

http://www.thehindu.com/2006/02/04/stories/2006020416080100.ht

http://www.wikkipedia.com

Joshi, Bhasker. (2011): Vegetational Analysis and Resource Utilization in some forest of Tarai and Bhabhar of Kumaun Adjacent to Kashipur. *Ph.D. Thesis*, Kumaun University, Nainital. India.

Joshi, Bhasker and Kumar, P. (2011): Resource Utilization and Anthropogenic Pressure in a part of Submontane forest of Outer Himalaya, Uttarakhand. *Environment Conservation Journal* 12(1&2): 43-47.

Komarek, E.V. (1968): Lightning and lightning fires as ecological forces. In: Proc. Ann. Tall Timbers Fire Ecol. Conf. 8. Tall Timbers Research Station. Tallahassee, Florida, USA. pp. 169-197.

Lotek Corp (2002): Retrieved from http://www.lotek.com, available Nov, 13th 2007.

Murphy, P. G. and Lugo, A.E. (1986): Ecology of tropical dry forest. *Annual Review of Ecology and Sytematics* 17: 67-88.

Narendran, K. (2001): Forest Fires: Origins and Ecological Paradoxes. *Resonance* 11: 34-41.

Phillips, J. (1965): Fire as master and servant : its influence in the bioclimatic regions of Trans-Saharat Africa. In: Proc. Tall Timbers Fire Ecol. Conf. 4. Tall Timbers Research Station. Tallahassee, Florida, USA. pp. 7-109.

Pyne S.J. (1994): Nataraja: India's Cycle of Fire. *Environmental History Review* 18(3): 1-20

Reich, P.B. (1995): Phenology of tropical forests: Patterns, causes and consequences. *Canadian Journal of Botany* 73: 164-174.

Roy, P. S. Forest Fire and Degradation Assessment using Satellite Remote Sensing and Geographic Information System. Satellite Remote Sensing and GIS Applications in Agricultural Meteorology pp. 361-400.

Saha S. and Hiremath A. (2003): Anthropogenic fires in India: A tale of two forests. *Fire Ecology* 11-12: 54.

Sahin, Y.G. (2007): Animals as Mobile Biological Sensors for Forest Fire Detection. *Sensors* 7: 3084-3099.

Verma, M. (2009): Valuation of forest ecosystem services in Uttarakhand Himalayas for setting mechamisms for compensation and rewards for ecosystem services for communities conserving forests of Uttarakhand State. XIII World Forestry Congress Buenos Aires, Argentina, 18-23 Octobber 2009.

Density, Diversity and Distribution of Earthworms in Pineapple Plantation (*Ananuscomosus*) Plots of Different Ages in West Tripura, India

—Animesh Dey, *India*
—P.S. Chaudhuri, *India*

ABSTRACT

A total of 13 species of earthworms were collected from four age groups (0-5 years, 15-20 years, 30-35 years and 40-45 years) of pineapple plantations. Among them 4 species belonged to the family *Megascolecidae* [*Metaphirehoulleti* (Perrier), *Metaphireposthuma* (Vailant), *Kanchuria* sp1, *Kanchuriasumerianus*Julka], 5 species to the family *Octochaetidae* [*Eutyphoeusgigas* Stephenson, *Eutyphoeusscutarius*Michaelsen, *Eutyphoeuscomillahnus* Michaelsen, *Eutyphoeusgammiei*(Beddard), *Eutyphoeus*sp.1], 3 species to the family *Moniligastridae* [*Drawidaassamensis*Gates, *Drawidapapillifer-papillifer* Stephenson, *Drawidanepalensis* Michaelsen] and one species to the family *Glossoscolecidae* [*Pontoscolexcorethrurus* (Muller)].

Out of 13 species, only 5 [*Drawidaassamensis*, *Drawidapapilliferpapillifer*, *Pontoscolexcorethrurus*, *Metaphirehoulleti* and *Eutyphoeusgigas*] were common to all the age groups of pineapple plantations. While *M. houlleti, M. posthuma* and *P. corethrurus* are exotic, the rest of the earthworm species are endemic to the Indian subcontinent. *D. assamensis* was the dominant earthworm species in all the age groups of pineapple plantation in respect of its density, biomass and relative abundance. While 30-35 years old pineapple plantation showed highest species richness (as indicated by presence of 11 earthworm species) the other age groups of plantations had only 7-8 earthworm species.

The overall earthworm densities and biomasses increased significantly ($p<0.01$) with increase in the age of pineapple plantation. A significant decrease ($p<0.05$) in Shannon diversity index and species evenness and significant increase ($p<0.05$) in Simpson's dominance index with increase in the age of plantation was worthy of note.

Keywords: Earthworm diversity, monoculture, pineapple plantation, plantation age, species richness.

Introduction

Pineapple (*Ananascomosus*(L.)Merr.) native to the Southern Brazil and Paraguay was introduced to India by Portuguese in 1548 A.D. It is one of the most delicious tropical fruit crops of commercial importance and widely cultivated in the hill slopes of Tripura, checking soil erosion. Pineapple – the only edible fruit crop of Bromeliaceae, is herbaceous and perennial that usually flowers from February to April. Fruits are harvested during mid May to mid July. The agro-climatic conditions prevailing in Tripura is ideal for commercial production of its three common varieties viz. Queen, Kew and Mauritius. The Queen and Kew cultivars of pineapple are good sources of various kinds of sugars, organic acids, vitamins and several enzymes including bromelains and peroxidases with immunomodulatory and tumor growth inhibitory property (Ghosh*et al.* 2008).

Earthworms are useful indicators of the health of soil ecosystem due to their role in soil fertility and plant productivity (Edwards and Bohlen 1996). They account for their highest biomass among tropical soil macro-fauna (Fragoso and Lavelle 1992). Although, in the tropics, studies on diversity, ecology and the role of earthworms have been carried out in the Savanna (Lavelle 1974), pasture (Dash and Patra 1977), mixed forest (Bhadauria *et al.* 2000), social forestry (Chaudhuri *et al.* 2008, 2009a, 2009b), different agro-climatic zones including coastal plains, hilly regions and interior plains (Kale 1997; Kale and Karmegam 2010; Najar and Khan 2011) and in the Eastern Himalayas, Khasi and Garo hills (Julka and Halder 1975; Julka 1976, 1977, 1981) of the Indian sub-continent, there are scanty records on diversity and distribution of earthworms and their role in the fruit crop plantations (Tiwari *et al.* 1992) of India—an enormous reservoir of biodiversity.

Thus the aim of our present investigation is to study the community characteristics and distribution of earthworms in pineapple plantation of different age groups in order to determine to what extent these artificial (agro) ecosystems are capable of conserving earthworm diversity.

MATERIALS AND METHODS

Study Area and Sites

The studies on the earthworm communities were conducted during April 2008 – September 2011 in the pineapple plantations (queen variety) of four different age groups: 1-5 years old, 15-20 years old, 30-35 years old and 40-45 years old plantations in Tripura having a total area of 10,491 sq. km. The state is almost encircled by Bangladesh except in the north-east where it meets its neighbouring states, Assam and Mizoram. For each age groups of plantations, 3 replicates were taken. Sampling of earthworms were done at different localities viz. Bamutia, Nandannagar, Shalbagan, Nutannagar, Bishalgarh, Bishramganj, Padmanagar, Jumerdhepa and Boiragibazar of west Tripura. The distance between the studied sites varied from 20-50 km.

Pineapple cannot tolerate water logged condition and are thus usually on undulating uplands, locally called tilla. The soils of well drained pineapple plantations were acidic in nature with loamy sand, loam or sandy loam texture. *Nepheliumlitche* (Sapindaceae) was the most abundant tree common to all age groups of pineapple plantation. Besides this, *Mangiferaindica* (Anacardiaceae), *Tecnonagrandis* (Verbenaceae) and *Casiatora*(Caesalpinaceae) were found in 15-20 years plantation. *Syzygiumcumini* (Myrtaceae) and *Casiasophera* (Caesalpinaceae) were restricted to 30-35 years and 40-45 years pineapple plantations. A few juvenile plants of *Nepheliumlitche* and *Mangiferaindica* were scatteredly distributed in 1-5 years plantation.

The year is divisible into summer (March-May), Monsoon (June-September), Autumn (October-November) and Winter (December-February). The study areas experienced a tropical climate with a mean annual rainfall of 2000 mm and temperature of 25°C.

Earthworm Sampling

Earthworms were collected during summer and monsoon of 2008-2011 by conventional digging and hand sorting (25 cm × 25 cm × 25 cm) (Dey*et al.* 2012). In each of the replicated study plots (three in number) under different age groups of pineapple plantations, 100 samples were taken from a generally plain terrain of 150 × 150 m^2 along transects with random origin. Each transect passed in between the rows of pineapple plantations. The distance between the neighbouring plants and two rows of pineapple were 30 cm and 60 cm respectively. A total of 300 samples were taken from each of the age group of plantations. Earthworms were only collected from the plain plots above and below the stiff slopes due to the difficulties of sampling in the latter. In the field, earthworms were counted and weighed on a electronic balance. Results were expressed in terms of biomass (fresh weight g m^{-2}) and density (ind. m^{-2}). Using the data available, relative abundance, frequency, index of dominance (Simpson 1949), species richness index (Menhinick 1964), index of general diversity (Shannon and Weaner 1963), species evenness (Dash and Dash 2009) of earthworm communities of the studied sites were determined. Sample data of all species collected during the study period from the four age groups of pineapple plantations were pooled to create species accumulation curve for determining sampling efficiency i.e. a plot with a number of species as a function of the number of individuals sampled (Sorensen *et al.* 2002). Raw data on species richness counts during the study period from each of the age group of pineapple plantations were pooled to provide rarefaction curves (Unterseher*et al.* 2008) for comparing estimated species richness among the four age groups of plantations. Steeper curves indicate more diverse communities. To determine the abundance pattern of the earthworm species, the rank abundance curve (Ramesh *et al.* 2010) was plotted using overall relative abundance of each species in the four types of studied sites. The common species are displayed on the left and rare species on the right side of the curve plotted for the earthworm species of four types of plantations.

Soil Analysis

Soil samples were dug from 0–15 cm depth. Composite soil samples comprising of 5 sub-samples were prepared for physico-chemical analysis. Soil samples were air dried, ground with mortar and pestle and sieved with 1 mm and 2 mm sieves. Soil samples were analysed for their moisture (gravimetric wet weight method), pH (1: 2.5 dilution method), soil organic matter (Walkley and Black 1934) and hand texture method (Daji 1996). Soil temperature was recorded in-situ at each sample plot at a depth of 15 cm.

Data Analysis

Variation in physico-chemical properties of soil and some biosynecological parameters viz. earthworm biomass, density, diversity, species evenness etc. among the four studied sites were tested using one way ANOVA. The correlation between soil parameters and earthworm density and biomass were calculated as a simple correlation coefficient (r), using STATPerl software.

RESULTS

Site Characteristics

Pineapple plantations of 1-5 years and 15-20 years age groups had loamy sand and loam soil respectively, while both 30-35 years and 40-45 years age groups had sandy loam soil respectively. In all the studied sites earthworm species were mostly distributed within 15 cm soil depth. Temperature, moisture, pH, organic matter differed significantly ($p<0.01$) among the different age groups of pineapple plantations (Table 5.1).

Table 5.1 : Physico-chemical properties of soil and biosynecological parameters of 4 pineapple plantations of different age group.

Parameters	1-5 years (Mean ± SE)	15-20 years (Mean ± SE)	30-35 years (Mean ± SE)	40-45 years (Mean ± SE)	F value	P value
Soil texture	Loamy sand	Loam	Sandy loam	Sandy loam	—	—
Temperature (°C)	26.62 ± 0.07	26.14 ± 0.07	25.83 ± 0.07	25.45 ± 0.07	45.68	<0.01
Moisture (%)	16.61 ± 0.29	18.84 ± 0.43	20.09 ± 0.35	22.33 ± 0.30	47.45	<0.01
pH	5.02 ± 0.04	4.81 ± 0.33	4.63 ± 0.04	4.25 ± 0.02	92.41	<0.01
Oxidizable carbon (%)	0.79 ± 0.01	0.99 ± 0.06	1.38 ± 0.03	1.45 ± 0.03	69.35	<0.01
Organic matter (%)	1.36 ± 0.02	1.93 ± 0.08	2.38 ± 0.06	2.48 ± 0.06	77.99	<0.01
Worm density	53.73 ± 2.57	77.2 ± 2.89	158.67 ±	191.07 ±	196.32	<0.01
(ind./m^2)	15.04 ± 1.83	23.78 ± 2.06	8.17	2.24	46.85	<0.01
Worm biomass (g/m^2)	7.0	7.0	41.92 ± 0.67	45.66 ± 3.19	—	<0.01
Species richness	1.24 ± 0.04	0.92 ± 0.02	11.0	8.0	51.35	<0.01
Shannon_H	0.35 ± 0.01	0.54 ± 0.02	0.67 ± 0.06	0.61 ± 0.03	146.31	<0.01
Dominance_D	0.71 ± 0.06	0.43 ± 0.05	0.69 ± 0.02	0.72 ± 0.01	23.68	<0.01
Evenness index	0.43 ± 0.04	0.43 ± 0.05	0.28 ± 0.04	0.27 ± 0.01	2.14	<0.01
Species richness index	—	—	0.37 ± 0.05	0.31 ± 0.02	—	—

Community Composition

A total of 13 species of earthworms were collected from the four age groups of pineapple plantation. Among them 4 species belonged to the family **Megascolecidae** [*Metaphirehoulleti* (Perrier), *Metaphireposthuma* (Vailant), *Kanchuria* sp1, *Kanchuriasumerianus* Julka], 5 species to the family **Octochaetidae** [*Eutyphoeusgigas* Stephenson, *Eutyphoeusscutarius* Michaelsen, *Eutyphoeuscomillahnus* Michaelsen, *Eutyphoeusgammiei* (Beddard), *Eutyphoeus*sp.1], 3 species to the family **Moniligastridae** [*Drawidaassamensis* Gates, *Drawidapapilliferpapillifer* Stephenson, *Drawidanepalensis*Michaelsen] and one species to the family **Glossoscolecidae** [*Pontoscolexcorethrurus* (Muller)]. Out of 13 species, only 5 species [*Drawidaassamensis, Drawidapapilliferpapillifer, Pontoscolexcorethrurus, Metaphirehoulleti* and *Eutyphoeusgigas*] were common to all the age groups of pineapple plantations (Table 5.2). *M. houlleti, M. posthuma* and *P. corethrurus* are exotic, where as the reminder are endemic to the Indian subcontinent. Density, biomass and relative abundance of different earthworm species are shown in Table 5.2. In respect of their density, biomass and relative abundance *D. assamensis* was the dominant earthworm species and *M. posthuma, Kanchuria* sp1, *K. sumerianus, E. gigas, E. scutarius, E. comillahnus, E. gammiei, Eutyphoeus*sp1 and *D. nepalensis* were the rare species (Table 5.2) of pineapple plantations. *M. houlleti* and *D. papilliferpapillifer* were the only epianecic (phytogeophagus) worms found in pineapple plantations, whereas the remaining species were endogeic (geophagus). Species accumulation curve showed an initial steep slope for samples of about 400 individuals followed by a gentle rise to reach a near saturation of species richness at overall abundance between 2800 and 3200 earthworms (Fig. 5.1).

Table 5.2 : Density, biomass, relative abundance and frequency of earthworm species in different age groups of pineapple plantation

Family and earthworm species	Age group (years)	Biomass ($g\ m^{-2}$)	Density (ind. m^{-2})	Relative abundance (%)	Frequency (%)
Megascolecidae					
M. houlleti*	1-5	1.25 ± 0.06	4.53 ± 0.27	8.52 ± 0.86	20 ± 1.44
	15-20	0.58 ± 0.19	3.33 ± 0.81	4.25 ± 0.89	15 ± 2.89
	30-35	1.64 ± 0.50	3.07 ± 0.87	1.89 ± 0.43	13.33 ± 4.64
	40-45	1.04 ± 0.09	4.40 ± 0.61	2.08 ± 0.13	15.83 ± 2.21
M. posthuma*	1-5	0.17 ± 0.01	0.53 ± 0.05	0.91 ± 0.09	1.67 ± 1.07
	15-20	0.00	0.00	0.00	0.00
	30-35	0.00	0.00	0.00	0.00
	40-45	0.00	0.00	0.00	0.00
Kanchuriasp 1	1-5	0.00	0.00	0.00	0.00
	15-20	0.08 ± 0.08	0.27 ± 0.13	0.36 ± 0.18	1.67 ± 0.83
	30-35	0.62 ± 0.09	1.20 ± 0.46	0.76 ± 0.30	3.33 ± 0.83
	40-45	0.15 ± 0.08	0.67 ± 0.35	0.35 ± 0.18	3.33 ± 1.67

...(Contd.)

Family and earthworm species	Age group (years)	Biomass (g m^{-2})	Density (ind. m^{-2})	Relative abundance (%)	Frequency (%)
K. sumerianus	1-5	0.00	0.00	0.00	0.00
	15-20	0.00	0.00	0.00	0.00
	30-35	0.15 ± 0.05	0.13 ± 0.03	0.08 ± 0.01	0.83 ± 0.03
	40-45	0.00	0.00	0.00	0.00
Octochaetidae					
E. gigas	1-5	0.09 ± 0.03	0.4 ± 0.04	0.77 ± 0.07	1.67 ± 1.07
	15-20	0.89 ± 0.26	0.67 ± 0.13	0.85 ± 0.15	3.33 ± 0.83
	30-35	1.11 ± 0.01	0.27 ± 0.02	0.17 ± 0.02	1.67 ± 0.02
	40-45	0.17 ± 0.09	0.67 ± 0.35	0.35 ± 0.19	3.33 ± 1.67
E. scutarius	1-5	0.00	0.00	0.00	0.00
	15-20	0.00	0.00	0.00	0.00
	30-35	0.30 ± 0.03	0.27 ± 0.02	0.15 ± 0.01	1.67 ± 0.05
	40-45	0.00	0.00	0.00	0.00
E. comillahnus	1-5	0.00	0.00	0.00	0.00
	15-20	0.00	0.00	0.00	0.00
	30-35	0.63 ± 0.06	0.40 ± 0.04	0.26 ± 0.01	1.67 ± 0.07
	40-45	0.18 ± 0.09	0.80 ± 0.46	0.43 ± 0.25	4.17 ± 2.21
Eutyphoeus sp1	1-5	0.00	0.00	0.00	0.00
	15-20	0.11 ± 0.11	0.27 ± 0.02	0.35 ± 0.04	1.67 ± 1.06
	30-35	0.16 ± 0.01	0.27 ± 0.07	0.15 ± 0.05	1.67 ± 0.05
	40-45	0.00	0.00	0.00	0.00
E. gammiei	1-5	0.04 ± 0.03	0.13 ± 0.01	0.23 ± 0.02	0.83 ± 0.08
	15-20	0.00	0.00	0.00	0.00
	30-35	0.00	0.00	0.00	0.00
	40-45	0.00	0.00	0.00	0.00
Moniligastridae					
D. assamensis	1-5	7.34 ± 1.01	26.13 ± 1.50	48.65 ± 1.80	60 ± 2.89
	15-20	15.12 ± 0.51	54.40 ± 1.41	70.56 ± 1.61	95 ± 2.88
	30-35	28.16 ± 0.39	130.93 ± 4.96	82.63 ± 1.12	95.83 ± 3.01
	40-45	38.58 ± 2.7	161.47 ± 2.91	84.50 ± 0.65	100 ± 0.00
D. papilliferpapillifer	1-5	1.76 ± 0.26	6.27 ± 0.48	11.63 ± 0.33	30 ± 2.89
	15-20	0.85 ± 0.22	4.53 ± 0.27	6.04 ± 0.59	17.5 ± 2.5
	30-35	2.36 ± 0.48	4.93 ± 0.93	3.07 ± 0.41	21.67 ± 4.17
	40-45	0.78 ± 0.03	3.33 ± 0.35	1.75 ± 0.20	14.17 ± 2.21
D. nepalensis *	1-5	0.00	0.00	0.00	0.00
	15-20	0.00	0.00	0.00	0.00
	30-35	0.44 ± 0.22	0.67 ± 0.35	0.40 ± 0.21	2.5 ± 1.44
	40-45	0.31 ± 0.16	1.33 ± 0.71	0.70 ± 0.38	4.17 ± 2.21
Glossoscolecidae					
P. corithrurus*	1-5	4.38 ± 0.45	15.73 ± 0.87	29.30 ± 1.14	55 ± 3.82
	15-20	6.04 ± 1.04	13.73 ± 1.87	17.72 ± 1.98	59.17 ± 3.01
	30-35	6.35 ± 2.27	16.53 ± 0.93	10.44 ± 0.48	74.17 ± 7.12
	40-45	4.44 ± 0.63	18.4 ± 1.51	9.62 ± 0.72	83.33 ± 6.82

mean ± se, * exotic species

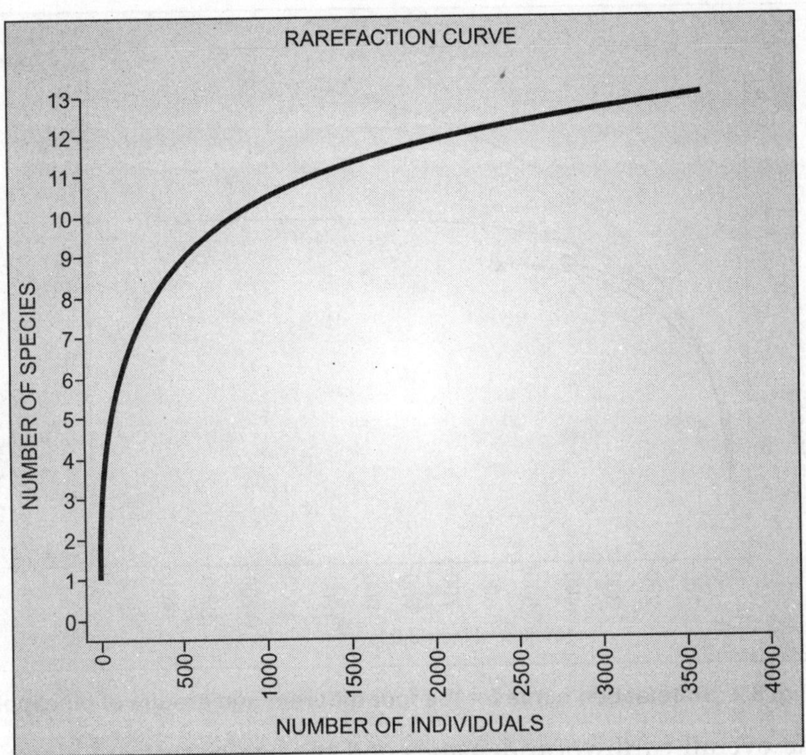

Fig. 5.1 : Species accumulation curve for earthworm species in pineapple plantations

Inter Habitat Variation in Community Characteristics

The survey showed varied number of earthworm species (species richness) found in different habitats. Seven species in 1-5 year age group (viz. *D. assamensis, P. corethrurus, D. papilliferpapillifer, E. gigas, M. houlleti, M. posthuma*and*E. gammiei*), seven in the 15-20 year age group (viz. *D. assamensis, P. corethrurus, D. papilliferpapillifer, E. gigas, M. houlleti, Eutyphoeus*sp.1 and *Kanchuria* sp1), eleven in the 30-35 years age group (viz. *D. assamensis, P. corethrurus, D. papilliferpapillifer, E. gigas, M. houlleti, Eutyphoeus*sp.1, *Kanchuria* sp1, *E. comillahnus, D. nepalensis, E. scutarius*and*K. sumerianus*) and eight species in the 40-45 year age group of plantations (viz. *D. assamensis, P. corethrurus, D. papilliferpapillifer, D. nepalensisE. gigas, M. houlleti, Kanchuria* sp1and *E. comillahnus*). The species richness index was highest in 30-35 year old plantation, while in the other age groups of plantation it varied from 7 to 8 (Table 1). Rarefaction curves from the four age groups of plantation initially showed a sharp rise (up to 5 species level) or approached towards asymptote gently in 1-5 year, 15-20 years and 30-35 years age groups of plantation (Fig. 2). Steepness of the rarefaction curve was highest in the 30-35 years old and lowest in the 15-20 years old plantation (Fig. 5.2).

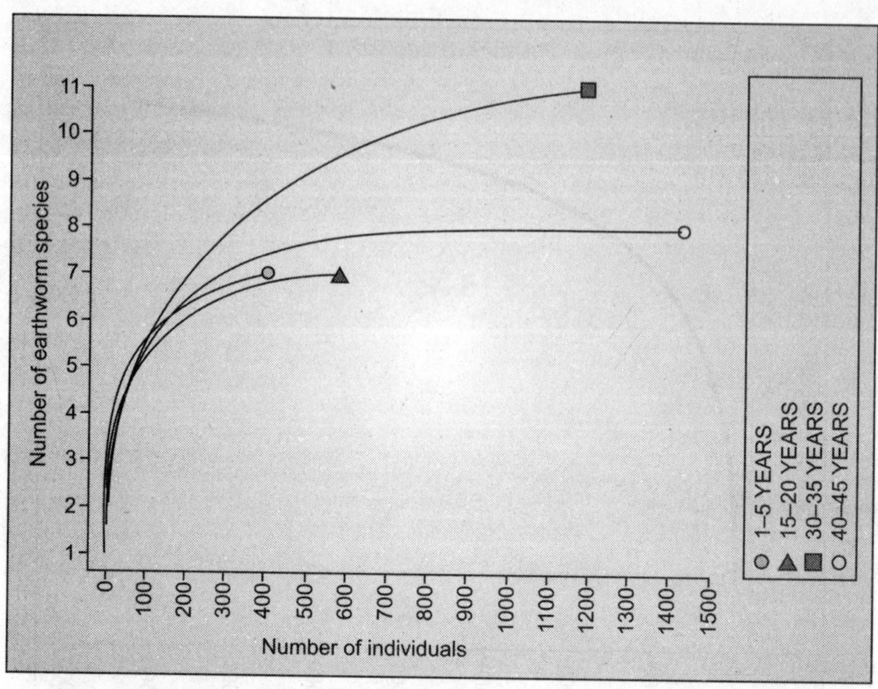

Fig. 5.2 : Rarefaction curve for the four different age groups of pineapple

The overall earthworm densities and biomasses differed significantly ($p<0.01$) among different age group of plantations. There was an increasing trend in overall biomasses and densities of earthworms with increase in plantation age (Table 5.1). Maximum earthworm density (191 ind m^{-2}) and biomass (45 g m^{-2}) were recorded in 40-45 year old pineapple plantation. The overall mean densities and biomasses of earthworms in the pineapple plantation were 120.17±32.62 ind m^{-2} and 31.6±7.30 g m^{-2} respectively. Lower population densities of some rare earthworm species viz. *E. gigas*, *E. comillahnus*, *D. nepalensis*and*E. scutarius* in young plantations and higher population densities of dominant species *D. assamensis* in aged plantations (Table 5.2 and Fig. 5.4) were noteworthy.Among the five common earthworm species of pineapple plantations, the density and biomass percent of *D. assamensis* gradually increased, whereas those of the others decreased with increase in age of the pineapple plantation (Fig. 5.3). Interestingly in 40-45 years old pineapple plantation, both densities and biomasses of *D. assamensis* accounted for more than 80 per cent densities and biomasses of all other earthworm species.

Relative abundance of *D. assamensis* increased significantly ($p<0.01$) from 48 per cent in 1-5 year age group of plantation to 70 per cent in 15-20 year old plantation and 82 per cent in the 30-35 year old plantation (Table 2). Increase in relative abundance of *D. assamensis* in 30-35 years plantation to 40-45 years old plantation was not however significant ($p>0.05$). In the rank abundance curve, *D. assamensis* occupied the highest rank followed by a few moderately abundant and large proportions of rare species of earthworms (Fig. 5.4).

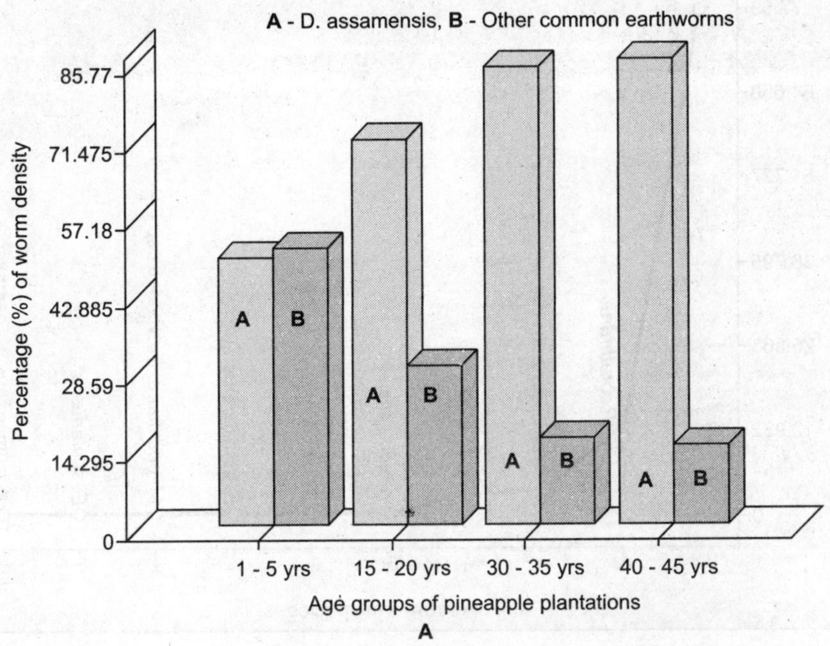

A

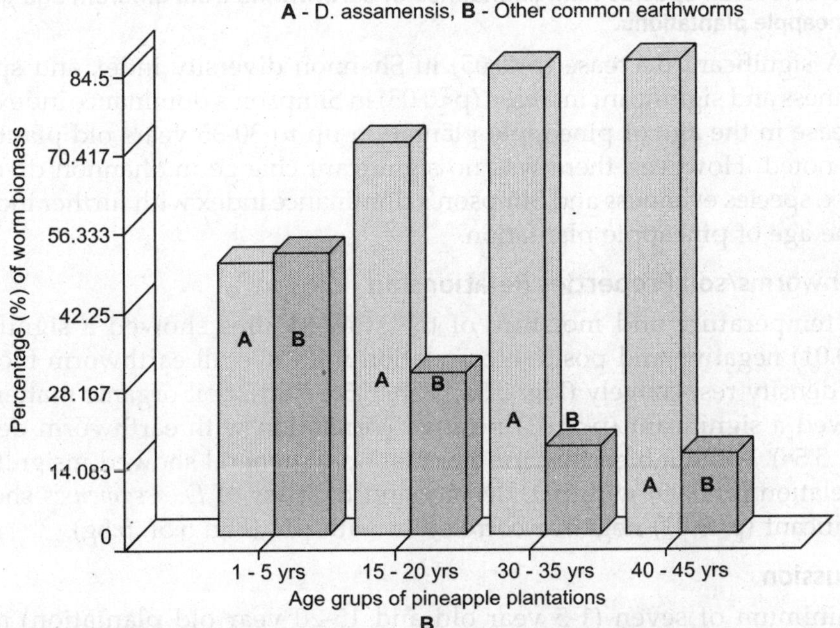

B

Fig. 5.3 (A) Density (%) and (B) biomass (%) values of *D. assamensis*and other 4 common species in different age groups of pineapple plantations compared.

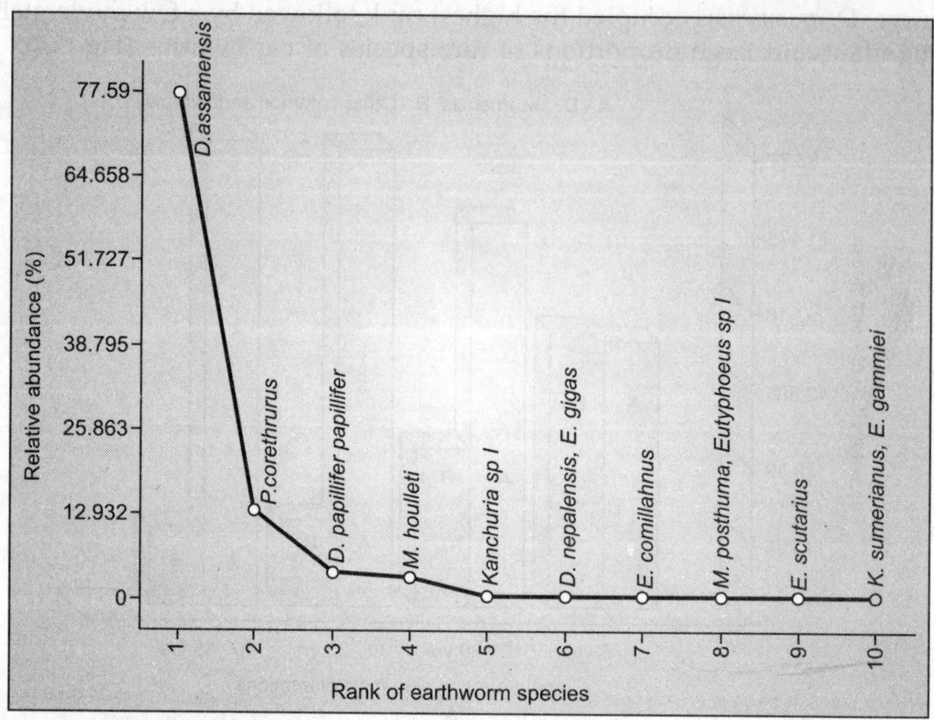

Fig. 5.4 : Overall species rank abundance of earthworms from different age groups of pineapple plantations.

A significant decrease ($p<0.05$) in Shannon diversity index and species evenness and significant increase ($p<0.05$) in Simpson's dominance index with increase in the age of pineapple plantation up to 30-35 years old plantation was noted. However, there was no significant change in Shannon diversity index, species evenness and Simpson's dominance index with further increase in the age of pineapple plantation.

Earthworms/soil Properties Relationship

Soil temperature and moisture of the studied sites showed a significant ($p<0.01$) negative and positive correlation with overall earthworm biomass and density respectively (Fig. 5.5a, 5.5b, 5.5c, 5.5d). Soil organic matter also showed a significant ($p<0.01$) positive correlation with earthworm density (Fig. 5.5e). Although earthworm population in general showed insignificant correlation ($p>0.05$) with pH, density and biomass of *D. assamensis* showed significant ($p<0.01$) negative correlation with pH (Fig. 5.5f, 5.5g).

Discussion

A minimum of seven (1-5 year old and 15-20 year old plantation) and a maximum of eleven (30-35 year old plantation) earthworm species are distributed in the studied sites among the 13 earthworm species found during

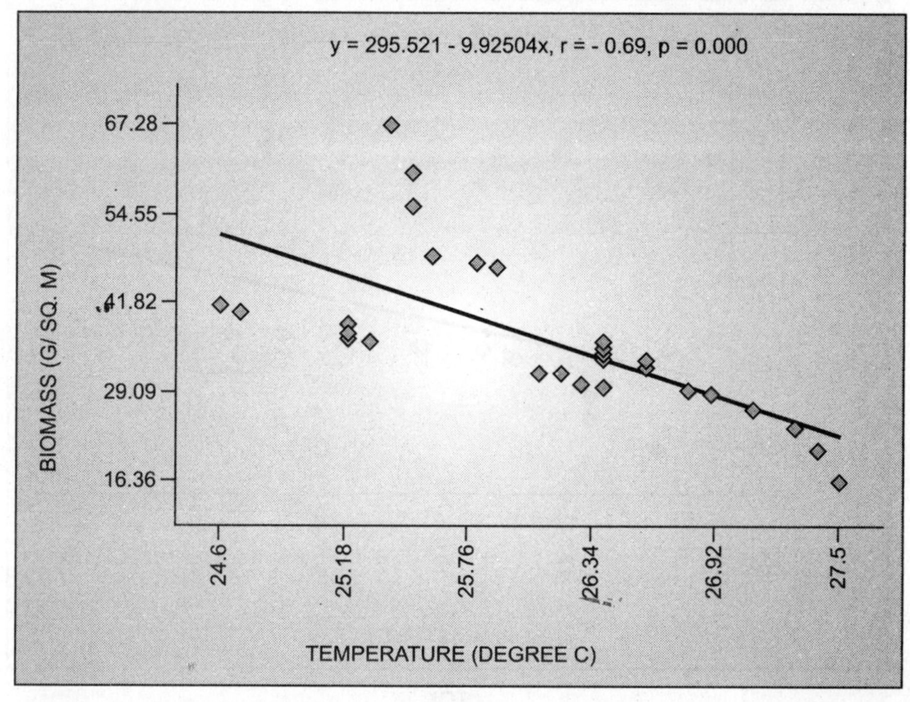
y = 295.521 - 9.92504x, r = - 0.69, p = 0.000
BIOMASS (G/ SQ. M)
67.28
54.55
41.82
29.09
16.36
24.6
25.18
25.76
26.34
26.92
27.5
TEMPERATURE (DEGREE C)

(A)

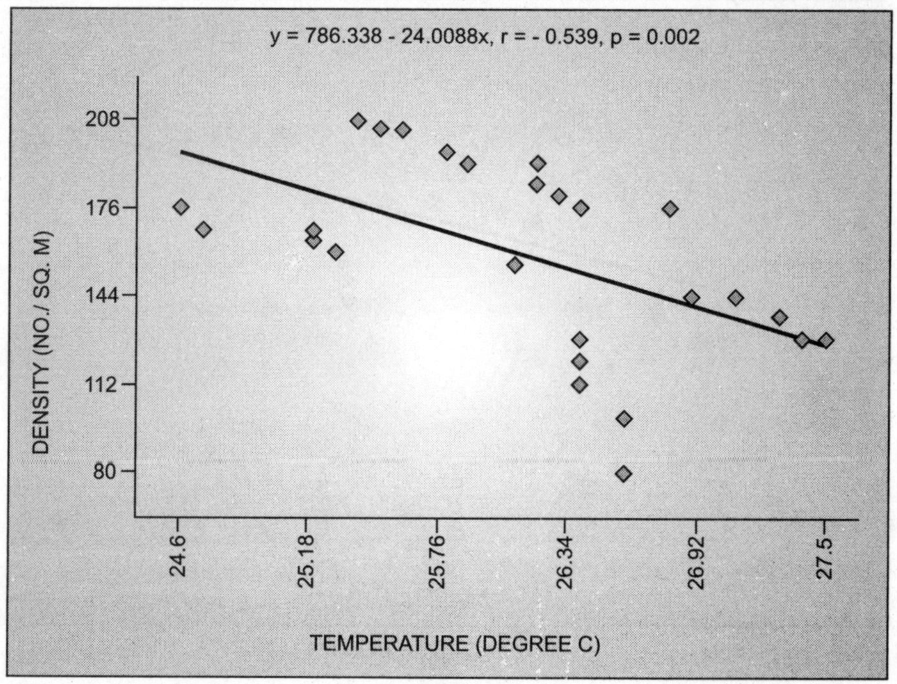
y = 786.338 - 24.0088x, r = - 0.539, p = 0.002
DENSITY (NO./ SQ. M)
208
176
144
112
80
24.6
25.18
25.76
26.34
26.92
27.5
TEMPERATURE (DEGREE C)

(B)

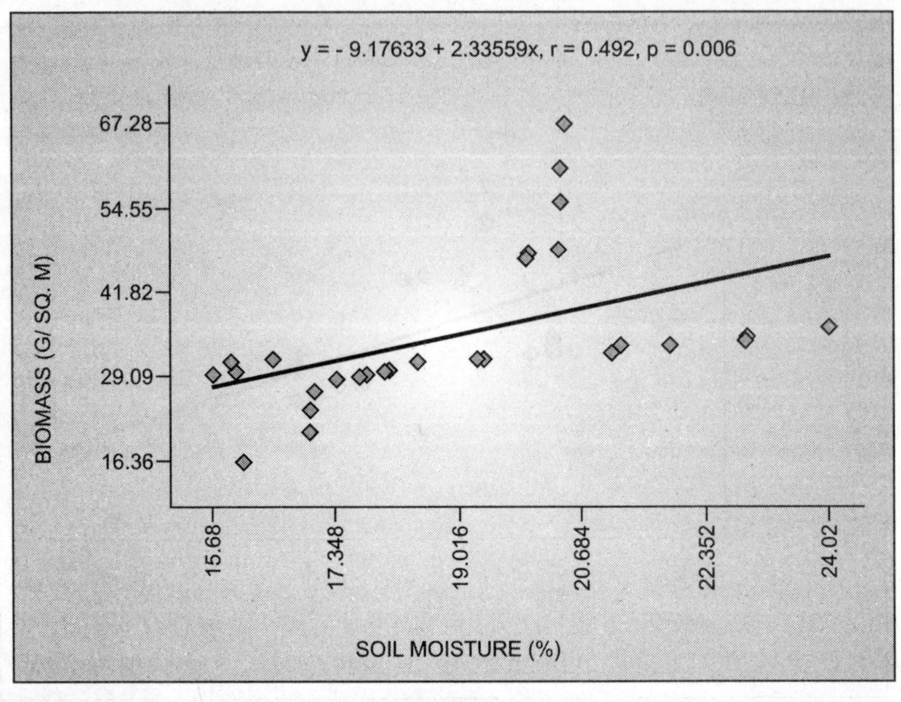
y = - 9.17633 + 2.33559x, r = 0.492, p = 0.006
67.28
54.55
41.82
29.09
16.36
BIOMASS (G/ SQ. M)
15.68
17.348
19.016
20.684
22.352
24.02
SOIL MOISTURE (%)

(C)

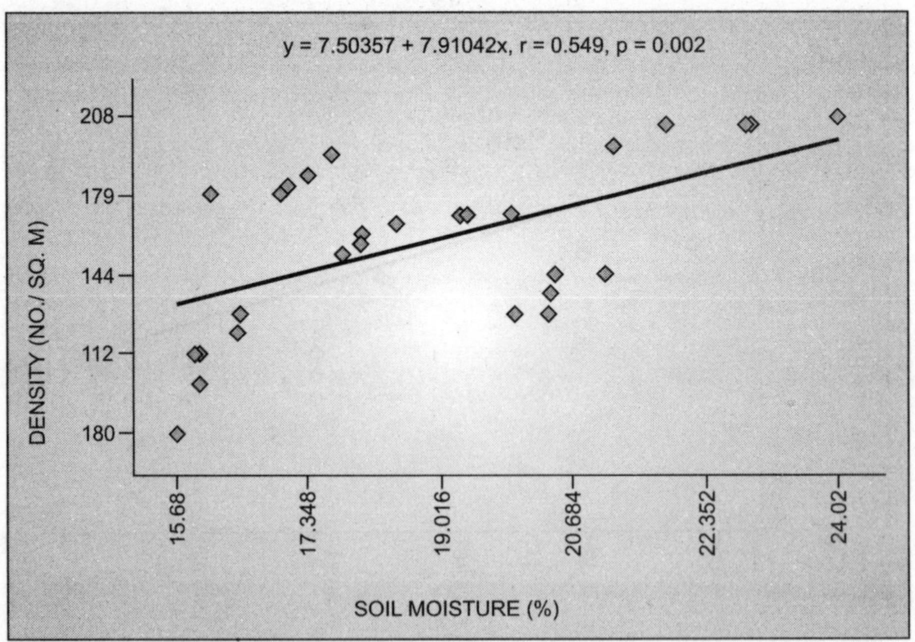
y = 7.50357 + 7.91042x, r = 0.549, p = 0.002
208
179
144
112
180
DENSITY (NO./ SQ. M)
15.68
17.348
19.016
20.684
22.352
24.02
SOIL MOISTURE (%)

(D)

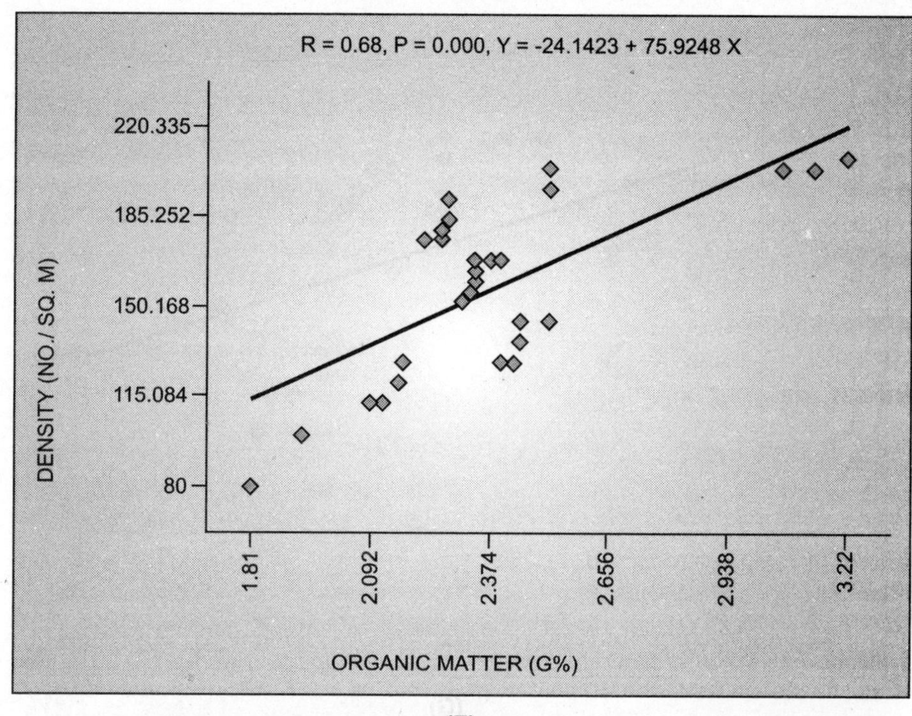
R = 0.68, P = 0.000, Y = -24.1423 + 75.9248 X
220.335
185.252
150.168
115.084
80
DENSITY (NO./ SQ. M)
1.81
2.092
2.374
2.656
2.938
3.22
ORGANIC MATTER (G%)

(E)

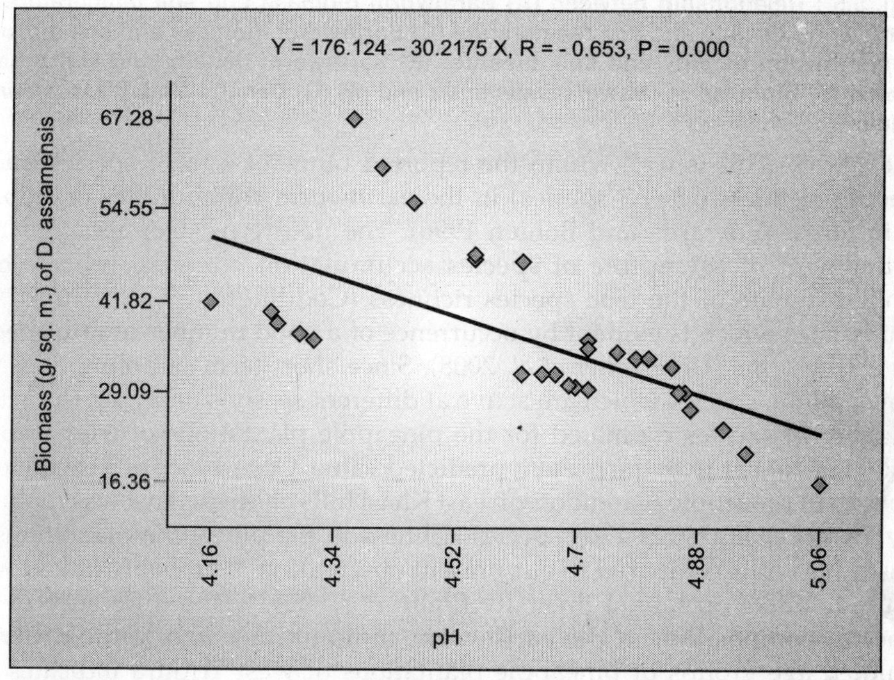
Y = 176.124 – 30.2175 X, R = - 0.653, P = 0.000
67.28
54.55
41.82
29.09
16.36
Biomass (g/ sq. m.) of D. assamensis
4.16
4.34
4.52
4.7
4.88
5.06
pH

(F)

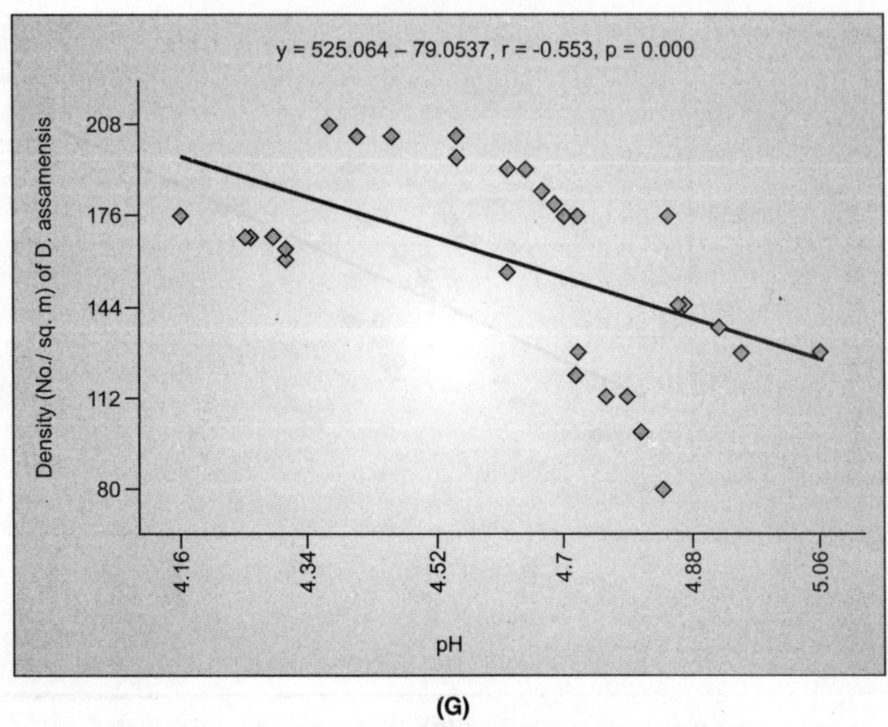

(G)

Fig. 5.5 : Relationship between (A) Earthworm biomass and soil temperature (B) Earthworm density and soil temperature (C) Earthworm biomass and soil moisture (D)Earthworm density and soil moisture (E) Earthworm density and soil organic matter (F) Biomass of *Drawidaassamensis* and pH (G) Density *Drawidaassamensis* and pH.

the survey. This is well within the reported range of 4 to 14 species (mean species richness 6.5±1.3 species) in the earthworm communities of tropical rain forest (Edwards and Bohlen 1996). The nature of steepness and non attainment of asymptote of species accumulation curve is indicative of underestimate of the true species richness (Coddington *et al.* 1996) of the study sites which is evident by occurrence of a good number of rare species of earthworms (Unterseher *et al.* 2008). Since short term sampling does not cover all the species which are active at different seasons of a year, the actual number of species estimated for the pineapple plantations of west Tripura might be higher than the present predicted value. Occurrence of 5 earthworm species in pineapple plantations in east Khasi hills of Meghalaya was reported by Tiwari *et al.* (1992). Less species richness in the pineapple plantations of east Khasi hills compared to our present observation is probably linked with altitude effect on faunal diversity (Palin *et al.* 2011). The difference in the species composition in the earthworm communities among the different studied age groups of pineapple plantations of west Tripura indicates the importance of habitat heterogeneity (β-diversity) in the diversity of earthworms as shown by Fragoso and Lavelle (1987) in the forests of Mexico. The steeper rarefaction curve observed for 30-35 years age group of plantation supports the occurrence of maximum number of species (11 species) including some less abundant or rare species of earthworm's viz. *K. sumerianus, Kanchuria* sp1, *E. scutarius, E. comillahnus, E. gigas* etc. in comparison to all other age groups of plantations. In fact, species richness estimates were highly influenced by rare species. The larger the number of rare species, the greater would be the difference between observed and the true species richness for the assemblages sampled (Dey *et al.* 2012).

A clear increasing trend in average biomasses and densities of earthworms with the increase in the age of pineapple plantation corroborates with the study of Gillot *et al.* (1995) and Chaudhuri and Bhattacharjee (2009), who also reported gradual increase in earthworm densities and biomasses in rubber plantations with increase in age of plantations. Significant increase in the earthworm density associated with the increasing age of *Eucalyptus* plantations was noticed by Mboukou-Kimbatsa and Bernhard-Reversat (2001). The mean earthworm densities (120.17±32.62 ind m^{-2}) and biomasses (31.6± 7.30 g m^{-2}) in pineapple plantations of Tripura are comparable to those of the tropical rain forest (Fragoso and Lavelle 1987; Leaky and Proctor 1987), natural forest and *Acacia* plantation (Blanchart andJulka 1997), rubber plantation (Chaudhuri *et al.* 2008). A four folds increase in densities and three folds increase in biomasses of earthworms in the 40-45 year age group plantation compared with the 1-5 year old plantation was probably due to a significant increase ($p<0.01$) in soil organic carbon and soil moisture and significant decrease ($p<0.01$) in temperature with increasing plantation age (Edwards and Bohlen 1996). Decaenas (2003) proposed that increased activity with the aging of plots was due to availability of trophic resource (i.e. dead roots, decomposed leaves) that sustained a high carrying capacity for the soil fauna.

D. assamensis was the only dominant species in all of our studied age groups of pineapple plantation in respect of its biomass, density, frequency and relative abundance. Tiwari *et al.* (1992) also reported *D. assamensis* as a dominant earthworm species in pineapple plantations in the east Khasi hills of Meghalaya. This is a reflection of a situation where one or a few factors dominate the ecology of a community (Magurann 1988). Factors contributing to the dominance in pineapple plantation may be individual plant species effect (Sarlo 2006) that favoured *D. assamensis* over other species of earthworms in addition to the competitive interaction with other earthworm species of pineapple plantations. The latter is important because density and biomass percent of *D. assamensis* increased and those of other earthworm species decreased with increase in plantation age. Recently Chaudhuri *et al.* (2008) and Nath andChaudhuri (2010) reported dominance of *P. corethrurus* and its invasion in man-made agro-ecosystems like rubber plantation. The highest rank of *D. assamensis* in the rank abundance curve reveals its survival superiority over other earthworm species of pineapple plantation.

The gradual decrease in the indices of Shannon diversity together with an increase in dominance is probably linked with the dramatic increase in the population density of dominant earthworm *D. assamensis* in pineapple plantations with increase in their age. According to Shakir and Dindal (1997), population density is negatively correlated with species diversity. These authors reiterated that the lower population density for the rare species were linked to high diversity and highest population densities for dominant species correlated with lower diversity. Thus lower population densities of rare octochaetid species such as *E. gigas, E. comillahnus* and *E. scutarius* in young plantations (1-5 year old) and higher population densities of dominant earthworm species, *D. assamensis* in aged plantations (30-35 year and 40-45 years old) were correlated with higher diversity in the former and lower diversity in the latter. In spite of higher species richness in 30-35 year old plantation (11 species) its diversity was lower compared to young plantations having a smaller number of species (7 species) due to dramatic increase in the densities of dominant species, *D. assamensis* in the former. Highest population density (191 ind m^{-2}) of dominant species, *D. assamensis* in 40-45 years old plantation attributed to its lowest diversity. According to Fragoso and Lavelle (1992) species diversity of earthworms in tropical rain forests ranges from 1.7 to 6.5. Thus species diversity of earthworms in pineapple plantation (0.61-1.24) is much less than that of tropical rain forest (3.6), natural forests in western ghat (2.5) and mixed forest (1.76) of Tripura (Fragoso and Lavelle 1992; Blanchart and Julka 1997;Chaudhuri and Nath 2011) but similar to that of monoculture rubber plantation (0.86) (Chaudhuri and Nath 2011).

Gradual decrease in the soil temperature with increase in plantation age not only improves soil moisture status but also leads to reduced oxidation of soil organic matter and favours its build up. Thus both moisture and temperature correlate strongly with earthworm density and biomass. Tiwari *et al.* (1992) and Lalthanzara *et al.* (2011) also found a significant correlation between earthworm populations and edaphic factors such as temperature and moisture. According to Edwards and Bohlen (1996) moisture and temperature of soil can act synergistically to influence earthworm population. Significantly ($p<0.01$) low density and biomass values of earthworms in the 1-5 year old plantations compared to mature plantations is probably due to high temperature and low moisture content of the soil due to direct solar radiation in the plantation floor in absence of canopy cover. Difference in canopy cover, quality and quantity of leaf litter, biotic resistance, variations in the edaphic factors etc. may have triggered changes in the abundance and community structure of earthworms among four plantation age groups. Significantly negative ($p<0.01$) correlation between pH and population density and biomass of *D. assamensis* indicates its acid tolerant characteristics. According to Spiers *et al.* (1986) acid tolerant earthworm species have a major role in the decomposer subsystem.

According to Sinha *et al.* (2003) and Dey *et al.* (2012), functional guild diversity of earthworm is lower in agro-ecosystems with homogeneous ecological niches, compared to forest ecosystems with varied ecological niches. A pineapple agro-ecosystem is largely dominated by endogeic earthworm species. Epianecic species forms a minor component of earthworm communities in pineapple plantation. Fragoso *et al.* (1999) also advocated that earthworm communities of tropical agro-ecosystem are composed mostly of endogeic species of earthworms.

In conclusion, *D. assamensis* was the dominant earthworm species of pineapple plantations in Tripura. The earthworm densities and biomasses increased significantly ($p<0.01$) with increase in the age of pineapple plantation. A significant decrease ($p<0.05$) in Shannon diversity index and species evenness and significant increase ($p<0.05$) in dominance index with increase in the age of plantation were remarkable.

Acknowledgements

The authors are thankful to Dr. Kevin R. Butt, University of Central Lancashire, UK, for linguistic improvement, Dr. R. Paliwal, Zoological Survey of India, Solan for identification of earthworm species and Head, Department of Zoology, M. B. B. College, Tripura for providing laboratory facilities.

REFERENCES

Bhadauria, T., Ramakrishnan, P.S. andSrivastava, K.N.(2000): Diversity and distribution of endemic and exotic earthworms in natural and regenerating ecosystems in the central Himalayas, India. *Soil Biology and Biochemistry*,32: 2045-2054.

Blanchart, E. andJulka, J.M.(1997): Influence of forest disturbance on earthworm (Oligocheata) communities in the Western Ghats (South india). *Soil biology and Bioiochemistry*,29: 303-306.

Chaudhuri, P.S. andBhattacharjee, S.(2009): Impact of rubber plantation on the earthworm communities in Tripura (India).In: Singh SM(Ed)Earthworm Ecology and Environment, International Book Distributing Co., Lucknow, pp. 97-110.

Chaudhuri, P.S., Nath, S. andPaliwal, R.(2008): Earthworm population of rubber plantation (*Heveabrasilensis*) in Tripura, India. *Tropical Ecology*,49(2): 225-234.

Chaudhuri, P.S., Nath, S., Bhattacharjee, S, andPaliwal, R.(2009a): Biomass, density of earthworm under rubber plantation (*Heveabrasilensis*) in Tripura, India. *The Bioscan*,4(3): 475-479.

Chaudhuri, P.S., Nath, S., Pal, T.K. andDey, S.K.(2009b): Earthworm casting activities under rubber plantations (*Heveabrasilensis*) in Tripura, India. *World Journal of Agricultural Sciences*,5(4): 515-521.

Chaudhuri, P.S. andNath, S.(2011): Community structure of earthworms under rubber plantations and mixed forests in Tripura, India.*Journal of Environmental Biology*, 32:537-541.

Coddington, J.A., Young, L.H. and Coyle, F.A.(1996): Estimating spider species richness in a southern Appalachian cove hardwood forest. *Journal of Arachnology*, 24: 111-128.

Daji, J.A.(1996):A Text Book of Soil Science, Media Promoters and Publishers Pvt. Ltd., Bombay.

Dash, M.C. and Patra, U.C.(1977): Density, biomass and energy budget of a tropical earthworm population from a grass site in Orissa, India. *Revue d"EcologieetBiologie du Sols*, 14: 461-471.

Dash, M.C. and Dash, S.P. (2009):Fundamentals of Ecology, Tata McGraw-Hill Education Pvt. Ltd., N. Delhi.

Decaens, T., Bureau, F. andMargerie, P.(2003): Earthworm communities in a wet agricultural landscape of the Seine Valley (Upper Normandy, France). *Pedobiologia*, 47:479-489.

Dey, A., Nath, S. andChaudhuri, P.S. (2012):Impact of monoculture (rubber and pineapple) practice on the community characteristics of earthworms in West Tripura (India). *NeBIO*, 3(1): 53-58.

Edwards, C.A. and Bohlen, P.J.(1996):Biology and Ecology of Earthworms. Chapman and Hall, London.

Fragoso, C. and Lavelle, P.(1987): The earthworm community of a tropical rain forest.In:Bonvicini- Pagliani AM, Omodeo P (Eds)On Earthworms,MucchiEditore, Itali, pp: 281-295.

Fragoso, C. and Lavelle, P.(1992): Earthworm communities of tropical rain forests. *Soil Biology and Biochemistry*,24: 1397-1408.

Fragoso, C., Lavelle, P., Blanchart, E., Senapati, B.K., Jimenz, J.J., Martinez, M.A., Decaens, T. andTondoh, J.(1999): Earthworm communities of tropical agro-ecosystem: origin, structure and influence of management practices. In: Lavelle P, Brusaard L, HendrixP (Eds.) Earthworm Management in Tropical Agro-ecosystems, CAB International, Wallingford, UK, pp: 27-55.

Ghosh, R., Chakraborty, J. andGhosh, D.(2008): Peroxidase activity of two cultivars (Kew and Queen) of ripe pineapple (*Ananascosmosus*) of Tripura. *Journal of Applied Bioscience*, 34(1): 106-109.

Gilot, C., Lavelle, P., Blanchart, E., Keli, J., Kouassi, P. and Guillaume, G.(1995): Biological activity of soil under rubber plantations in Cote d' Ivorie. *ActaZoologicaFennica*,196: 186 - 189.

Julka, J.M. (1976): Studies on the earthworm collected during the Daphabum expedition in Arunachal Pradesh, India. *Recordings of Zoological Survey of India*, 69: 229-239.

Julka, J.M.(1977): Contribution to the knowledge to the earthworm fauna (Oligochaete:Annelida) of Meghalaya. *Newsletter of Zoological Survey India*, 3(6): 398-400.

Julka, J.M. (1981): Taxonomic studies on the earthworms collected during the Subansiri Expedition in Arunachal Pradesh, India. *Recordings of Zoological Survey of India*, 26:1-37.

Julka, J.M. andHalder, K.R.(1975): Record of *Pheretimamalacagates* (Oligochaeta:Megascolicidae) from Andaman Islands. *Newsletter of Zoological Survey of India*,4: 65-66.

Kale, R.D.(1997): Earthworms and Soil.*Proceedings of National Academy of Science, India*, 67(B): 13-24.

Kale, R.D. andKarmegam, N.(2010):The Role of Earthworms in Tropics with Emphasis on Indian Ecosystems. *Applied and Environmental Soil Science*, 1 – 16.

Lalthanzara, H.S.,Ramanujam, N. andJha, L.K.(2011): Population dynamics of earthworms in relation to soil physico-chemical parameters in agro-forestry systems of Mizoram, India. *Journal of Environmental Biology*, 32: 599-605.

Lavelle, P.(1974): Les vers de terredelasavanne de lomto, in analyse d'un Ecosystem Tropical Humide: La Savanne de Lampo (Cote d'Ivoire). *Bull. De Liasion de chercheurs de Lamto*,5: 133-136.

Leaky, R.J.G. and Proctor, J.(1987): Invertebrates in the litter and soil at a range of altitudes on GunugSilam. *Journal of Tropical Ecology* 3:119-129.

Magurran, A.E.(1988):Ecological Diversity and its Measurement. Chapman and Hall, London.

Mboukou-Kimbatsa, L.M.C. and Bernhard-Reversat, F.(2001): Effect of exotic tree plantations on invertebrate soil macro fauna.In:Bernhard-Reversat F (Ed)Effect of Exotic Tree Plantations on Plant Diversity and Biological Soil Fertility in Congo, Svana: with special reference to Eucalyptus,Centre for International Forestry Research, Bogor, Indonesia, pp: 49-55.

Menhinick, E.F.(1964): A comparison of some species diversity indices applied to samples of field insects. *Ecology*, 45: 859-861.

Najar, I.A. and Khan, A.B.(2011): Earthworm communities of Kashmir valley, India. *Tropical Ecology*, 52(2): 151–162.

Nath, S. andChaudhuri, P.S.(2010): Human- induced biological invasions in rubber (*Heveabrasilensis*) plantations of Tripura (India) - *Pontoscolexcorethrurus* as a case study. *Asian Journal ofExperimental Biological Science*, 1(2): 360–369.

Palin, O.F., Eggleton, P., Malhi, Y., Girardin, A.J., Davila, A.R. and Parr, C.L.(2011): Termite Diversity along an Amazon-Andes Elevation Gradient, Peru. *Biotropica*, 43(1): 100-107.

Ramesh, T., Hussain, K.J., Selvanayagam, M., Satpathy, K.K. and Prasad, M.V.R.(2010): Patterns of diversity, abundance and habitat associations of butterfly communities in heterogeneous landscapes of the department of atomic energy (DAE) campus at Kalpakkam, South India. *International Journal of Biodiversity and Conservation*,2(4): 75-85.

Sarlo, M.(2006): Individual tree species effects on earthworm biomass in a tropical plantation in Panama. *Caribbean Journal of Sciences*, 42(3): 419-427.

Shakir, S.H. andDindal, D.L. (1997): Density and biomass of earthworms in forest and herbaceous micro-ecosystem in central New York, North America.*Soil Biology and Biochemistry*, 29: 275-285.

Shannon, C.E. andWeaner, W.(1963):The Mathematical theory of communication.University of Illinois Press, Urbana, pp:117.

Simpson, E.H.(1949): Measurement of diversity. *Nature* (London), 163: 688.

Sinha, B., Bhadauria, T., Ramakrishnan, P.S., Saxena, K.G. andMaikhuri, R.K. (2003): Impact of landscape modification on earthworm diversity and abundance in the Himalayan sacred landscape, Garhwal Himalaya. *Pedobiologia*, 47:357-370.

Sorensen, L.I., Coddington, J.A. andScharff, N.J.(2002):Inventorying and estimating sub-canopy spider diversity using semi-quantitative sampling methods in an Afromontane forest. Environmental Entomology, 31(2):319–330.

Spiers, G.A., Gagnon, D. andNason, G.E.(1986): Effects and importance of indigenous earthworms on decomposition and nutrients cycling in coastal forest ecosystems. *Canadian Journal of Forest Research*, 16: 983-989.

Tiwari, S.C., Tiwari, B.K. and Mishra, R.R.(1992): Relationship between seasonal populations of earthworms and abiotic factors in pineapple plantations. *Proceedings of National Academy of Science India. Sec. B (Biological Science)*,62(2): 223-226.

Unterseher, M., Schnittler, M., Dormann, C. andSickert, A.(2008): Application of species richness estimators for the assessment of fungal diversity. *FEMS Microbiology Letters*, 282: 205-213.

Walkley, A. and Black, I.A.(1934): Determination of organic carbon in soil. *Soil Sciences*,37: 29-38.

Solid Waste Disposal and Management

A Review

—**Vibha Bhardwaj, *India***
—**Neelam Garg, *India***

ABSTRACT

Solid waste management is a polite term for garbage management. As long as humans have been living in settled communities, solid waste, or garbage, has been an issue, and modern societies generate far more solid waste than early humans ever did. Daily life in industrialized nations can generate several pounds of solid waste per consumer, not only directly in the home, but indirectly in factories that manufacture goods purchased by consumers. Solid waste management is a system for handling all of this garbage; municipal waste collection is solid waste management, as are recycling programs, dumps, and incinerators.

To the great benefit of archeology, early solid waste management consisted of digging pits and throwing garbage into them. This created a record of the kinds of lives that people lived, showing things like what people ate, the materials used to make eating utensils, and other interesting glimpses into historic daily life. When human cities began to be more concentrated, however, solid waste management became a serious issue. Houses that did not have room to bury their garbage would throw it into the streets, making a stroll to the corner store an unpleasant prospect. In response, many cities started to set up municipal garbage collection, in the form of rag and bone men who would buy useful garbage from people and recycle it, or waste collection teams which would dispose of unusable garbage.

Key words: solid waste, environmental pollution, incinerators, disposal

Introduction

Environmental pollution is the major problem associated with rapid industrialization, urbanisation and rise in living standards of people. For developing countries, industrialization was must and still this activity very much demands to build self reliant and in uplifting nation's economy. However, industrialization on the other hand has also caused serious problems relating to environmental pollution. Therefore, wastes seem to be a by-product of growth. The country like India can illaffordto loses them as sheer waste. On the other hand, with increasing demand for raw materials for industrial production, the non-renewable resources are dwindling day-by-day. Therefore, efforts are to be made for controlling pollution arising out of the disposal of wastes by conversion of these unwanted wastes into utilizable raw materials for various beneficial uses. The problems relating to disposal of industrial solid waste are associated with lack of infrastructural facilities and negligence of industries to take proper safeguards. The large and medium industries located in identified (conforming) industrial areas still have some arrangements to dispose solid waste. However, the problem persists with small scale industries. In number of cities and towns, small scale industries find it easy to dispose waste here and there

and it makes difficult for local bodies to collect such waste though it is not their responsibility. In some cities, industrial, residential and commercial areas are mixed and thus all waste gets intermingled. Therefore, it becomes necessary that the local bodies along with State Pollution Control Board (SPCB) work out requisite strategy for organising proper collection and disposal of industrial solid waste. Management of Industrial Solid Waste (ISW) is not the responsibility of local bodies. Industries generating solid waste have to manage such waste by themselves and are required to seek authorisations from respective State Pollution Control Boards (SPCBs) under relevant rules. However, through joint efforts of SPCBs, local bodies and the industries, a mechanism could be evolved for better management.

The Problems

Assessment of industrial solid waste management problem greatly varies depending on the nature of the industry, their location and mode of disposal of waste. Further, for arriving at an appropriate solution for better management of industrial solid waste, assessment of nature of waste generated is also essential. Industries are required to collect and dispose of their waste at *specific disposal sites* and such collection, treatment and disposal is required to be monitored by the concerned State Pollution Control Board (SPCB) or Pollution Control Committee (PCC) in Union Territory. The following problems are generally encountered in cities and towns while dealing with industrial solid waste:

- There are no specific disposal sites where industries can dispose their waste;
- Mostly, industries generating solid waste in city and town limits are of small scale nature and even do not seek consents of SPCBs/PCCs;
- Industries are located in non-conforming areas and as a result they cause water and air pollution problems besides disposing solid waste;

- Industrial estates located in city limits do not have adequate facilities so that industries can organise their collection, treatment and disposal of liquid and solid waste;
- There is no regular interaction between urban local bodies and SPCBs/ PCCs to deal such issues relating to treatment and disposal of waste and issuance of licenses in non-conforming areas.

Industrial Solid Waste

The major generators of industrial solid wastes are the thermal power plants producing coal ash, the integrated Iron and Steel mills producing blast furnace slag and steel melting slag, non-ferrous industries like aluminum, zinc and copper producing red mud and tailings, sugar industries generating press mud, pulp and paper industries producing lime and fertilizer and allied industries producing gypsum.

DESCRIPTION OF IMPORTANT INDUSTRIAL SOLID WASTE

Coal Ash

In general, a 1,000 MW station using coal of 3,500 kilo calories per kg and ash content in the range of 40-50 per cent would need about 500 hectares for disposal of fly ash for about 30 years' operation. It is, therefore, necessary that fly ash should be utilized wherever possible to minimize environmental degradation. The thermal power plant should take into account the capital and Operation/maintenance cost of fly ash disposal system as well as the associated environmental protection cost, vis-a-vis dry system of collection and its utilisation by the thermal power plant or other industry, in evaluating the feasibility of such system. The research and development carried out in India for utilisation of fly ash for making building materials has proved that fly ash can be successfully utilized for production of bricks, cement and other building materials. Indigenous technologies for construction of building materials utilizing fly ash are available and are being practiced in a few industries. However, large scale utilisation is yet to take off. Even if the full potential of fly ash utilisation through manufacture of fly ash bricks and blocks is explored, the quantity of fly ash produced by the thermal power plants is so huge that major portion of it will still remain unutilized. Hence, there is a need to evolve strategies and plans for safe and environmentally sound method of disposal.

Integrated Iron & Steel Plant Slag

The Blast Furnace (BF) and Steel Melting Shop (SMS) slags in integrated iron and steel plants are at present dumped in the surrounding areas of the steel plants making hillocks encroaching on the agricultural land. Although, the BF slag has potential for conversion into granulated slag, which is a useful raw material in cement manufacturing, it is yet to be practiced in a big way. Even the use of slag as road subgrade or land-filling is also very limited.

Phosphogypsum

Phosphogypsum is the waste generated from the phosphoric acid, ammonium phospate and hydrofluoric acid plants. This is very useful as a building material. At present very little attention has been paid to its utilisation in making cement, gypsum board, partition panel, ceiling tiles, artificial marble, fiber boards etc.

Red Mud

Red mud as solid waste is generated in non-ferrous metal extraction industries like aluminum and copper. The red mud at present is disposed in tailing ponds for settling, which more often than not finds its course into the rivers, especially during monsoon. However, red mud has recently been successfully tried and a plant has been set up in the country for making corrugated sheets. Demand for such sheet should be popularised and encouraged for use. This may replace asbestos which is imported and also banned in developed countries for its hazardous effect. Attempts are also made to manufacture polymer and natural fibres composite panel doors from red mud.

Lime Mud

Lime sludge, also known as lime mud, is generated in pulp & paper mills which is not recovered for reclamation of calcium oxide for use except in the large mills. The lime mud disposal by dumping into low-lying areas or into water courses directly or as run-off during monsoon is not only creating serious pollution problem but also wasting the valuable non- renewable resources. The reasons for not reclaiming the calcium oxide in the sludge after recalcination are that it contains high amount of silica. Although a few technologies have been developed to desilicate black liquor before burning, none of the mills in the country are adopting desilication technology.

Waste Sludge and Residues

Treatment of industrial wastes/effluents results in generation of waste sludge/residues which, if not properly disposed, may cause ground and surface water pollution.

Potential Reuse of Solid Wastes

Research and Development (R&D) studies conducted by the R&D Institutions like Central Building Research Institute, Roorkee (CBRI) and the National Council for Building Research, Ballabgarh (NCBR) reveal that the aforesaid solid wastes has a very good potential to be utilised in the manufacture of various building materials.

WASTE MANAGEMENT APPROACH

A two-tier approach should be thought of for waste management, e.g., (*a*) prevention & (*b*) control of environmental pollution. Prevention aims at minimisation of industrial wastes at source, while the latter stresses on treatment and disposal of wastes.

Prevention- A Waste Minimisation Approach

Reduction and recycling of wastes are inevitably site/plant specific. Generally, waste minimisation techniques can be grouped into four major categories which are applicable for hazardous as well as non-hazardous wastes. These groups are as follows :

Inventory Management and Improved Operations

- Inventorisation and tracing of all raw materials;
- Purchasing of fewer toxic and more non-toxic production materials;
- Implementation of employees' training and management feedback; and
- Improving material receiving, storage, and handling practices.

Modification of Equipment

- Installation of equipment that produce minimal or no wastes;
- Modification of equipment to enhance recovery or recycling options;
- Redesigning of equipment or production lines to produce less waste;
- Improving operating efficiency of equipment; and
- Maintaining strict preventive maintenance programme.

Production Process Changes

- Substitution of non-hazardous for hazardous raw materials ;
- Segregation of wastes by type for recovery ;
- Elimination of sources of leaks and spills ;
- Separation of hazardous from non-hazardous wastes ;
- Redesigning or reformulation for products to be less hazardous; and
- Optimizations of reactions and raw material use.

Recycling and Reuse

- Installation of closed-loop systems;
- Recycling off site for use; and
- Exchange of wastes.

Waste minimization at source may be achieved within the industry through application of various approaches described above.

Waste Management at Source

A specific example worth-mentioning in this context is removal of fly ash through coal beneficiation process at the mine head in view of high ash content. It is evident that the larger the volume of waste and the longer the distance oftransportation of raw material (coal), the bigger will be the economic benefit in favour of coal beneficiation instead of carrying the filthy fly ash. However, benefitcost analyses have to be made before taking appropriate decision.

It is possible to cut down waste generation at source by simple, inexpensive measures modifying production processes, through changes in raw materials/product design and by employing recovery/recycling and reuse techniques.

To avoid treatment through utilisation of waste, it is important from the environmental pollution view point as well as for the benefit of entrepreneurs to recycle and reuse the wastes generated by adoption of certain process change or by use of low/no-waste generation technology.

Waste minimisation can be practised at various places in the industrial processes. Waste minimisation requires careful planning, creative problem evolving, changing in attitude, some times capital investment, and most important a real commitment. More often than not, investment on waste minimisation and recovery pays off tangibly within a short time.

CURRENT PRACTICE OF INDUSTRIAL SOLID WASTE MANAGEMENT

Collection and Transport of Wastes

Manual handling of industrial waste is the usual practice in developing countries; there are very few mechanical aids for waste management. Wastes are shovelled by hand into storage containers and loaded manually into lorries. The people undertaking salvaging do so mainly by hand, picking out useful items, usually not even wearing gloves. Although there may not be a health risk in handling clean waste paper, people handling or salvaging waste without protective clothing are at risk when waste is mixed with chemicals. Apart from the likelihood of cuts caused by broken glass or sharp metals, sorting through waste contaminated with hazardous chemical materials could cause skin burns, excessive lacrimation, or even loss of consciousness; chronic hazards include respiratory problems from dust inhalation, and potential carcinogenicity from toxic chemicals present in discarded containers or surface deposits in other waste. Personnel handling waste from tanneries or hide processors may also be exposed to such diseases as anthrax. Necessary precautions will reduce and minimise hazards associated with manual handling of industrial wastes. Personnel handling hazardous wastes should wear appropriate protective clothing. Mechanical methods for handling waste should be adopted wherever possible, and people should be educated about the dangers of manual handling ofhazardous waste.

Storage & Transportation

The storage of industrial solid waste is often one of the most neglected areas of operation of a firm. Very little attention is paid to proper storage and heaps of mixed waste piled against a wall or on open ground are a common sight in many factories. Concrete bays or disused drums are also often used for storage. Whereas the sludges originating from holding tanks or interceptors do not present storage problems as no separate sludge storage is required, because the sludge is retained in the tank until sufficient quantities are collected. Waste is rarely covered, protected from vermin or pretreated in any manner. There are no restrictions on access and employees are often encouraged to sort out through such wastes and take away any useful material or articles they find. Waste is regarded as an unwanted product by firms and very often no senior person is assigned for its control.

Transportation of industrial waste in metropolitan areas of developing countries is generally not by purpose-built vehicles such as skip-carrying lorries, but by open trucks. The wastes are not covered during transportation. It is typical for a firm not to have any standing arrangements with one contractor, but to allow collection by whoever is the contractor quoting lowest rates. It is rare for special arrangements to be made for hazardous wastes; they are usually collected together with the other wastes. Contractors who carry hazardous waste do not need to be licensed, and consequently, there is little control over either the types of firms engaged in carrying hazardous waste or the vehicles used. Drivers are not given a list of precautions to be taken; there is no manifest or labeling system of wastes during transport. Fly-tipping is often prevalent and wastes are often taken to disposal sites inappropriate for the type of waste concerned.

Disposal of Industrial Solid Waste

Industrial waste, whilst presenting the same disposal problems as domestic waste, also contains hazardous waste, thereby exacerbating the difficulties of disposal. Fortunately, the types of industrial wastes generated in a municipal area of a developing country are such that there are not usually large quantities of particularly hazardous wastes for disposal. In the past there has been little control over the disposal of industrial wastes; indeed, it has only been during the last decade that even developed countries have brought in legislation to curb the uncontrolled and environmentally unacceptable practices that were widespread. Without such legislation disposal is almost always by uncontrolled landfill at sites which often pose a threat of water pollution due to leachates.

HEALTH CONSEQUENCES OF POOR INDUSTRIAL WASTE DISPOSAL

The solid waste generated from industrial sources contains a large number of chemicals, some of which are toxic. The waste is considered toxic, if the concentration of the ingredients exceeds a specified value. Although the levels of some ingredients may occasionally exceed the permissible level, the waste as such is considered to be toxic only if the average value of ingredients exceeds the toxicity level. Various criteria and tests have been devised by different agencies to determine the toxicity of a given substance. It is necessary to know the properties of the waste so as to assess whether its uncontrolled release to the environment would lead to toxic effects on humans or other living organism in ecosystem. This evaluation is carried out using criteria such as toxicity, phytotoxicity, genetic activity and bio-concentration. The potential toxic effects also depend on quantity of the toxic constituents. Substances are classified as hazardous or otherwise depending on the dose, exposure, and duration of exposure. For a chemical to affect

human health it must come in contact with or enter the human body. There are several ways in which this can happen.

Skin contact: Chemicals that cause dermatitis usually do so through direct contact with skin. Some chemicals like corrosive acids can damage the skin by a single contact while others, like organic solvent, may cause damage by repeated exposure.

Inhalation: Inhalation is the most common source of workplace exposure to chemicals and the most difficult to control. Air pollutants can directly damage respiratory tract or gets absorbed through lung and cause system/ systemic effects. An adult male will breathe about 10 cubic meters of air during a normal working day.

Ingestion: Ground water and sub soil water contamination from leachates from refuse dumps and poorly managed landfill sites can result in ingestion of toxic chemicals by population groups who live far away from the factory sites and decades after the garbage has been dumped.

There are very few studies conducted in India on specific health problems resulting from accidental exposure to toxic industrial solid waste. There had been reports that sacks, cardboard cartons and paper envelopes contaminated with chemicals packed in them were burnt and the irritating fumes from these caused respiratory problems. There had also been reports of skin or respiratory irritation following exposure to corrosives chemicals. There has been no efforts to systematically investigate and obtain reliable epidemiological data on health consequences of exposure to hazardous industrial wastes in different States. Wastes from slaughter house is potentially infectious. All precautions to ensure that potential pathogens to not gain a foot hold in the workers in the slaughter house and in the general population, have to be taken during collection, storage and disposal of the slaughter house waste. Wastes from non hazardous industries can at times produce health problems, not only among the workers and handlers of waste, but also among general population. One example of this category is the cotton dust. Cotton waste are generally non hazardous; however they may, in susceptible individuals provoke respiratory allergic reactions; allergy may be due to inhalation of dust containing cotton wastes or fungus or other contaminants in the waste dust.

COLLECTION, STORAGE TREATMENT & DISPOSAL OF WASTES

Waste Segregation

Many wastes are mixtures of hazardous and non-hazardous wastes. Much of their contents may even be water. By segregating key toxic constituents, isolating liquid fraction, keeping hazardous streams away from non-hazardous wastes, generator can save substantial amounts of money on disposal or find new opportunities for recycling and reuse of wastes. The Ministry of Environment, Government of India, had identified toxicity of different chemicals, through the 'Manufacture, Storage and Import of Hazardous Chemicals Rules, 1989' in exercise of power conferred by Section 6, 8 and 25 of Environment Protection (E.P). Act, 1986, and had notified mandatory requirements for its management. In India quantum of generation of wastes (solid/liquid and hazardous/non-hazardous) for different industry has not been detailed, which is necessary for wastes exchange system or for adopting treatment/ disposal alternatives for different wastes segregated.

Collection, Storage and Transport

The unsatisfactory state of storage of hazardous wastes can be remedied to a large degree by such low-cost measures as restricting access, fencing off the storage area to minimise any wind-blown nuisance, providing separate covered storage for putrifiable of hazardous wastes, and ensuring regular and frequent collection. There are certain measures a municipal authority can take to control the transportation of industrial wastes, even if it does not want to become actually involved itself. For instance, contractors should be licensed after ensuring that they are technically competent and environmentally aware and should be allowed to handle industrial wastes. Labeling and coding of hazardous waste load can be made mandatory so that in the event of an accident, the emergency services know how to handle a spillage. Municipal authorities can be given the responsibility to monitor the contractors to minimise cases of fly-tipping and ensure that industrial wastes are disposed at the appropriate sites. If a municipal authority can also collect industrial waste; industries must pay the charge which will be based on the quantity and nature of the waste. This might minimise the quantity of waste produced by industry and at the same time the programme will become financially viable and self sustaining. The principle 'the polluter pays' should be adhered to in all such cases.

Combined Treatment Facilities

Small-scale industries, which contribute about more than half of the total production, also generate huge quantity of wastes. The small-scale industries are not in a position to treat their solid wastes or liquid effluent because of space, technical know-how and financial constraints. It is, therefore, deemed that in a cluster of small-scale industries the different wastes are characterized, identified, quantified and stored for treatment through a combination of recycling, recovery and reuse of resources such as, raw material, bio-gas, steam and manure, besides providing an efficient service facility, to make the system less expensive. The combined effluent treatment plants (CETP) are to be operated by the local bodies, where the cost of construction, operation and maintenance need to be shared by individual industries depending upon the quality and quantity of wastes generated. However, such common treatment facility may require pre-treatment at individual industry to the extent specified by the State Pollution Control Board. With regard to availability of wastes along with their identification, quantum of waste generated should also be ascertained so that technology development/adoption can be considered on economic grounds for a small-scale or organised sector of industry. If economics justify movement of wastes over longer distances for a centralised plant, specific subsidies for storage, collection and transportation could be considered. CETPs are being successfully operated in Gujarat and Andhra Pradesh and such facilities should be promoted in other States. Small scale industries having waste characteristics similar to those of near by large industry having waste treatment facilities can take help in treating their wastes on payment basis.

Disposal Methods

Depending upon the characteristics of the wastes, different types of disposal methods can be used for hazardous and non-hazardous industrial wastes. The most predominant and widely practised methods for wastes disposal are : (*a*) Landfill, (*b*) Incineration and (*c*) Composting.

For thousands of years, man has disposed the waste products in a variety of ways, the disposal method might reflect convenience, expedience, expense, or best available technology. There were no major ecological or health hazards associated with these practices until the last century. Explosive increase in the amount of chemical waste produced and the indiscriminate dumping of hazardous industrial waste in the last few decades has created health and ecological crisis in many areas of the world. In many instances, leachate from the wastes dumped by one generation haunts the later generation in the form of ground water and subsoil water contamination. The recent discovery of volatile organic chemicals from landfills and industrial disposal ponds is disturbing because many of these chemicals are known or suspected carcinogens and are not removed easily by natural geochemical processes. The risk of the contamination of groundwater supplies due to leachates from landfills depends on several factors; toxicity and volume of the contaminant generated at each site, the nature of the geologic medium underlying the site, and the hydrologic conditions dominant in the area. In the past, the least expensive and most widely used waste management option for both municipal and industrial waste has been the sanitary landfill, where wastes are compacted and covered with earth. In any geographic area other than arid zones, the fill is subjected to percolating rainwater or snowmelt which eventually flows out from the bottom of the landfill site and moves into the local groundwater system. Leachate is a liquid that is formed as infiltrating water migrates through the waste material extracting water-soluble compounds and particulate matter. The mass of leachate is directly related to precipitation, assuming the waste lies above the water table. Much of the annual precipitation, including snowmelt is removed by surface run off and evaporation; it is only the remainder that is available to form leachate. Since the landfill covers to a large extent and controls leachate generation, it is exceedingly important that the cover be properly designed, maintained and monitored in order to minimise leachate production. Fortunately, many substances are removed from the leachate as it filters through the unsaturated zones, but leachate may pollute groundwater and even streams. These leachates, can contain large amount of inorganic and organic contaminants. At some sites, the leachate is collected and treated. But even in the best engineered sites, some leachate escapes into the groundwater system because no permanent engineering solution has been found to isolate the leachate completely from the groundwater. It is now recognised that the interaction between leachate and soil are actually very complex and depend both on the nature of soil and on the leachate. When leachate percolates through solid wastes that are undergoing decomposition, both biological materials and chemical constituents are picked up. Recent research in the United Kingdom (U.K) has, however, shown that chemical and biological phenomena in landfill such as microbiological process; neutralisation; precipitation and complexion; oxidation and reduction; volatilisation; adsorption reduce the quantity and quality of polluting leachate from landfill site and achieve some degree of onsite treatment or immobilisation. In spite of all these, the leachate often pose severe disposal problem at a landfill site. Two of the most economic but efficacious purification methods are spraying over grassland or percolation through an aerobic bed of sand or gravel. In general, it has been found that the quantity of leachate is a direct function of the amount of external water entering the landfill. In fact, if a landfill is constructed properly, the production of measurable quantities of leachate can be eliminated. When sewage sludge is to be added to the solid wastes to increase the amount of methane produced, leachate control facilities must be provided. In some cases leachate treatment facilities may also be required. The pollution of static water ditches, rivers or the sea can occur when a sanitary landfill adjoins a body of water. The normal source of the leachate causing this pollution is rain falling on the surface of the fill, percolating through it, and passing over an impermeable base to water at a lower level. The quantity of leachate can be substantially increased when upland water drains across the site of the landfill, but the worst case is when a stream crosses the site. The solutions to these problems lie in appropriate site engineering such as :

(*i*) diversion or culverting of all water courses which flow across the site,

(*ii*) diversion of upland water by means of drainage ditches along appropriate contours, (*iii*) containment of leachate arising from precipitation by the construction of an impermeable barrier where necessary, such as a clay embankment adjoining a river,

(*iv*) grading the final level of the site so that part of precipitation is drained acrosssurface, reducing percolation below the level needed to produce a leachate.

Works of this nature will obviously add to the cost of a sanitary landfill project. However, when capital expenditure is spread over the life of the project, the cost/ton of waste disposed might be less than for any alternative method of disposal. Furthermore, some of these forms of expenditure, such as culverts or river walls, represent capital assets of continuing value when the reclaimed land is handed over for its final use, perhaps for agriculture or recreation. Incineration of hazardous industrial waste has been advocated in developed countries. Guidelines for safe incineration of hazardous chemical waste have been drawn up by United States Environmental Protection Agency. Incineration of hazardous waste is a process requiring sophisticated expensive incinerators and a high degree of technological expertise for satisfactory operation. The capital cost of incinerator is high, especially if it is intended for hazardous wastes and gas scrubbing equipment is required. Some wastes such as oils and organic solvents can be readily treated by incineration. If financial constraints come in the way of purchasing sophisticated incinerators then the utilisation of open pit incinerator under careful technical supervision can be considered as an option.

Landfill

The owner or operator of a facility must follow the design and operating criteria stipulated by the regulatory agencies. However, depending upon the characteristics of the waste, the landfill system with leachate collection system has to be designed with necessary facility for ground water quality monitoring.

Landfill means a disposal facility or a part of a facility where hazardous waste is placed in or on land and is not a land treatment facility, a surface impoundment or an injection well. Landfill cell means a discrete volume of a hazardous waste landfill that uses a liner to provide isolation of wastes from adjacent cells or wastes. Examples of landfill cells are trenches and pits.

Incineration

Depending upon the categories of waste and its potential hazards, following incineration methods are adopted :

(*i*) Destruction of hazardous waste by thermal process using incinerator or any other method; and

(*ii*) Burning of hazardous waste in boiler or in industrial furnace in order to destroy them and/or for any recycling purpose and/or energy source.

The first category of incinerator requires special attention. In India there are very few incinerators installed on a large scale. It is important to have a central incinerator facility in the remote areas of different regions for incinerating hazardous wastes which may be operated by a corporate body. However, before taking a step in burning hazardous wastes through incinerator it is essential to stipulate standards to be achieved after incinerating such material. The hazardous wastes in the region to be treated can be centrally collected and transported to the facilities. In this process of central facility of treatment, the polluter has to pay for treatment facility depending on the quantity and quality of wastes generated. In the second category of incineration, there are a number of cement industries and thermal power plants where the wastes can be burnt after considering the nature and quantity of wastes. However, in this case it is to be seen that the gaseous emission through stack does not affect the ambient air quality adversely. The operating agency will find that the incineration is a costly alternative, but sometimes it is the only alternative. It reduces the volume of waste requiring the landfill capacity, is suitable for most clinical, commercial and house-hold wastes, is the only suitable disposal option for certain waste (practical or legal point of view) and can recover heat system. Incinerator means any enclosed device using controlled flame combustion. In designing an incinerator the operating agency should take into consideration the thermal feed rate, waste feed rate, organic chlorine feed rate (where relevant), minimum combustion gas temperature, minimum combustion gas residence time, primary and secondary combustion units, removal of Hydrochloric acid (HCl), Suspended Particulate Matter (SPM) and other air pollutants, minimum oxygen concentration in secondary chamber, controlling fugitive emissions (by keeping combustion zone totally sealed or by maintaining the combustion zone pressure negative), stack height, eventuality of alternative fuel, eventuality of change in waste containing Principal Organic Hazardous Constituent (POHC). The operating agency should convey these criteria to the SPCBs for any comments and if there is any change subsequently in the gadget or geometry, the same too must be informed or authorisation got so amended. This will enable them to take a new trial burn if necessary. Incineration is not an open burning. Open burning means the combustion of any material without the following characteristics :

1. Control of combustion air to maintain adequate temperature for efficient combustion.
2. Containment of the combustion reaction in an enclosed device to provide sufficient residence time and mixing for complete combustion Control of emission of the gaseous combustion products as per regulations.

Open burning on land is not a method for disposal as it does not have a status of either incinerator or landfill. The operating agency should assure the SPCBs that they will undertake only controlled method and it is open for their inspection any time of combustion, emissions, attendant units (like pumps valves, conveyors) or housekeeping. In general, industrial incinerators comprise a storage pit, fuel tanks, a furnace (generally of a rotary kiln type), a heat recovery boiler, off gas purification [possibly a scrubbing water treatment unit, and even Electro Static Precipitator (ESP) in good installations], an induced draft (ID) fan, a reheating unit (if necessary) and a stack (incidentally, even co-generation is possible). In a reported experience of Bayer, AG, Germany, the plant temperature in rotary kiln is maintained at 1000-12000C, with oxygen concentration kept at 11% by volume, and detention of 4 seconds. The detention is 18 seconds in after burner chamber. In the waste heat recovery boiler, the temperature comes down to 320- 3500C, the HCI, SO2 is washed down. PCBs are found destroyed. If the operating agency desires to get rid of organics like halogenated solvents, petroleum refinery waste, vinyl chloride monomer, plastics, pesticides, off-spec pharmaceuticals etc. with a chemical destruction efficiency of 99.99%, then incineration will be his only choice, regardless as to whether he feeds as gas, liquid, semi-solid, or solids. Operating agency has to put only selected crew to run this unit as the precautions are necessary at every place right from unloading the incoming tankers (preferably with nitrogen blanket), segregated storing as per high or low British Thermal Unit (BTU) value. Some, if arriving in a mixed form, has to be sent to a specific gravity based separators through vibratory screen, as also a separate storage for high or low pH wastes. This helps in blending, because the success of operating agency's incinerator cannot be ensured, if the feed is non-uniform in quality and quantity. In this system, organics are destroyed and the inorganics are converted. The clays, dissolved salts or silica are released within the incinerator flue gas and the same ash is required to be trapped and then disposed of in the landfill. The volume reduction be estimated and recorded. The operating agency should also record the temperatures at various points (actual against designed) such as say (1) initial temperature in the primary chamber 14000 C, (2) after injecting aqueous waste as 8000 C, (3) after passing through scrubber/ spray dryer, (4) after fabric filter 2000 C in the stack. In the stack, the emission monitoring be done for levels of oxygen, unburnt hydrocarbons, sulfur dioxide and opacity (- a measure of particulate matters going up the stack) and record the same, in computer. The residence time in seconds also be recorded. The operating agency should keep a safety and security in its plant to boast that nothing moves in the premises without permission, even the rain water (which is collected as run-on, analysed, pH adjusted or settled and then pumped run to allow it out).

Manifest System

In the management of solid and liquid industrial wastes it is very important to incorporate a manifest system by which the chain responsibility of generator, carrier and receiver is to be realised. This system will help the regulatory agency as nodal agency, where finally the copy of the manifest will be sent, to know whether the actual wastes generated are transported to the facilities where it is to be disposed off. In this process of waste management, all the three, viz. pollution generator, carrier and receiver, will have to take authorisation from the nodal agency. It is felt that in India also for the management of industrial wastes, whether they are hazardous and non-hazardous, a manifest system has to be framed to identify.

Post Treatment

The post treatment precautions to be undertaken by the operating agency depend much on what treatment he has offered to the subjected hazardous waste. The treatment given to the waste shall be complete and not half-way. If physico-chemical-biological treatment is successfully given, the outgoing post-treatment streams will be three fold. The oil may be sold or sent for incineration, the sludge after dewatering be sent to secure landfill and the water after analysis may join a stream on permission from the SPCB or may be used on adjoining land by irrigation. Operating agency to maintain a full record. If the treatment-disposal is a secured landfill, if post-treatment leachate appear, the same be collected and recycled into the operating agency's facility for re-treatment. One will find that leachate exhibits very high polluting and hazardous characteristics.

If incineration or thermal treatment is adopted, the captured post-treatment ash be sent for burial and scrubber water be sent back into the facility for treatment. Operating agency at every step should maintain a computerised record. If recovery is a treatment method, it converts a hazardous waste into a nonhazardous non-waste. This post-treatment, is acceptable to the customers and can be so sold. It may be a hazardous chemical, but no more a hazardous waste.

Back-transport

There can be only three types of back-transport. Number one, where there is a manifest discrepancy, number two where the waste sent by generator to operating agency facility is not as per contract and number three, when a renovated material after recovery returns back to a customer. The former two be avoided, while the third one is a welcome step. It will be a good practice if the operating agency keeps a discipline of collecting the waste by himself from the generators' premises. Operating agency can get an opportunity of supervising the waste before loading or even adjusting the form of waste. This will avoid any eventuality of returning. The returning not only involves engaging the transport tankers for one trip during which three normal trips would have been performed, it also means increase of risk. It is, however, also true that operating agency should not accept such material which he cannot handle such as say PCBs, coming suddenly to him unawares. If the return becomes necessary due to discrepancy in the manifest then the operating agency has a room to use his discretion. If the discrepancy is marginal and the material can be accepted by writing a note, he may preferably do so rather than relaying the hazardous waste back all along.

If the operating agency has an acceptable recovered material and a demand for the same, he should make its analysis on Gas Chromatograph (GC) and send the examination report to prospective customer by fax and on his acceptance message the goods be sent. This transport should be done in clean tankers. Dirty tankers should not be pressed for this service, as else unacceptable contamination may take place. The outgoing recovered waste is no more a hazardous waste and hence, manifest system will not be needed. However, it still is a hazardous chemical and whatever obligations under Manufacture, Storage and Import of Hazardous Chemical Rules, 1989 are placed on transport, will have to be studied and followed by the operating agency.

Monitoring

Monitoring and laboratory examination is important in many fields, but more so in the field of hazardous waste management. In monitoring we collect a sample and from its analysis we infer about the universe (i.e. full batch). Monitoring will tell the operating agency about the dividing line between hazardous and nonhazardous waste, about the treatability of the hazardous waste, about incompatibility of different wastes, about the performance efficiency of hazardous waste treatment and disposal facility, about the impact, about the quality of the recovered material, and about the post-closure effects if any. Monitoring gives a final signal if something is going wrong in the facility of operating agency, giving an opportunity of rectification. Monitoring becomes handy in investigation of complaints and during the time of any accidental leakages or spills. The operating agency, therefore, should have an excellent set up of materials and methods. Monitoring should commence one year before the facility is brought in existence by the operating agency, should continue while the facility is in use, to know the migration kinetics and contemporary concentrations, to take a decision as to whether it is a time to abandon a particular site, and till five year after it is abandoned to see that the "ghost" does not reappear as mere 'cradle to grave' is not sufficient precaution, it should be "cradle to grave to ghost". In consultation with the SPCBs, the operating agency will have to draw samples of air, water groundwater, leachate waters, soils, ash, solid wastes and aesthetics. The periodicity and station selection be done carefully and the following locations might prove appropriate:

(*a*) **Air:** upwind, downwind, three stations at 120m around the facility, distance depending on stack height and location of any particular sensitive feature. This is for ambient. Samples be selected in stack, vents and ducts.

(*b*) **Surface waters :** upstream and downstream in the stream adjoining local nullah, upstream in the rivulet, on both the banks, upper stream and benthal deposits, and add as per sanitary survey.

(*c*) **Groundwater :** From wells specially dug one upgradient and at least three on down gradient, and deep enough.

(*d*) **Soil :** Surrounding soil at ground level be sampled in a circular grid.

(*e*) **Vegetative cover :** Whether mal-effect is occurred and if yes, in what direction.

(*f*) **Biological indicator :** by planting sensitive plants in all directions and at different distances and to note periodically as to what is the health status of each plant, providing the operating agency with information as to what further precautions are required to be taken.

Among all the above, ground water monitoring is a more serious and complicated matter of which the operating agency has very little experience. The groundwater monitoring is of great significance to such operating agency, who are engaged in land treatment, land application, sanitary landfills, secured landfills, surface impoundment or composting. This monitoring is more significant when the groundwater is popularly used either for agricultural or personal purposes. However, it may be of low or no significance if it is found that the operating agency facility is an engineered structure, does not receive or contain free liquids, is designed and operate to exclude liquid, rains, other run-on or run-off, has both inner and outer layers of containment enclosing the waste, and has an eye on leak detection, i.e. there is no potential for migration of liquid from regulated units to the uppermost aquifer (during the facilities active life and to some extent thereafter). This monitoring is also not significant, if there is no groundwater. This is the first stage of self-examination that the operating agency should keep his findings recorded, supported by expert documents that he should gather by contacting universities. There are three types of groundwater monitoring, depending on its purpose, viz. (i) detection monitoring, (ii) assessment monitoring and (iii) compliance monitoring. The detection monitoring is to determine whether land disposal facility has leaked hazardous waste or constituents into an underlying aquifer in quantities sufficient to cause a significant change in groundwater quality. This can be found out within the first year itself. But if it is detected within say three months, one should not wait for one year, but should immediately begin the assessment monitoring. In detection monitoring, only a few indicator parameters may be analysed to establish, if migration is occurring. The indicator parameters used may include specific conductance, total organic carbon, total organic halogen or any specific waste constituents which the operating agency receives.

Assessment monitoring is a more aggressive programme, if a significant change is discovered in groundwater quality during the detection monitoring.

In the place of non-specific, generally, specific chemicals are estimated and verticalhorizontal concentration profiles are attempted. Rate and extent of contaminant migration is studied. This study will lead to design corrective steps to be taken by operating agency.

The success of corrective steps so designed and implemented should be reflected in compliance monitoring. The goal of the compliance monitoring programme is to ensure that leakage of hazardous constituents into the groundwater does not exceed acceptable limits. The operating agency will know from his experience that these hazardous constituents will be no different than the list of hazardous chemicals given in the Manufacture, Storage and Import of Hazardous Chemicals Rules, 1989 in its Schedule I, Part II as amended in 1999. The State Boards may not normally announce these limits in the Authorisation. However, if assessment monitoring finds the presence of hazardous chemicals, corresponding standards will be prescribed so that the groundwater remains usable. The corrective action programme by operating agency should include, to remove or treat the constituents specified within an agreed time-frame. The corrective action programme does not terminate, till correction is seen in the groundwater quality. The operating agency will keep in mind that the groundwater monitoring does not mean a generalised blanket analysis. Specific parameters are required to be selected as a three tier system, viz. (*i*) indicator parameters, (*ii*) groundwater quality and (*iii*) drinking water quality. These can be :

(*i*) Indicator parameters : to know the pollutant grossly; they are pH, colour, specific conductance, Total Organic Carbon (TOC) and Total Organic Halogen.

(*ii*) Groundwater quality parameters : to know its suitability for other (nondrinking) purposes like agriculture; they are chloride, iron, manganese, phenols, sodium, sulfates etc.

(*iii*) Drinking water suitability parameters for its obvious purpose as a source; they are Arsenic, Barium, Cadmium, Chromium, Fluoride (temperature dependent), Lead, Mercury, Nitrate, Selenium, Silver, Endrin, Lindane, Methodxy chlor, Toxaphene, Radio-activity and Coliform bacteria.

For a groundwater quality understanding, there should be sampling points (well) on hydraulically upgradient and a minimum of three on the downgradient, for a small facility of operating agency. However, the number required may increase depending on the complexity of facilities, of geography and of geology. The monitoring well must give a true picture of the groundwater and nothing else. The monitoring wells must be cased in a manner that maintains the integrity of the monitoring well bore hole. The casing must be screened or perforated and, if necessary, packed with sand or gravel to enable sample collections at depths were appropriate aquifer flow zones exist. The annular space (the space between the bore hole and the well casing) above the selected sampling depth must be sealed with a suitable material, such as bentonite slurry or grout. The operating agency shall keep a frequency of sampling as once in three months normally, unless the circumstances compel to do it more often to develop confidence. They should continue even after abandoning the site for a fixed period. All this should be done by the operating agency in constant consultation with the SPCBs. It may not be out of place to mention that 175 wells are reportedly monitored monthly by a U.S.A. operating agency, CECOS (M/S.Chemical and Environmental Conservation Systems Inc.) for their secure chemical landfilling at Niagara Falls site, spending a quarter million dollars a year (1986) to check and ensure that groundwater does not become contaminated.

Record Keeping

The operating agency should remember that no job is complete unless paper work is complete. The record keeping and reporting is especially important when dealing with hazardous waste. The operating agency should maintain the minimum record as is required by the hazardous waste rules, but should additionally keep other records like health statistics, insurance, cost analysis and whatever may be required by other departments. The statutory authorities sometimes demand only an annual figure. However, to arrive at, the operating agency has to have a daily record.

LEGISLATION FOR MANAGEMENT OF HAZARDOUS WASTE AND CATEGORISATION OF HAZARDOUS WASTE

In exercise of the powers conferred under the Environment (Protection) Act, 1986 (29 of 1986), the Central Government has made the Hazardous Waste (Management & Handling) Rules, 1989 and published in the official Gazette No.S.O.594(E), dated 28.7.1989. These Rules define the Hazardous Wastes and provide specific schedule in which wastes are listed for application of the rule. The rules have been further amended in 1999 called Hazardous Waste (Management and Handling) Rules, January 6, 2000. The occupier generating hazardous waste has obligation to take all practical steps to ensure that such wastes are properly handled and disposed off without any adverse effect, which may result from such wastes. The occupier shall also be responsible for proper collection, transportation, treatment, storage and disposal of these wastes, either by himself or through the operator of a facility. The occupier shall submit application to the SPCB for grant of authorisation for handling of hazardous wastes. The SPCB shall not issue an authorisation unless it is satisfied that the operator of a facility or an occupier, as the case may be, possesses appropriate facilities, technical capabilities and equipment to handle hazardous wastes safely. The State Govt./U.T. Administration, or a person authorised by it, is required to undertake a continuing programme to identify the sites and compile and publish periodically an inventory of disposal sites within the State/UT for the disposal of hazardous wastes. An environmental impact study shall be undertaken before final identification of a site as waste disposal site. Import of hazardous waste from any country to India shall not be permitted for dumping and disposal of such wastes. However, import of such wastes may be allowed for processing or re-use as rawmaterial, after examining each case on merit by the SPCB or by an officer authorised in this behalf.

HANDLING OF HAZARDOUS CHEMICALS

It has been observed that there is always potential risk due to handling and transportation of toxic/ hazardous chemicals and particularly in residential areas. Storage of such chemicals in residential and commercial areas should be closely monitored. The MoEF have notified the Manufacturer, Storage and Import of Hazardous Chemical Rules, 1989 (as amended on January 20, 2000) and according to these rules, activities relating to handling and transportation of hazardous chemicals should be regulated. However, this subject is not under the purview of local bodies but, they can provide assistance to the concerned agencies whenever needed.

INDUSTRIAL LOCATION

There are certain types of industries though they are small sized/tiny but, cause considerable pollution when they are located in residential areas. Such industries quite often do not seek s 'Consents' from SPCBs and even not 'licensed' by the local authorities. Therefore, SPCBs and Municipal authorities should review and interact with each other to ensure that industries do not come up in nonconforming areas. From solid waste generation point of view, small industries dispose variety of solid waste like, packaging materials, oil sludges, scraps, paints, metallic/non-metallic containers, metallic sludges, etc. Municipal authorities while providing services in residential and commercial areas when find that there are industries which discharge solid waste, should bring out information to the knowledge of SPCBs so that necessary actions are taken. In commercial areas, service units like flour mills, automobile service stations should be properly served notices by the concerned administration to the effect that such units should dispose their solid waste as per norms laid by Pollution Control Boards/ municipal authorities.

MANAGEMENT OF INDUSTRIAL SOLID WASTES-COORDINATION (SPCBs & LOCAL BODIES)

Urban local bodies are constantly in the field and they are well aware of the local situation. They also know sources of waste generation and areas under their control. In order to organise proper collection, transportation and disposal of industrial solid waste, there is need to set up co-ordination between SPCBs, local bodies and industrial departments. Following guidelines are suggested to follow :

(*i*) Urban local bodies should identify the areas from where industrial solid waste is generated.

(*ii*) Inventorisation of industries could be attempted through SPCBs or industries department for characterization of wastes.

(*iii*) SPCBs may take necessary actions for issuance of consents/ Authorizations to the industries under relevant Acts and Rules.

(*iv*) Urban local bodies may undertake collection, transportation and disposal of solid waste on cost recovery basis as per existing rules and may identify suitable sites for final treatment and disposal of industrial solid waste as per existing rules and regulations.

REFERENCES

Akolkar, A.B. 2005. Status of Solid Waste Management in India, Implementation NStatus of Municipal Solid Wastes, Management and Handling Rules 2000, Central Pollution Control Board, New Delhi.

Allen AR, Dillon AM, O'Brien M., 1997. Approaches to landfill site selection in Ireland. Engineering Geology and the Environment. Balkema, Rotterdam pp 1569-1574.

Amar M Dhere, Chandrasekhar B Pawar, Pratapsingh B Pardeshi and Dhanraj A Patil, 2008. Municipal solid waste disposal in Pune city – An analysis of air and groundwater pollution Current science 95, 6,773-777.

Jilani T, 2002, State of Solid Waste Management in Khulna City. Unpublished Undergraduate thesis, Environmental Science Discipline, Khulna University Khulna, pp. 25-85.

Kontos THD, DP Komilis and C.P Halvadakis 2003).Siting MSW Landfills in Lesvos Island with a GIS-based methodology. Waste Management and Research, 21(3), 262–277.

MeBean E A, Rovers F A and Farquhar G J, Solid Waste Landfill Engineering and Design, Prentice Hall, NJ, 1995, p. 380.

Suchitra M, 2007. Outside: Burnt or buried, garbage needs land. Down To Earth, 15 March, pp. 22–24.

Susi Abraham and Madana Kumar CK, 2001. Minor water bodies in Kottayam Municipality area: A bio ecological study.

Miles SB and HO CL, 1999. Applications and Issues of GIS as Tool for Civil Engineering Modeling. J. Comp.City. Engrg. ASCE 13:144-152.

Navalgund RR and Kasturirangan K, 1983. The remote sensing satellite – A programme overview. Proc. Indian Acad. Sci. Engg. Sci. –Remote Sensing – III, 6, 313–336.

Ozeair Abessi, Mohesn Saeedi, 2009. Site Selection of a Hazardous Waste Landfill Using GIS Technique and Priority Processing, a Power Plant Waste in Qazvin Provincc Caso Example. Environmental sciences,6,4,121-134.

Savage GM, LF Diaz and GC Golueke, 1998. Guidance for Land Filling Waste in Economically Developing Countries. Washington DC, USA: United States Environmental Protection Agency, National Risk Management Research Laboratory, Cincinnati, OH, EPA 600/ R-98-040.

Suchitra M, 2007. Outside: Burnt or buried, garbage needs land. Down To Earth, 15 March, pp. 22–24.

Susi Abraham and Madana Kumar CK, 2001. Minor water bodies in Kottayam Municipality area: A bio ecological study.

Species Distribution in Different Elevational Zones

A Case Study in Forest Habitat of Nainital (Western Himalayas) India

—Kamal Kant Joshi, *India*
—Dinesh Bhatt, *India*
—Tribhuwan Chandra, *India*

INTRODUCTION

Biodiversity

The earth is home to rich and diverse array of living organisms. These living organisms are independent with one another but precisely linked with each other by complex laws of nature. This relationship with one another and their physical environment constitute our planet's biodiversity. The word biodiversity is a contraction of 'biological diversity'. Biodiversity has been defined by many ecologists and politicians associated with governmental and non governmental organization (e.g. McNeely *et al.*, 1990; Heywood and Watson, 1995; Groombridge 2000).

As mentioned in the US Biodiversity Act (1990) the definition of Biodiversity may be "Biological diversity means the full range of variety and variability with in and among living organisms and the ecological complexes in which they occur and encompasses ecosystem or community diversity, species diversity and genetic diversity". Biodiversity is generally considered an 'Umbrella term' referring to organisms found within the living world. The term biodiversity only really came into public vocabulary around 1988 (MaNeely, 1994) and it came into sharp focus only after the Convention of Biodiversity (CBD) which was agreed upon by around 157 governments at the Earth submit in Rio De Janeiro, Brazil in June, 1992.

Biodiversity can be focused on three levels: ecosystem diversity, species diversity and genetic diversity; all these are interlinked but are not synonymous: maintenance of the ecosystems diversity implies maintenance of the species (or at least the most important species), which constitute that ecosystem; however, it is perfectly feasible to maintain species independent of the ecosystems or habitats in which they normally occur. Similarly, maintenance of genetic diversity with in a species self evidently implies maintenance of that species. Species diversity does not distribute uniformly across the globe. Some habitats, particularly in tropical forests among the terrestrial ecosystem have a great number of species diversity and density to others. Therefore, some countries which are wholly or partially located in the tropical and subtropic regions are known as mega diversity countries (McNeely *et al.* 1990).

Myers (1992) defined the centre of diversity as merely an area with high species richness and many centers of diversity have been recognized on global, regional and local scales. On a global scale, four important analyses merit mentioning: (*i*) Mayers' Hotspots (*ii*) IUCN's centre of plant diversity (*iii*) Mega diversity centre (*iv*) Diversity zones (Barthlott *et al.*, 1996). On the basis of species diversity and richness countries are recognized as mega diversity centre or countries. So far 12 mega diversity countries have been identified and India is one of them.

This biodiversity is the natural biological capital of the earth and presents important opportunities for all nations. It provides goods and services essential to support human livelihood aspiration and enables society to adapt to changing needs and circumstances. The protection of these assets and their continued exploration through science and technology offer the only means by which the nation of the world can hope to develop sustainability.

Biodiversity Status in the World

Biodiversity is not distributed evenly on Earth. It is consistently richer in the tropics and in other localized regions such as the California Floristic Province and on the other hand in the Polar regions we generally finds fewer species. Flora and fauna diversity depends on climate, altitude, soils and the presence of other species. Biodiversity rich areas are known as hotspots and these regions are with a high level of endemic species. Most of these hotspots are located in the tropics and most of them are forests. These biodiversity hotspots were first identified by Dr. Norman Myers (1988). Our earth is a relatively unexpected planet biologically.

However it is unfeasible to describe all species currently because of the huge number of species on the earth. In the past many scientists estimated a number of species in major groups (Myers *et al.*, 1979; Myers, 1988; Barnes, 1989; May, 1990). However, almost nothing is known about species ranges and rates of species turnover geographically, so global estimate are very uncertain. And what is more intriguing is that a large fraction of the species will disappear before they have been named or described, because the present rate of inventorying or description of new species is quite low as regard to the present rate of extinction of species.

A large numbers of the earth species are formally classified as rare or endangered or threatened species. However, most scientists estimate that there are millions more species actually endangered which have not yet been formally recognized. There are about 30 million insects, 15,210 mammals, reptiles and amphibians; 9225 birds, 21000 fishes, about 4,80,000 plants and 3 million other invertebrates and microorganisms (Solbrig, 1993). Current crude estimates range from 13 million to as high as 14 million species in our globe, while 1.75 million species have been recorded scientifically (Heywood *et al.*, 1995) (Table 7.1).

Table 7.1 : Species Number of Major Taxonomic Groups of Organism in the World

Group	Described species number	Estimated species number	Described/ Estimated species number %
Viruses	400,000	40,000,000	1.0
Bacteria	400,000	100,000,000	0.4
Fungi	7,200,000	150,000,000	5.3
Protozoans	4,000,000	20,000,000	20.0
Algae	4,000,000	40,000,000	10.0
Nematodes	2,500,000	40,000,000	6.3
Molluscs	7,000,000	20,000,000	35
Crustaceans	4,000,000	15,000,000	26.7
Arachnids	7,500,000	75,000,000	10.0
Insects	95,000,000	800,000,000	11.9
Plants (Embryophytes)	27,000,000	32,000,000	84.4
Vertebrates	4,500,000	5,000,000	90.0
Others	11,500,000	25,000,000	46
Total	**175,000,000**	**1,362,000,000**	**12.8**

Sources: Heywood *et al.*, (1995)

Biodiversity in India

India is situated at the tri junction of the three realms namely Afro tropical, Indo Malayan and Paleo - Arctic. This assemblage of three distinct realms is the cause of rich and unique biological diversity. India stands 10th in the world, 4th in Asian in plant diversity and ranks 10th in the number of endemic species of higher vertebrates in the world. India occupies only 2.4 per cent of the world's land area but its contribution to the world's biodiversity is approximately 8 per cent of the total numbers of species, which is estimated to be 1.75 million. Of these 1, 26, 188 have been described in India (Table 7.2).

Table 7.2: Summary of Animal Biodiversity Threats in India

	Number of Indian species (% of world total)	% of Indian species evaluated	Species threatened in India as % of those evaluated	Number extinct (% of those evaluated)
Mammals	386 (7%)	59%	41%	4 (1.8%)
Birds	1219 (12%)	Unknown	7%	Unknown
Reptiles	495	73%	46%	Unknown
Amphibians	207 (4%)	79%	54%	Unknown
Fresh water fishes	700	46%	7%	Unknown

Based on (Kumar *et al.*, 2000)

The species recorded includes flowering plants (angiosperms), mammals, fish, birds, reptiles and amphibians and constitute 17.3 per cent of the total whereas nearly 60 per cent of Indian bio wealth is contributed by fungi and insects (Khoshoo, 1996). At present India has 5 world heritage sites (*Kaziranga NP, Keoladeo Ghana NP, Manas Wildlife Sanctuary, Nanda Devi Biosphere Reserve, Sundarban NP*), 12 biosphere reserves (Augustamalai and Ankleshwar are proposed) and 6 Ramsar wetlands; amongst the protected areas India has 88 national parks and 490 sanctuaries covering an area of 1.53 lakhs Km^2. (MoEF 2000). There are 10 biogeographical zones in India (Fig. 7.1), these unique and endemic biodiversity ranks to India a Hotspot of the world. In these biogeographical zones Himalayan region is rich of endemic species.

As mentioned earlier, India is recognized as a country uniquely rich in all aspects of biodiversity. For any one country in the world, it has perhaps the largest array of environmental conditions by virtue of its tropical location, varied physical features and climatic type. Indian has the widest variety of biomes. Groves are unique tradition which have been responsible for preserving pockets of biodiversity in various parts of the country, such groves occur mainly in the Western Ghats and North Eastern India. The Trans Himalayan regions with due geographical condition and sparse vegetation are the richest in faunal community and migratory birds in the world. Due to decline of quality and quantity, deforestation, grazing and wood cutting pressure in this region species become exotic.

According to Bird Life International majority of the world's 217 endemic bird areas (EBAs) occurs in tropical countries. India represents about five hot biodiversity endemic bird area. These are: Western Himalaya, Central Himalaya, Eastern Himalaya, Assam plain and Western Ghats. There are nine Bio-Zone with birding areas in India, (Fig. 7.1) these are Trance Himalaya, Himalaya, Gangatic plain, Desert, Semi arid, Deccan Peninsula, Western Ghats, Coastal area and Island.

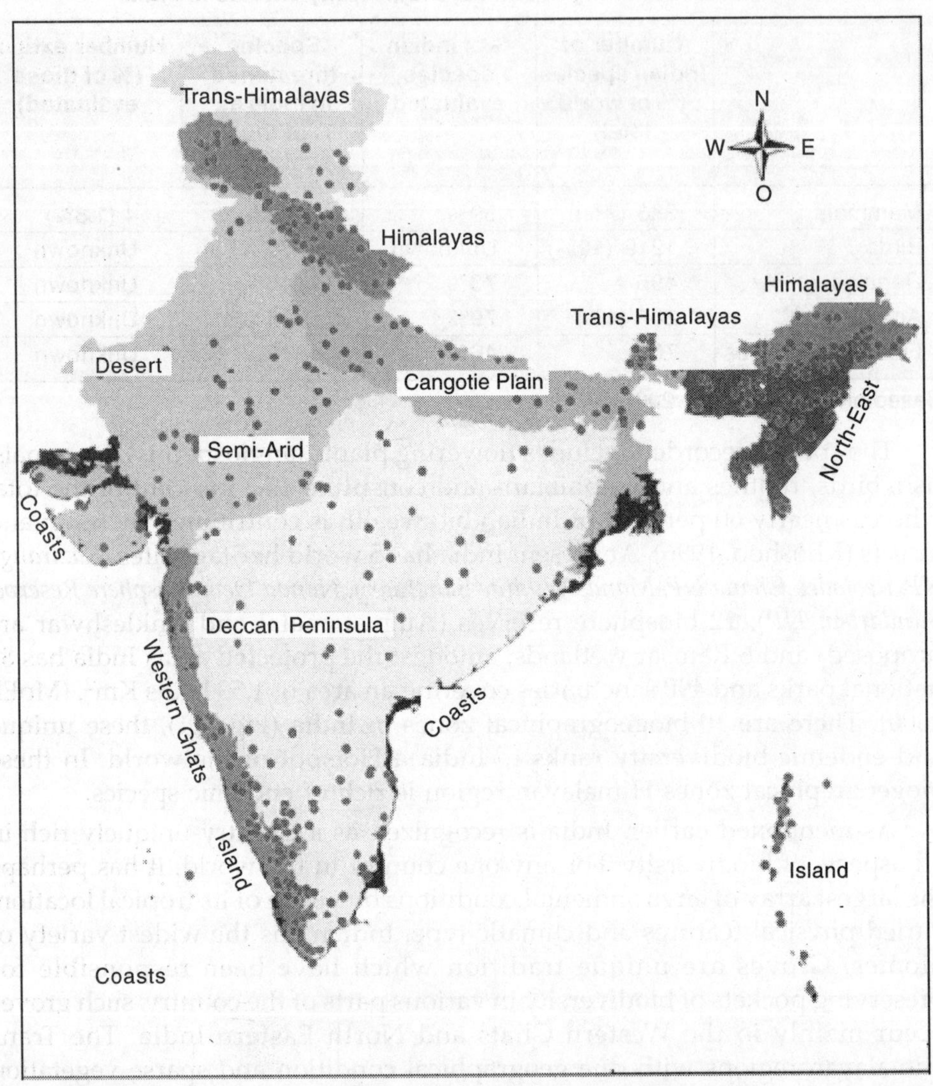

Fig. 7.1 : Bio zones with birding areas of India

The Himalayan ranges are about 2500 Km long, extending from 73° East to 97° East longitude and from 27° North to 37° North latitude and covering an area of approximately 2,36,000 Km^2 and these ranges are pull out from few hundred to over 8000m asl, it is known as the outer Himalaya, middle Himalaya and the inner or great Himalaya ranges. Thus there are three factors (longitude, latitude and altitude) which provide various microclimate and ecological niches for plants and animals (Khoshoo, 1987). The Western Himalaya extends from Jammu-Kashmir, Himachal Pradesh, and Uttarakhand up to the western border of Nepal; the forest cover of this region from

4.9 per cent (J&K) to 63.13 per cent (Uttarakhand) (Anonymous, 1991). In the Western Himalayan (Kumaun) region of Uttarakhand, Kumaun and Garhwal (Uttarakhand) hills covered with 65 per cent of forest land. Forest habitats of this region provide good shelter for faunal wealth. Due to the poor accessibility and weather conditions less work has been done in this region about faunal diversity. However, records of the Government agencies (ZSI, WII) help to understand the diversity of this region; there are 124 species of pisces, 19 species of amphibian, 69 species of reptiles, 521 species of birds and 51 species of mammals surviving in the Kumaun and Garhwal region (Arora and Kumar, 1995).

Although the scientific description of Western Himalayan bird species are available in several valuable contributions by the most experienced field ornithologists such as Jerdon (1862-64), Hudson (1930), Baker (1922-31), Ali and Ripley (1968-78), etc. However, thereafter there is no systematic study in this area about avian diversity and status except few biologists (Bisht *et al.*, 1986, Chandola *et al.*, 1987, Bisht *et al.*, 1991 and Sultana 2000).

India has not received enough attention though active research is being pursued on other aspects of avian biology. Although of late a few studies have been conducted to measure the avian diversity (Gaston, 2000; Price, 1979; Johnsingh *et al.*, 1987, Daniels *et al.*, 1993, Joshua and Johnsingh, 1994; Pramod *et al.*, 1997; Kunte *et al.*, 1999; Sharma, 2001 and Singh, 2005). These published work gives us baseline data for birds in certain habitats and can be used for future comparisons. In temperate areas such as Europe and USA studies of birds have been a major area of research in community ecology. Birds are among the most well studied and documented groups of animals. Sibley and Monroe (1990) recognized 9,672 species of birds in the world. They are regarded as good indicators of biodiversity because their distribution is well known and they are sensitive to environmental change.

Despite the fact that being mobile, several bird species show a restricted distribution, depending on the availability of habitats within which they can survive. India is third one in bird species diversity (ICBP, 1992).

BIODIVERSITY ESTIMATION

The global magnitude of exact biodiversity is poorly understood. In the context of species richness, in particular this fact has been much lamented. Biodiversity is a broad concept, so a variety of objective measures have been created in order to empirically measure biodiversity. Each measure of biodiversity relates to a particular use of the data. The under developed state of listings of the world's species has been contrasted with more advanced catalogues of star and galaxies (May, 1990) and the lack of a definite estimate of the overall number of species has been contrasted with the estimates of the numbers of star of the Milky Way (Wilson, 1985). Similarly, global biodiversity is very often considered in terms of global number of species in each of the different taxonomic groups. Fossil records provide us necessary background of biodiversity as well as origin of diversity. Fossil generic and family diversity trends are considered useful proxies for species diversity trends (Sepkoski, 1992: Gaston *et al*. 1995). Inevitably some groups are much less well known than others, perhaps as many as 75% of species remains to be formally described and there is no catalogue of global biodiversity yet available and estimates of the total number of species on earth vary by an order of magnitude (May, 1990, 1992, 1994). Describing the species abundance distribution of an assemblage is one thing: providing a synoptic measure of its diversity represents a rather different challenge. Estimation of the diversity of any community are based upon a restricted sample of the community members, estimates of species richness and equitability are recorded in relation to the number of individual sampled and are thus a function of the number of species present and their relative abundance (Pielou, 1966; Hill, 1973; Magurran, 1988). Richness of species is an important component of biodiversity assessment (Jenkins, 1992). The species richness estimates the cataloging of all species occurring in an area, region and habitat types. Other extrapolations have used the relationship between number of species and their body size (May, 1990). Most studies report densities by species which could potentially be summed to give the total number of individuals in the area; Terborgh *et al*. (1990) studied on the densities of forest birds in tropical and temperate region. The total number of individuals and the species richness of a taxon in assemblages are related both theoretically and empirically (Kobayashi and Kimura, 1994). Species richness can be defined as the number of species of a given taxon in the chosen assemblage, biological species concept and the cohesion concept followed through the avian biologist (Templeton, 1996). Diversity statistics are conventionally classified as either species richness measure (McIntosh, 1967) or heterogeneity measures. Heterogeneity measures are those that combine the richness and evenness components of diversity. Evenness measures were later developed (Lioyd and Ghelardi, 1964) in an attempt to distil the evenness component of diversity into a single number. Evenness measures assess the disappearance of the observed pattern from the expected pattern in a hypothetical assemblage. The species richness estimation can be expressed as numerical species richness, which is the number of species per specified number of individuals or biomass or species diversity, which is the number of species per specified collection area or unit. The most widely used diversity index is the Shannon-Weaver information to measure the species diversity (H') (MacArthur, 1961). The species diversity is a better tool for ecologists who are interested to understanding the mechanisms of certain ecological phenomena, such as environment disturbance and species distribution etc.

Species richness data may provide relatively little ecologically significant information. Such data is also important for prioritizing conservation strategies since they allow identification of geographic region of the world. Biodiversity is usually plotted as taxonomic richness of a geographic area, with some reference to a temporal scale. Whittaker, (1972) described three common metrics used to measure species-level biodiversity. Species richness, Shannon index and Simpson index are the most primitive of the indices available.

Alpha diversity refers to diversity within a particular area, community or ecosystem, and is measured by counting the number of taxa within the ecosystem, Beta diversity is species diversity between habitat or ecosystems; this involves comparing the number of taxa that are unique to each of the ecosystems and Gamma diversity is a measure of the overall diversity for different ecosystems within a region (Magurran, 1988). The concept of species richness (i.e. the number of species) gives as much information that is related to biodiversity as the concept of species diversity. This has led to both terms being used interchangeable, which in turn leads to a confusion of the concepts and the ecologists apply more direct approaches to the study of species numbers relations by relying on direct measures of the number of species rather than apply several diversity indices that are simple derived variables (Laishangbam and Bhatt, 2005).

SPECIES DISTRIBUTION ALONG ELEVATIONAL GRADIENTS

The broad scale geographical changes are the significant for species distribution. The distributional patterns of species specify the potential membership of communities and guilds in any locality. Distributions are based on presence – absence information but the absence of a species from an area may reflect a distributional fact or a simple failure to record its actual presence in census (MacArthur, 1972). Other factors which may influence the species distribution Cody (1985), listed these reasons: 1. the lack of suitable habitat 2. barriers that prevent dispersal to the area 3. competitive interaction with a closely related. 4. diffuse competition with several somewhat similar species 5. the absence of critical resources such as a specific food type. 6. an area too small to contain an individual territory 7. climate factors producing physiological stress 8. historical factors 9. chance. The climate stresses may exert strong and direct influence on the distribution of species. The species differ in their tolerance of harsh breeding; winter conditions and small climate changes would alter their distributional patterns. Physiological adaptation and tolerances may also constrain the distributions of bird species. Physical and ecological factors such as local climate, ecotones, competition and habitat structure and heterogeneity play a prominent role in determining species diversity (Terborgh, 1977, 1985; Ricklefs and Schluter, 1993; Huston, 1999; Lomolino, 2001). Migration also plays an important role for species distribution of that area. The patterns of bird species diversity, is much higher in the tropics than in temperate zone (Cody 1975, 1986, Diamond, 1971, 1973, and 1975). Many tropical birds migrate to the temperate zone for a relatively brief time to breed and raise their young in this way for some time species diversity and abundance rises in the temperate region (MacArthur 1959). Many physical conditions in addition to temperature also change along the altitudinal and latitudinal gradients with significant effect on bird distributions. In terrestrial ecosystem, species diversity generally decreases with increasing altitude. This phenomenon is most apparent at extremes of altitude, with highest regions at all latitudes having very low species diversity. There are many examples showing gradients of species richness with altitude although amongst vertebrates this has been demonstrated for bird species in New Guinea (Brown, 1988). Several hypotheses have been proposed to explain the dramatic increase in distribution of species richness along the latitudinal gradient towards the equator and more generally the richness of tropical countries. (Brown, 1971; Pianka, 1966; Krebs, 1972; Rohde, 1978; Schall and Pianka, 1978; Dimaond, 1989; Wiens, 1989). Most studies have focused on the species distribution and their relationship with elevation gradient and habitat types in humid tropical forest (Rahbek, 1995; Stotz *et al.*, 1996; Stotz, 1998; Colwell and Lee, 2000; Brown, 2001; Lomolino, 2001; Blake and Loiselle, 2000; Lawrence R. Heaney, 2001; Shankar Raman *et al.*, 2001; Lee, 2004; McCain, 2003; Kattan and Franco, 2004; Colwell *et al.*, 2004; Tzung Su Ding, 2005; Barbara, 2005; Christy M. Mccain, 2007) as well as avian species distribution (richness and diversity) vary in different habitats i.e. forest , urban, agriculture, fragment forest, and river habitat (Johnsingh and Joshua, 1994; Pramod, 1997; Sharma, 2001; Stuart, 2001; Wang Zhijun, 2003; Green, 2004; Pablo *et al.*, 2004; Ivan A Diaz, 2005; Castellatta *et al.*, 2005; Singh, 2005). According to Wiens (1989) vegetation structure is one of the key features to influence the avian species abundance at the local level. The species composition and distribution influence through the ecological and habitat disturbance, in the tropical regions most of the bird communities' distribution changed due to the habitat disturbance by natural or human made (Terborgh and Weske 1969, Schemske and Brokaw, 1981). In avian community the special feature that would determine the guilds and species in a habitat are feeding sites, perching sites, nest sites and predation etc. (Cody, 1986). Similarly the distribution and abundance of many bird species are determined by the configuration and composition of the vegetation that comprises a major element of their habitat (Morrison *et al.*, 1992; Block and Brennan, 1993, Estades, 1997). As vegetation changes along complex geographical and environmental gradients any particular bird species may appear, increase in abundance, decrease, and disappear as habitat becomes more or less suitable for its persistence. The avian community quantified aspects of species richness, species diversity and feeding guilds which are related to structural variables of the habitat such as floristic, foliage density, canopy cover, vertical height density etc (James, 1971; Schroeder, 1987; Kropil, 1996; Pramod, 1996; Chakraverthy, 1997; Sharma, 2001; Singh, 2005; Manhaes *et al.*, 2005).

SEASONAL CHANGES IN AVIAN DIVERSITY

There are ancient records of the seasonal appearances and disappearances of foods. Early naturalist were not certain whether birds migrate or hibernate. Dorst (1997) observed avian species such as cranes, dove, larks, swallows moved seasonally from the steppes of Asian to the marshes of the Nile, later proposed a general appreciation of the phenomenon of bird migration. The capability of flight makes birds one of the most mobile terrestrial organisms, enabling a few bird species to travel more than 20,000 km annually. Many migrating birds travel thousands of kilometers each year from their breeding to wintering areas and back, crossing deserts, mountains and seas. This long distance travel is hazardous for bird species because of its loss of energy costs, risk of exposure, exhaustion and other physical calamities. As a result of which more than half migratory birds never return their destination. Stiles, (1978) found that the abundance of food in summer season is the cause of bird migration from temperate to tropical regions. Mayer (1988) found that shore birds migrate due to lack of nest/roosting site and adequate food supply from Latitude to Longitude or temperate to tropical; but some bird species population migrate and some do not. Partial migration evolves when local conditions promote opportunistic movement of birds to better condition in nearby regions. In the tropical region, fruit eating and nectar feeding birds wander locally in search of their unpredictable sources of food. With in India there are certain Himalayan endemics that evidently fly non stop on their annual migration to the hills of the South Western Ghats i.e. Thrush, Chats, Flycatcher, Ducks etc. species whose migration routes evidently lie along the eastern and western ghats are fairly common in the south Indian hills during winter but are very seldom met with on passage in the intervening country (Ali, 1981). The Himalayan chains of mountain play a very important role in the migration of birds from one place to another. Observations carried out by different naturalists over the past 30 years show that there is seasonal migration across the Himalaya. (Grimmet *et al.*, 1998 and Kery, 2000). Altitudinal migration is another interesting feature of bird species, many altitudinal migration birds appears in low altitude during winter seasons for feeding and suitable climate. There are certain bird species such as Asian paradise flycatcher (*Terpsiphone paradise*), Verditer flycatcher (*Eumyias thalassina*), Pied crested cuckoo (*Clamator jacobinus*), Eurasian cuckoo (*Cuculus canorus*) and long tail minivet (*Pericrocotus ethologus*) which visit in Western Himalayan region in summer season for breeding and back to resident region in early winter season.

Blue Whistling thrush (*Myophonus caeruleus*)

CASE STUDY IN NAINITAL FOREST UTTARAKHAND

Topography of Study Area

To understand the species distribution along elevation a study was carried out in different elevational zones of forest and urban habitats in Nainital district of Uttarakhand for a period of two years during January 2005 to December 2006. The Nainital district occupies the southern portion of the Kumaun division (latitude 28^0 44′ N and 30^0 49′ N and 78^0 45′ E and 81^0 01′ E longitude). The Nainital district is of irregular shape bounded on the north by Almora and a pportion of Garhwal. Geographically the Nainital district is a most heterogeneous, the northern portion consists of hill and the southern portion consists of the alluvial plain called Bhabar (Valdia and Bartarya, 1980).

The study was conducted along different altitudes; Site A (Nainital; 1900m - 2450m asl), Site B (Bhowali; 1450m - 1700m asl) and Site C (Haldwani; 350m - 500m asl) (Fig. 2).

Study Site A (Nainital; 1900-2450m asl)

• **Forest habitat:** The forest habitat surveyed in present study comes under the Naina forest range of Nainital forest division along the elevation 2098m to 2450m asl (N 29° 23′ 47.7″ - 29° 24′ 12.7″ to E 79° 26′ 26.3″- 79°26′ 47.1″). The study site is rich with fuel and fodder trees; local people use this floral wealth for daily needs (Plate 1).

Plate 1: a view of Nainital forest habitat (site A)

Vegetation: There are four species Rainj (*Quarcus lannginosa*), Banj (*Q. inacana*), Karkshul (*Q. semicarpifolia)*, Tilonj (*Q. dilatala*) Oak, Himalayan cypress (*Cupresus torulosa*), and Deodar (*Cedrus deodarus*) are present in the study area. Among Oak *Q. inacana* (Banj) is most common. The conifer species constitutes the most valuable section of the timber trees in this area.

Fauna: The wide range of climate and elevation furnishes the animals from the hill (Nainital) to Bhabar plain (Haldwani). The common wild species in the study site are Kakar (*Cervulus aureus*), Himalayan antilope (*Antilope duvaucelii*), Himalayan langoor *(Prebytis entellus)*, Hare *(Lepus nigricollis)*, Wild cat (*Felis chaus*), Fox *(Vulpes vulpes)* and Red face monkey (*Macaca mulatta)*. The Nainital forest is rich with summer migratory and resident bird species. Many bird species visit during summer from the different part of the India.

Study Site B (BHOWALI; 1450-1700m asl)

• **Forest habitat:** The forest habitat surveyed in the present study comes under the Shyamkhet forest range of Nainital forest division (elevation 1450m asl to 1601m asl; N 29° 22′ 11.7″ - 29° 22′ 31.6″ to E 79° 32′ 10.3″ - 79° 32′ 18.3″). This site is rich in fuel and fodder trees in which Chir Pine (*Pinus roxburghii*) and Banj oak (*Q. inacana*) species are dominant. Gollu dev temple foot track pass away from the study site (Goludhar), occasionally local people used this track to reach the temple. The Bhagtura area of forest habitat is being used for building construction (Plate 2).

Plate 2: A View of Bhowali forest (site B)

Vegetation: The Chir Pine (*Pinus roxburghii*) is the most dominant species in the study area. Deodar (*Cedrus deodara*) and Banj (*Q. inacana*) species are also planted with this by the forest department. The shrubs Lantana (*Lantana camarana*) are wide spread in the study area.

Fauna: The faunal wealth of the study area is very varied and diverse due to variation in the climatic and elevation ranges. Some important and visible species are: Himalayan langur *(Prebytis entellus)*, Hare *(Lepus nigricollis)*, Wild cat (*Felis chaus*), Fox *(Vulpes vulpes)*, Red face monkey (*Macca mullata*) and Porcupine *(Hyatrix indica)* and a number of avian species.

Study Site C (HALDWANI; 350 - 500m asl)

Forest habitat: Immediately below the foot of the Nainital hills is known as Bhabar belt. This belt is waterless forest land. The forest habitat of the study site comes under the Bhakra range of Nainital forest division. Towards the hills valuable trees such as Sal (*Shorea robusta*), Sain (*Terminalia tomrntosa*) and Haldu (*Adive cordifolia*) were found (Plate 3). The study area lays between 350m asl and 440m asl elevation (N 29° 11′ 26.1″ - 29° 11′ 38.2″ to E 79° 27′ 49.3″ - 79° 26′ 48.3″). The forest habitat study was carried out in Bhakra range and covered about 16 ha area. This forest habitat is protected by the forest department and local people use there vegetation as fodder and fuel.

Vegetation: The Sal (*Shorea robusta*), Sain (*Terminalia tomrntosa*), Haldu (*Adive cordifolia*), Dhauri (*Lagerstroemia parviflora*), Shisham (*Dalbergia sissoo*) and Khair (*Acacia catechu*) are dominant species in the study area, as well Eucalyptus (*Eucalyptus globulus*) and Sal (*Shorea robusta*) species are planted by the forest department in the study site. The shrub Lantana is widely spread in the study area. The seed of this plant species are often used by a number of avian species.

Plate 3: Showing Transect Line in Haldwani Forest (site C)

Fauna: The important avian includes Spotted dear (*Muntos muntijuk*), Himalayan goat (*Nemorahaedus goral*), Red face monkey (*Macaca mulatta*), Porcupine (*Hystrix indica*), Mangoose (*Herpestes edwardsi*), Jackal (*Canis aures indicus*) and snakes like Cobra (*Naja naja*) and Karit (*Bungarus caerules*) are reported in the study area. ▫

Bird Species Survey

Birds were surveyed by the variable line transects (fixed – width line transects 40 m × 1000 m) method (Bibby *et al.*, 1992) used for measuring birds abundance (Fig. 7.3). Observations of bird species in each habitat were made 3-4 times

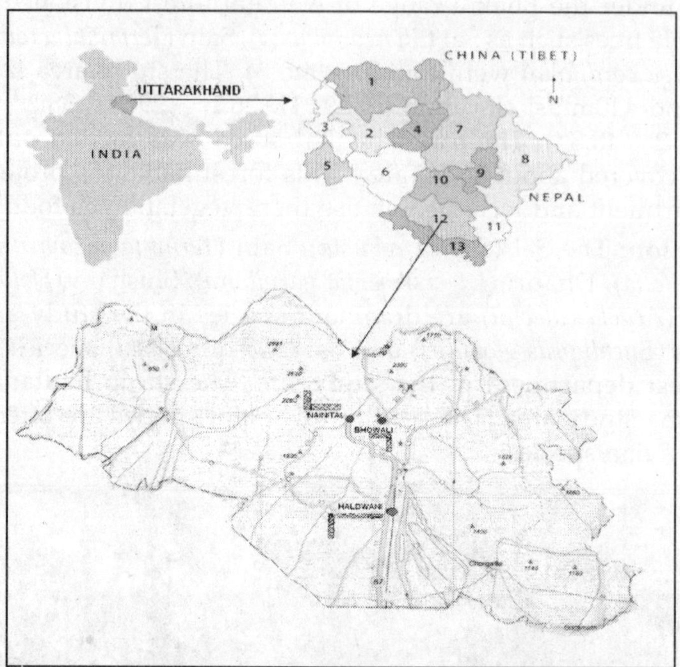

Fig. 7.2 : Study location (▭▭▭▭▭▭▭▭▭) map of Nainital District (Western Himalaya)

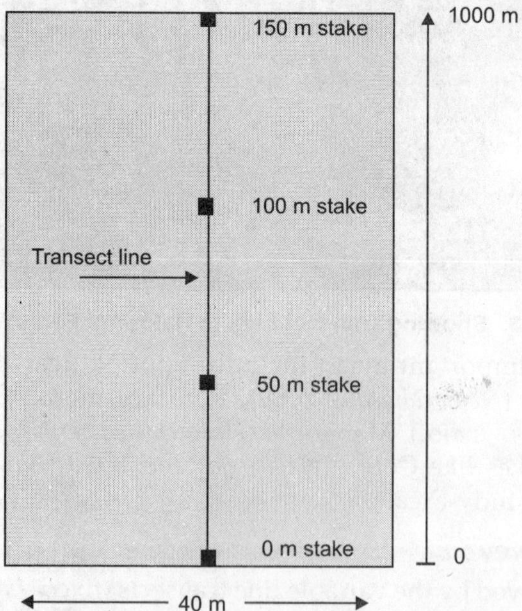

Fig. 7.3 : Schematic diagram of line transect surveys and each transect was marked by stakes at 50 m intervals for vegetation sampling.

in a week on foot with the use of binocular (10 × 4). Geographical location of the site was recorded using GPS (e-trex vista). Transects were walked with constant speed (1km/h) during 7-10 AM and/or 4 - 6 PM in summer season. In Site C (Haldwani) I used the bicycle with constant speed. In winter seasons survey were carried out between 8.30 - 10.30 AM and/or 3.00 - 5.00 PM. Field guide books (Ali and Ripley 1998 and Kazmierczak 2001) were used for identification of bird species and some time birds were identified by their vocalization.

ANALYSIS OF DATA

After collection of raw data, most of the analytical work and calculations were completed by computer software package i.e. PAST, BIODIVERSITY PRO and Microsoft excel.

Bird Species Diversity

The Shannon's index (H') was used in the present study. This index is relatively easy to interpret the species distribution, based on information theory, less sensitive to species richness and sample size. The values of the Shannon's index fall between 1.5 and 3.5 and rarely 4 (Magurran, 1988).

Shannon's Index (H'): $H' = -\sum_{i=1}^{s}\left(\frac{N_i}{S}\right)\ln\left(\frac{n_i}{N}\right)$

Where,

n_i is the total number of individual of the ith of species in the sample.

N is the total number of individuals.

Bird Species Richness

A number of indices have been proposed to measure species richness. To analyze the species abundance I used Mergalef richness index (Magurran, 1988). Species richness shows the functional relationship between species (S) and the total number of individuals observed (N).

Species richness: $R = \frac{S-1}{\ln N}$

Where,

S is the total species in a sample and

N is the total number of individual in a sample

Feeding Guild Structure

Feeding guild structure that exploit the same class of environment resources in a similar way (Root, 1967) by birds are helpful to understand the suitable food chain in the habitat. Such type of information provides help for bird species habitat management. In the present study we determined the avian guilds structure in forest and urban habitats. The guild categories can be divided into six main divisions namely, Insectivore, Carnivore, Omnivore, Nectarivore, Frugivore and Granivore. These feeding guilds again may be sub-divided into a number of sub-feeding guilds on the basis of field observations (observation >70%): Insectivore (bark gleaning insectivore, foliage gleaning insectivore, sallying insectivore, under-story insectivore, grass land insectivore); Carnivore (sallying carnivore, aerial carnivore, terrestrial carnivore, wading carnivore); Omnivore (terrestrial omnivore, Arboreal terrestrial omnivore); Fruitivore, (Fruitivore-omnivore), Granivore (Granivore seed eater, Terrestrial granivore insectivore, Frugivore granivore insectivore-seed eater) and Nectarivore (nectar-seedeater, nectar-insect eater). The feeding habits of each species were observed during sampling as well as the literature (Ali and Ripley 1998, Grimmett, *et al.*, 1998) was also consulted in the study.

Migration and Species Distribution

During the study period we recorded the species presence/absence data in different seasons of the study sites and used the literature (Kazmierczak, 2001, Grimmett *et al.*, 1998) to know the status of birds.

Rare Species

Some of the avian species may be categorized as 'rare' of the study area. In the present study we used the Gaston (1994) criteria to define the rarity. According to this criterion those avian species which were recorded in lowest abundance or below 5 individuals sighted during sampling were categorized as rare avian species of the sampling sites.

Finding

A total of 160 bird species belonging to 24 families were recorded in forest habitat. Out of these 79 species were found exclusively in the forest habitat and 81 species were common in forest and their adjoine area. Among these 79 exclusive species, maximum numbers of species 31; 39.24 per cent were found in site B (Bhowali, 1450 m to 1610 m asl) and minimum 21; 26.26 per cent at site A (Nainital, 2098 m to 2450 m asl). The low altitude site C (Haldwani, 350m to 410m asl) supported 27; 34.17 species (Fig. 7.4).

Among the 24 families Muscicapidae (32.09%) was the largest family followed by Picidae (18.20%), Phasianidae (7.31%) and Accipitridae (4.82%).

Species Distribution in Different Elevational Zone

A total 88 species were recorded from the site A (Nainital). Out of these, 26 species were exclusively found in forest. In site B (Bhowali), out of 106 bird species 39 were exclusively found in forest habitat while in the site C (Haldwani) out of 95 species 34 species were exclusively found in forest habitat (Table 7.3).

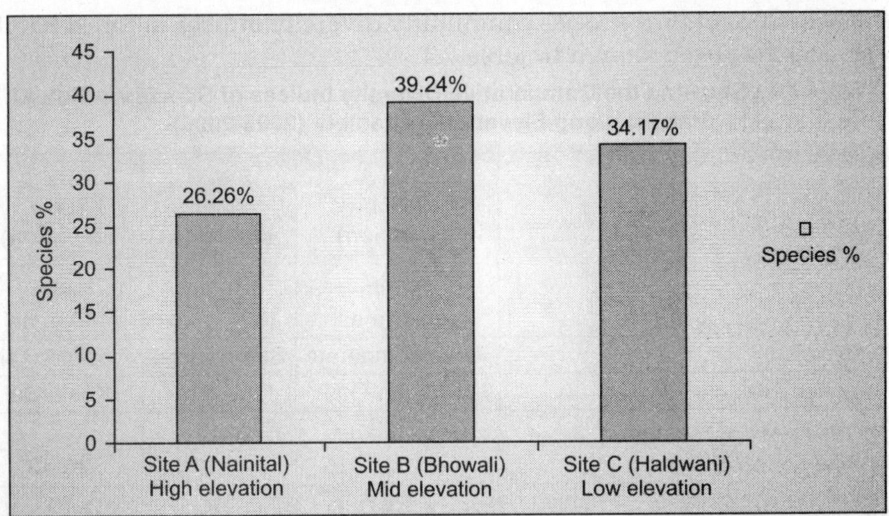

Fig. 7.4: Showing the distribution of exclusive forest species (in percentage) among the study sites

Table 7.3 : Distribution of Avian Species in Forest Habitats Along Different Elevation Zones

Siteelevational zones	Exclusive species in the forest area	Common species in forest and their adjoin area	Total species
Site A (Nainital)	26	62	88
Site B (Bhowali)	39	67	106
Site C (Haldwani)	34	61	95

In site A (Nainital), mean species diversity and richness was recorded 2.91 ±0.21 and 4.17 ±0.74 respectively. In site B (Bhowali), mean species diversity and richness was recorded 3.09 ±0.27 and 5.11 ± 0.99 respectively, and in site C (Haldwani), mean species diversity and richnes was recorded 3.02 ±0.15 and 5.06 ±0.43 respectively.

The species richness and diversity were recorded maximum at site (B) as compared to the other sites. The distribution of bird species community among the sites shows that 26, 39 and 34 species were exclusive to forest habitat of site A, B and C respectively. However, sixty two species in site A, 67 species in site B and 61 species in site C were common with urban habitats. On comparing the bird community composition among forest habitats of among the sites significant higher composition was observed at mid elevation (Bhowali) than the high elevation (Nainital) (t=2.75, df= 11, $P<0.05$) and lower composition was found at the low elevation (Haldwani) than the mid elevation (Bhowali) (t=0.21, df=11, $P>0.05$), however, the differences was not significant.

The assessment of bird species community diversity indices in forest habitats of the sites has been shown in table 7.4.

Table 7.4 : Showing the Comparative Diversity Indices of Species in Forest Habitat along Elevational Gradient (2005-2006)

	Site A (High elevation)	Site B (Mid elevation)	Site C (Low elevation)
Elevation (m asl)	2098m- 2450 m asl	1450m- 1601 m asl	344m- 440 m asl
Forest types	Moist temperate	Sub tropical	Tropical moist
Dominant Tree species	Deodar, Oak	Pine, Oak	Khair, Sal
Shannon's diversity index (*H'*)	3.72	3.86	3.77
Species richness (*R*)	10.21	11.67	10.43
Exclusive species in forest habitat	26	39	34
Rare species (n<5)	17	13	13
Species individuals (N)	5029	8064	8170
(1/d) dominance value	13.74	12.28	13.32

Feeding Guild Structure

The species were classified into 6 feeding guilds and further classified into 18 sub feeding guilds. The details of their feeding guilds have been given in the following tables 7.5 (a, b).

Table 7.5(a) : Showing the Major 6 Feeding Guilds of Avian Species in the Study Sites

Main feeding guilds	Sub feeding guilds	Nainital	Bhowali	Haldwani
Insectivore	6	58 (65.90%)	58 (54.71 %)	51 (53.68 %)
Omnivore	2	9 (10.22 %)	13 (12.26 %)	14 (14.73 %)
Frugivore	2	7 (7.95 %)	9 (8.49 %)	14 (14.73 %)
Carnivore	4	6 (6.81 %)	8 (7.54 %)	7 (7.36 %)
Granivore	2	6 (6.81 %)	15 (14.15 %)	7 (7.36 %)
Nectarivore	2	2 (2.27 %)	3 (2.83 %)	2 (2.10 %)

Table 7.55(b) : Showing the species sub feeding guilds in the study sites

Main feeding guilds	Sub feeding guilds	Site A (Nainital)	Site B (Bhowali)	Site C (Haldwani)
Insectivore				
	Aerial insectivore	22 (25%)	20 (18.86%)	19 (20%)
	Bark gleaning insectivore	9 (10.22%)	7 (6.60%)	12 (12.63%)
	Foliage gleaning insectivore	6 (6.81%)	6. (5.66%)	2 (2.10%)

Main feeding guilds	Sub feeding guilds	Site A (Nainital)	Site B (Bhowali)	Site C (Haldwani)
	Sallying insectivore	9 (10.22%)	10 (9.43%)	9 (9.47%)
	Under-storey insectivore	8 (9.09%)	9 (8.49%)	5 (5.26%)
	Grass land insectivore	4 (4.54%)	6 (5.66%)	4 (4.21%)
Omnivore				
	Terrestrial omnivore	4 (4.54%)	7 (6.60%)	6 (6.31%)
	Arboreal terrestrial omnivore	5 (5.68%)	6 (5.66%)	8 (8.42%)
Granivore				
	Granivore seed eater	4 (4.54%)	9 (8.49%)	4 (4.21%)
	Frugivore granivore insectivore seed eater	2 (2.27%)	6 (5.66%)	3 (3.15%)
Frugivore				
	Frugivore seed eater	4 (4.54%)	6 (5.66%)	10 (10.52%)
	Frugivore insectivore	3 (3.40%)	3 (2.83%)	4 (4.21%)
Carnivore				
	Sallying carnivore	1 (1.13%)	4 (3.77%)	4 (4.21%)
	Arboreal terrestrial carnivore	2 (2.27%)	1 (0.94%)	1 (1.05%)
	Terrestrial carnivore	1 (1.13%)	3 (2.83%)	1 (1.05%)
	Wading carnivore	2 (2.27%)	0	1 (1.05%)
Nectarivore				
	Nectarivore insectivore	1 (1.13%)	1 (0.94%)	1 (1.05%)
	Nectarivore	1 (1.13%)	2 (1.88%)	1 (1.05%)

Discussion

In terms of species distribution along the elevational zones, species abundance value was higher at mid elevation (site B, Bhowali, 1450m – 1601m asl) than the site C (low elevation, Haldwani 344m- 440m asl) and site A (high elevation, Nainital, 2098m- 2450m asl). The mean species diversity and richness in each study site in each year were observed almost same during the study period. However, the species diversity was fluctuating along the elevations in different seasons as a result of migrations between summer breeding areas and winter feeding areas. The highest diversity therefore was recorded in the summer season (April and June) at high elevation (sites A, 2450 m asl) and mid elevation (site B, 1600 m asl); while low elevation (site C, 440 m asl) was observed with highest species diversity in winter (November). It was found (on the basis of present/ absent data) that a number of bird species such as Long tail minivet (*Pericrocotus ethologus*), Grey back shrike (*Lanius tephronotus*), Grey headed canary flycatcher (*Culicicapa ceylonensis*), Blue-capped rock thrush (*Monticolus cinclorhynchus*), Himalayan bulbul (*Pycnonotus leucogenys*), Blue whistling thrush (*Myophonus caeruleus*) and Common swallow (*Hirundo rustica*) migrated from the higher elevation site to lower elevation site in winter season. In the same manner, during summer season these bird species migrate to higher elevation from lower elevation causing increase in abundance/ diversity at Site A. The presence of summer visitors like Asian paradise flycatcher (*Terpsiphone paradisi*), Verditer flycatcher (*Eumyias thalassina*), and Pied crested cuckoo (*Clamator jacobinus*) at study sites also contribute to the avian diversity of the area. These species visit here in summer season from the southern part of India. Species abundance and diversity also fluctuate through the migration of species in the month of July and August (Johnsingh and Joshua, 1994). It was observed that the altitudinal winter migratory birds disappeared in the last week of November and the same species appeared as visitor in the summer season by early March.

Species abundance fluctuates in different seasons in the entire year in general in the India subcontinent. A number of migratory birds from Palaearctic zone visit the Indian subcontinent during winter every year increasing the species richness temporarily. Some studies have shown (MacArthur, 1959, Weins, 1989) that many tropical birds migrate to the temperate zone also for a brief time to breed. These tropical birds become major component of temperate bird species diversity, greatly increasing the temperate bird diversity during the summer breeding season.

In this study it was found that insectivore species were dominant in forest habitat, indicating rich abundance and easy availability of insects in the forest habitat. The variation in bird community consistent with the distribution of food resources was reported by Lefebvre and Poulin, (1997) also. Some studies conducted in the Indian subcontinent (Johnsingh *et al.*, 1994; Kropil, 1996; Sharma, 2001; Singh, 2004) have also shown that the insectivore guild is dominant in the forest habitat.

According to Thiolly *et al.* (1988), each forest type has its own species. The distribution and abundance of many bird species are determined by the configuration and composition of the vegetation that comprises a major element of their habitat (Cody, 1985; Morrison, 1992; Block and Brennan, 1993). Among the avian species of forest habitat in all the sites the Large billed crow (*Corvus macrorhynchos*), Himalayan bulbul (*Pycnonotus leucogenys*) and Red vented bulbul (*Pycnonotus cafer*) were estimated dominant species which indicating that forest of the study sites are rich in food availability. It is interesting to know that the abundance of Red jungle fowl (*Gallus gallus*) was good in forest habitat of site C showing less human interruption/ poaching in this area. During our observation also we found least anthropogenic activities except occational cattle grazing aand fodder collection by local people in the reserved forest. Bird species diversity and abundance in forest stands can be predicted by the presence of forest structural elements (canopy emergent trees, logs, snags and understorey cover) in the forest habitat (Diaz *et al.*, 2005). To keep this thought a case study also proposed in the same study area.

REFERENCES

Ali S, 1981. The Himalayan in Indian Ornithology, Him. Asp. Change. ed. Lall & Moddie.16-31.

Ali S, Ripley D, 1998. Birds of India and Pakistan. Bombay: Oxford University Press.

Anonymous, 1991. The state of forest Report 1991. Forest Survey of India Ministry of Environment and Forests Government of India, New Delhi.

Arora GS, Kumar A, 1995. Faunal resources in the Western Himalaya. In Studies on the Himalayan Ecosystem. Document on Himalayan Ecosystem. 223–230.

Baker EC, Stuart 1922-31. Fauna of British India: Birds Vols. 1- 8., Taylor and Francis, London.

Barbara A, Michael A, Richardson, Felip N, Sato-adames, 2005. Separating the effects of forest types and elevation on the diversity of litter invertebrate communities in a humid tropical forest in Puerto Rico. *J. of Animal Biology.* 74: 926-936.

Barnes HL, 1989. Cross-Generational Coalitions, Discrepant Perceptions and family functioning. In David H, Olson, Candyce S. Russell, Douglas H, Sprenkle ed. cricunplex Model: systemic Assessment and Treatment of families (pp. 175-198). Binghamton, New York: The Howorth Press.

Barthlott W, Lauer W, Placki A, 1996. Global distribution of species diversity in vascular plants: Towards a world map of Phytodiversity. *Erdkunde.* 50: 317 -327.

Bibby CJ, Burgess ND, Hill DA, 1992. Bird census techniques. London, United Kingdom: Academic press. 257.

Bisht M, Lakhera P, Chandola SA, 1986. Behavioural ecology of white Kaleej pheasant (*Lophura leucomelanus*) Garhwal Himalaya Proc. of XIX. International Ornithological congress: 835.

Blake JG, Loiselle BA, 2000. Diversity of birds along an elevational gradient in the Cordillera Central, Costa Rica. The Auk. 117: 663–686.

Block MW, Brennan LA, 1993. The habitat concept in ornithology. *Current Ornithology.* 11: 35-91.

Brown JH, 1971. Mammals on mountaintops: non equilibrium insular biogeography. *Am. Nat.* 105: 467–478.

Brown JH, 1988. Species diversity. In: Myers, A.A and Gillet, P.S. ed. Analytical Biogeography. Landon: Chapman and Hall.

Brown JH, 2001. Mammals on mountainsides: elevational patterns of diversity. *Glob. Ecol. Biogeogr.* 10: 101 – 109.

Castellatta M, Thiolly JM, Sodhi NS, 2005. The effects of extreme forest fragmentation on the bird community of Singapore Island. *Biol.Cons.* 121 (1): 135-155.

Chakraverthy AK, 1997. The western Ghats Malaned where coffee, cardamom and paddy cultivation sustain bird diversity in Karnataka, India. Indian *J. of biodiversity* vol.1, 3, 7-27.

Christy M. McCain, 2007. Could temperature and water availability drive elevational species richness patterns? A global case study for bats. *Global Ecol. Biogeogr.* 16: 1-13.

Cody ML, 1975. Towards a theory of continental species diversity: Bird distributions over Mediterranean habitat-gradients. In: Cody MI, Diamond JM ed. Ecology and Evolution of communities Harvard University Cambridge: Press. 214-254.

Cody ML, 1985. Habitat selection in birds. New York, Academic Press.

Cody ML, 1986. An Introduction to Habitat selection in birds. In: Cody ML, ed. Habitat selection in birds. New York: Academic Press. 4-46.

Colwell RK, Lee DC, 2000. The mid – domain effect: geometrical constraints on the geography of species richness, *Treands Ecol. Evol.* 15: 70-76.

Colwell RK, Rahbek C, Gotelli NJ, 2004. The mid domain effect and species richness patterns: what have we learned so far? *Am. Nat.* 163: 1-23.

Daniels RJR, Joshi NV, Gadgil M, 1992. On the relationship between bird and woody plant species diversity in the Uttara Kannada district of south India. Proc. Natl. Acad. Sci. 89: 5311-5315.

Diamond JM, 1971. Comparison of faunal equilibrium turnover rates on a tropical island and temperate island. Proc. Natn. Acad. Sci. 68: 2742.

Diamond JM, 1972. Comparison of faunal equilibrium turnover rate on a tropical island and a temperate island. Proc. Natn. Acad. Sci., 68. 2742.

Diamond JM, 1975. Assembly of species communities. In M.L. Cody and J.M diamond eds. Ecology and evolution of communities. Cambridge: Harvard University press. 342-444.

Diamond JM, 1989. The present, past and future of human-caused extinctions. Philosophical Transactions of the Royal Society of London Series B, 325: 469-477.

Diaz IA, Armesto JJ, Reid S, Sieving KE, Willson MF, 2005. Linking forest structure and composition: avian diversity in successional forests of Chile Island, Chile. *Biol. Cons.* 123: 91-101.

Dorst J, 1997. The life of birds Vol. II New York: Columbia University Press.

Erwin TL, 1982. Tropical forests: their richness in Coleoptera and other arthropod species. Coleopt. Bull. 36: 74-5.

Estades CF, 1997. Bird-habitat relationship in a vegetational gradient in the andes of central Chile. *The Condor.* 99: 719-727.

Gaston KJ, 1994. Rarity, population and community biology. Series – 13 London: Chapman & Hall.

Gaston KJ, 2000. Global patterns in biodiversity. *Nature.* 405: 220-226.

Gaston KJ, Williams PH, Eggketib P, Humphires CJ, 1995. Large scale patterns of biodiversity: Spatial variation in family richness, Proc. Roy. Soc. London. 260: 149-154.

Green RE, Newton I, Shultz S, Cunningham AA, Gilbert M, Pain DJ, Prakash V, 2004. Diclofenac poisoning as a cause of vulture population declines across the Indian subcontinent. *J. Appl. Ecol.* 41: 793-800.

Grimmett R, Inskipp C, Inskipp T, 1998. Birds of the Indian subcontinent. New Delhi: Oxford University Press.

Groombridge B, 1992. Global biodiversity: Status of the Earth's Living Resources. Compiled by the world Conservation Monitoring Centre. London: Chapman and Hall.

Groombridge B, Jenkins MD, 2000. Global Biodiversity: Earth's living sources in the 21st centaury UK: World Conservation Monitoring Committee. 246.

Heywood VH, Watson RT, 1995. Global Biodiversity Assessment UNEP. UK: Cambridge University Press.

Hill MO, 1973. Diversity and evenness: a unifying notation and its consequences. *Ecology*. 54: 427 – 31.

Hudson C, 1930. A list of some birds of seven hills of Nainital, U.P. *J. Bombay Nat. Hist. Soc.* 34: 821 – 827.

Huston MA, 1999. Local processes and regional patterns: appropriate scales for understanding variation in the diversity of plants and animals. *Oikos*. 86: 393-401.

in a thorn scrub habitat in south India. *Trop. Ecol.* 28: 22-34.

Ivan A Diaz, Armesto JJ, Reid S, Sieving KE, Willson MF, 2005. Linking forest structure and composition: avian diversity in successional forests of Chiloe Island, *Chile. Biol. Conser.* 123: 91-101.

James FC, 1971. Ordinations of habitat relationship among breeding birds. Wilson / bull. 83: 215-236.

Jenkins M, 1992. Species Diversity: An Introduction. In: Groombridge B, ed. Global Biodiversity, Status of the Earth's living resources. London: Chapman and Hall. 40-46.

Jerdon TC, 1862-64. Birds of India, 2 vols (3 parts). Culcutta.

Johnsingh AJT, Martin NH, Balasingh J, Chelladurai V, 1987. Vegetation and avifauna

Johnsingh ATJ, Joshua J, 1994. Avifauna in three vegetation types on Mundanthurai Plateau, South India. *J. Trop. Ecol.* 10: 323-335.

Kattan GH, Franco P, 2004. Bird diversity along elevation gradients in the Andes of Colombia. *J. Biogeogr.* 13: 451–458.

Kazmierczak K, 2001. A field guide to the Birds of India. United Kingdom: Pica Press.

Kery M, Mathies D, Sapillman HH, 2000. Reduced fecundity and offspring performance in small population of the decling grassland plants Primula veris and Gentiana lutea. *J. Ecol.* 88: 17-30.

Khoshoo TN, 1987. Ecodevelopment of Alkaline Land: Banthra – A case study. National Botanical Research Instt. CSIR, Lucknow. 1 – 141.

Khoshoo TN, 1996. Biodiversity in the India Himalayas: conservation and utilization. In: Sheggi P, ed. Banking on Biodiversity. Kathamndu: International Centre for Integrated Mountain Development.

Kobayashi S, Kimura K, 1994. The number of species occurring in a sample of a biotic community and its connections with species – abundance relationship and spatial distribution. *Ecol. Res.* 9: 281-294.

Krebs CJ, 1972. Ecology. The experimental analysis of distribution and abundance. Harper and Row, New York.

Kropil R, 1996. Structure of the breeding bird assemblage of the fir-breech primeval forest in the west Carpathians (Badin natural reserve). *Folia Zoologica*. 45: 311-324.

Kunte K, Jogleker A, Utkarsh G, Pramod P, 1999. Patterns of butterfly, bird and tree diversity in the Western Ghats. *Curr. Sci.* 77(4): 577-586.

Laishangbam S, Bhatt D, 2005. How relevant are the concepts of species diversity and species richness? *J. Biosci.* 30 (5): 557-560.

Lawrence RH, 2001. Small mammal diversity along elevational gradients in the Philippines: an assessment of patterns and hypotheses. *G. Ecol. Biogeogr.* 10: 15-39.

Lee PF, Ding TS, Hus FH, Geng S, 2004. Breeding bird species richness in Taiwan: distribution on gradients of elevation, primary productivity and urbanization. *J. Biogeogr.* 31: 307 - 314.

Lefebvre G, Poulin B, 1997. Bird communities in Panamanian black mangrove: potential effects of physical and biotic factor. *J. Tropic. Ecol.* 13: 97-113.

Lloyd M, Ghelardi RJ, 1964. A table for calculating the 'equitability' component of species diversity. *J. Anima. Ecol.* 33: 217-255.

Lomolino MV, 2001. Elevation gradients of species density historical and prospective views. *Global Ecol. Biogeogr.* 10: 3-13.

MacArthur RH, 1959. On the breeding distribution pattern of North American migrant birds. *Auk.* 76: 318-325.

MacArthur RH, 1972. Geographical ecology: patterns in the distribution of species. New York: Harper & Row.

MacArthur RH, MacArthur J, 1961. On bird species diversity. *Ecology.* 42: 594-598.

Magurran AE, 1988. Measuring Biological Diversity. Australia: Blackwell publishing.

MaNeely JA, 1994. Critical Issues in the implementation of the conservation on biological diversity. Widening perspectives on Biodiversity, IUCN. 7-10.

Manhaes MA, Ribeiro AL, 2005. Spatial Distribution and diversity of bird community in an urban area of Southeast Brazil. Brazilian Archives of Biology and Technology. 48: 285-294.

May RM, 1990. How many species? Phil. Trans. R. Soc. Lond. B 330: 293-304.

May RM, 1992. How many species inhabit the earth? *Sci. Am.* 267: 42-48.

May RM, 1994. Conceptual aspects of the quantification of the extent of biological diversity. Phil. Trans. R. Soc. Lond. B 345: 13-20.

McCain CM, 2003. North American desert rodents: A test of the Mid-Domain effect in species richness. *J. Mammal.* 88: 967-980.

McNeely JA, Miller KR, Reid WV, Mittameier RA, Werner TB, 1990. Conserving the world's Biological Diversity Washington, D.C. and Gland, Switzerland: WRI, world conservation Union, World Bank WWF-US and conservation International.

Morrison MC, Marcot BG, Mannan RW, 1992. Wildlife habitat relationships concepts and applications. Madison, University of Wisconsin Press.

Morrison ML, 1992. Bird abundance in forests managed for timber and wildlife resources. *Biol. Conserve.* 60: 127-134.

Myers N, 1988. Threatened biota: 'hot spots' in tropical forests. *Environmentalist.* 8: 187-208.

Myers N, 1992. Future Operational Monitoring of Tropical Forests: An Alert Strategy. Joint research centre, commission of the European Community, Ispra, Italy.

Pablo MV, Javier AS, 2004. Avian responses to fragmentation of the Maulino Forest in central Chile. *Oryx.* 38 (4): 383-388.

Pianka ER, 1966. Latitudinal gradients in species diversity: a review of concepts. *Am. Nat.* 100: 33-46.

Pielou EC, 1966. Species diversity and pattern diversity in the study of ecological succession. *J. Theo. Biol.* 10: 370-383.

Pramod P, 1996. Ecology studies of bird communities of silent valley and neighboring forests Ph.D Thesis Calicut University.

Pramod P, Joshi NV, Ghate U, Gadgil M, 1997. On the hospitability of western Ghats Habitats for bird communities. Curr. Sci. 73(2): 122-127.

Price TD, 1979. The seasonality and occurrence of birds in the Eastern Ghats of Andhra Pradesh. *J. Bombay Nat. Hist. Soc.* 76: 379 - 422.

Rahbek C, 1995. The elevation gradient of species richness: a uniform pattern. *Ecography.* 18(2): 200 -205.

Ricklefs RE, Schluter D, 1993. Species diversity: regional and historical influences. In: Ricklefs RE, Schluter D ed. Species diversity in ecological communities: historical and geographical perspective. Cambridge: University of Chicago Press. 350-363.

Rohde K, 1978. Latitudinal gradients in species diversity and their causes. 1. Review of hypotheses explaining gradients. *Biol. Zbl.* 97: 393-404.

Root R, 1967. The niche exploration pattern of the Blue – grey Gnatcatcher. *Ecol. Monographs.* 37: 317-350.

Schemske DW, Brokaw N, 1981. Tree falls and the distribution of under storey birds in a tropical forest. *Ecology.* 72: 1763-1774.

Schroeder RL, 1987. Community models for wildlife impact assessment: a review of concepts and approaches. U.S.F.W.S. Biol. Rep. 87: 41.

Sepkoski JJ, 1992. Phylogenetic and ecology patterns in the phanerozoic history of marine biodiversity. In: Eldridge N ed. Systematic, Ecology and the Biodiversity Crisis. New York: Columbia Univ. Press. 77-100.

Shall JJ, Pianka ER, 1978. Geographical trends in numbers of species. Science. 201: 679 686.

Shankar Raman TR, Joshi NV, 2001. Bird community structure along an elevational gradient in a tropical rainforest. In: Ganeshaiah KN, Umashankar R, Bawa KS ed. Tropical ecosystems: structure, diversity and Human welfare. Proceedings of the international conference on Tropical Ecosystems. New Delhi: Oxford IBH. 701-706.

Sharma RK, 2001. Avian diversity and vegetation association in four distinct habitat types in Haridwar. Ph.D. dissertation. Gurukul Kangri University Haridwar, Uttarakhand.

Sibley CG, Monroe BL, 1990. Distribution and Taxonomy of Birds of the world. New Haven: Yale University Press.

Singh LS, 2004. Avian diversity and vegetational association in four distinct landscape elements in Bishnupur district and adjoining area of Manipur. Ph.D. dissertation. Gurukul Kangri University Haridwar, Uttarakhand.

Solbrig OT, 1993. All of US – 1 – Sept.

Stiles TG, 1978. Patterns of fruit presentations and seed dispersal in bird disseminated woody plants in the eastern deciduous forests. *Am. Nat.* 116: 670-688.

Stotz DF, 1998. Endemism and species turnover with elevation in montane avifauna in neotropics: implications for conservation. In: Mace GM, Balmford A, Ginsberg JR ed. Conservation in a changing world. Cambridge: University Press. 161-180.

Stuart FC, Erika SZ, Valerie TE, Rosamonal LN, Peter MV, Heather LR, David UH, Sandra L, Osvaldo ES, Sarah EH, 2000. *Nature.* 405: 234-241.

Sultana A, Khan JA, 2000. Birds of Oak forests in the Kumaun Himalaya, Uttar Pradesh India. *Forktail.* 16: 131-146.

Templeton AR, 1996. Translocation in conservation. In: Szaro, R.C. and Johnston, D.W. Biodiversity in Managed Landscapes. Oxford Univ. Press,Oxford, pp. 314-325.

Terborgh J, 1977. Bird species diversity on an Andean elevational gradient. *Ecology.* 58: 1007-1019.

Terborgh J, Robinson SK, Parker III TA, Munn CA, Pierpont N, 1990. Structure and organization of an Amazonian forest bird community. *Ecol. Monogr.* 60: 213-38.

Terborgh J, Weske J, 1969. Colonization of secondary habitats by Peruvian birds.

Thiolly JM, Meyburg BU, 1988. Forest fragmentation and the conservation of raptors: a survey on the island of Java. *Biol. Con.* 44: 229-250.

Tzung-Su ding, Hsiao-weiYuan, ShuGeng, Yao-Sung Lin and Peiten lee, 2005. Energy flux body size and density in ratio to bird species richness along an elevation gradient in Tiawan. *Glob. Ecol. Biogeogr.* 14: 299-306.

Valdiya KS, Bartarya SK, 1980. Geology of Kumaun Lesser Himalaya. Dehradun: Wadia Institute of Himalayan Geology. 291.

Wang Z, Young SS, 2003. Differences in bird diversity between two swidden agricultural sites in mountainous terrain, Xishuangbanna, Tunnan, *China. Bio. Conser.* 110: 231-243.

Whittaker RH, 1972. Evolution and measurement of species diversity. Taxon. 21: 213-251.

Wiens A, 1989. The ecology of bird communities volume I. Foundation and patterns. UK: Cambridge University press.

Wilson EO, 1985. The biological diversity crisis. *Bio Science.* 35: 700-706.

Evaluation of the Effect of Integrated Rice-fish Farming in the Tarai Region of Uttarakhand

—B.C. Joshi, *India*
—A.K. Upadhyay, *India*
—S.C. Joshi, *India*

ABSTRACT

A trial on rice-cum-fish farming was conducted in Tarai region during June – October, 2010. The rice variety Jalnidhi was grown for 150 days and the combination of five species of fish i.e. rohu, catla, mrigal, silver carp and common carp were stocked at the rate of 5000 fingerlings per hectare and grown for 5 months. The rice harvest from the rice-cum-fish field was on average 12.68 per cent higher than that from the rice-only field. Without providing any artificial feed the total fish production was satisfactory (329.81kg/ha in 150 days). The physico-chemical characteristics of water found within the optimal range for the growth of carps.

Key Words: Rice, Fish, Integration, Physico-chemical Characteristics, Production.

Introduction

Rice cum fish farming is almost an old farming practice. It is suggested that fish culture in rice fields was practiced in India from about 1500 years ago (Tamura, 1961; Coche, 1967). The combination of rice and fish farming shows a mutual relationship between rice and fish. It requires very little input and provides off-season employment to farm labours (Hora and Pillay, 1962). The rice field is gracious to many fish both for spawning and for pasture. The swamped rice field contains significant quantity of decaying plants which give rise to huge amount of plankton and in fact serves rich food for fry and fingerlings. In paddy field the shallow water spawners and the nest builders get favourable conditions of breeding. The adhesive eggs laid by fish on green plants facilitate more oxygen for developing embryo.

On the other hand fish feed on organisms which grow in fields and on many injurious insects and their larva, thus saving the crop from harmful organisms and promoting better rice yield. By culturing herbivorous fish, the weed growth can be controlled to a considerable extent and the expenses on labour for weeding can also saved. It is also possible to control the growth of molluscs and breeding of mosquitoes, thus reducing public health hazards. Movement of fish in flooded rice fields increases tillering, which is helpful in higher rice production (Coche, 1967). Greater depth of water maintained in fields prevents pests like rodents from digging holes in bunds, and floods their existing holes.

For the efficient integration of rice with fish culture, the physicochemical and biological factors of the rice field play major role in overall metabolism, water quality and aquatic production. The selection of fish species for culture should according to the physicochemical and biological environment of the rice field. It is, therefore necessary to have a proper knowledge of the important physical and chemical properties the system.

Rice-cum-fish culture method ensures a more economic utilization of resources and increases the income without increasing expenses, (Hickling 1962). Very little extra labour is required to take care of fish, as it can be attended to at the same time as the rice. Fish is often called swimming fertilizer factory as it fertilize through its fecal matter (Sinha, 1985). Thus, in integrated farming nothing goes waste; the byproduct of one system becomes the input for other. Certain species of fish like common carp act like a biological plough and overturns the submerged soil thus making available more nutrient as well as oxygen to the paddy plant. The present investigation is mainly aimed to assess the effect of an integrated farming system on the yield of the two crops.

MATERIAL AND METHOD

The rice-cum-fish farming trial conducted at farmer's field near Pantnagar for the period of 150 days during June – October, 2010. Tarai region was chosen for the trial because its agro-climatic conditions are suitable for both rice and fish production.

Geographical Location and Climatic Condition of Experimental Sites

Pantnagar is situated at 29°N latitude, 79°E longitude & altitude of 243.84 m above sea level, in Tarai belt of Shivalik range of Himalayan foot hills. The climatic condition of Pantnagar is humid, sub-tropical & is characterized by very hot & dry summer & extremely cold condition. The fog generally occurs with winter towards the end of December & may continue till February end. The monsoon normally commences during the third week of June ceases by the end of September. The metrological information of rainfall, relative humidity, seasonal atmospheric temperature and insolation period during experiments is given in Table 8.1.

Table 1: Monthly Fluctuation in Meteorological Condition during the Course of Investigation

Month	Temperature °C		Rel. Humidity		Rainfall (mm)	Wind speed	Insolation Period	Evap. (mm)
	Max.	Min.	Max.	Min.				
May	35.4	23.6	72	40	112.2	12.6	08.3	8.4
June	35.1	25.1	76	47	056.0	12.1	07.9	6.8
July	32.9	26.1	87	65	297.0	11.5	04.7	5.1
Aug.	32.6	25.2	88	66	328.2	9.2	06.9	4.6
Sept.	32.3	23.1	90	63	103.8	8.1	08.1	4.2
Oct.	30.9	17.9	90	52	029.8	3.6	08.3	3.2

Plate 1: Rice – Fish farming land preparation measures

Experimental Design

Two plots of 0.1 hectare (40m×25m) and 0.11 hectare (44m x 25 m) were prepared and marked as T_1 and T_2 respectively. The T_1 plot was irrigated rice plot and T_2 was integrated rice and fish plot in which one trench of 100 m^2 (10m × 10m) size was constructed at centre for the shelter of fish during low water level in rice field. Surrounding the plot T_2, a peripheral dyke is constructed which create a confinement for fish, which prevents entry of water and unwanted organisms from out side also helps in preventing the escaping of cultured fish from the area.

Pre-transplantation Land Management

The field for rice cultivation is prepared by ploughing it 3-4 times during April –May. After ploughing the field is leveled evenly so that every part of it will be uniformly irrigated. During land preparation 1000 kg cow dung, 6.2 kg monosuperphosphate, 1.5 kg urea and 1.6 kg potash was applied in each plot. Top dressing by 1.5 kg urea was done in each trial during active tillering stage and panicle initiation stage.

Transplantation and Maintenance

The Jalnidhi variety of rice was chosen for the trials in view of its long cycle and height. The rice plant gain sufficient height to culture with fish. Seedlings were prepared by germinated seeds sown in the month of May at the bed of 10 m length and 1.25 m breadth. The 25-30 days old seedlings were transplanted in the month of June in lines with 2- 3 seedlings per hill and the spacing was kept 20 cm between each plant. Deweeding was done during the whole cultivation period of paddy when it was become necessary. The level of water for the entire paddy cultivation period was maintained at below the half height of the paddy plant. Harvesting of paddy was done after 150 days in the month of October. During harvesting water depth was reduced in the plot by opening the outlet.

Plate 8.2: Examination of Rice – Fish farming plot.

Plate 8.3: A close view of rice crop

Fish Stocking and Management

Five species combination of fishes was taken for the experiment. Three species of Indian Major Carps i.e. Rohu, Catla and Mrigal and two species of exotic carps i.e. Silver Carp and Common Carp was reared as per the ratio given in Table 8.2. Fingerling size (10 - 15 cm length and 12.1 – 12.8 gm weight) of fish seed was stocked at the rate of 5000 nos. /hectare (includes total area of pond and plot).

Table 8.2: Species combination of fishes taken for integrated rice cum fish farming.

S. No.	Fish species	Percentage of 5 species composition (numbers/ hectare)
1.	*Catla catla* (Bahu, Dhekera, Bhakua)	15 (750)
2.	*Labeo rohita* (Rohu)	20 (1000)
3.	*Cirrhinus mrigala* (Mrigal, Nain)	20 (1000)
4.	*Cyprinus carpio* (Common Carp)	20 (1000)
5.	*Hypophthalmichthys molitrix* (Silver Carp)	25 (1250)

Prestocking Pond Management

The fish pond/trench preparation was done during the preparation of paddy field i.e. during April – May. The pond was left for 10-15 days in sun to kill fish parasite, their larvae and disease producing organisms. All the aquatic weeds were manually removed from the pond. Well grounded Quick lime (CaO) @ 200 kg/ha was broadcasted all over the pond bottom after drying as a prophylactic measure and for fast mineralization (Khanna and Singh, 2005). The pond was then manured with cow dung @ 5 tonnes/hectare respectively i.e 500 kg. Half of the total quantity of manure was applied after two days of liming i.e. 250 kg and the remaining was applied in two subsequent installments i.e.125 kg each (Joshi, 2008). After one week of liming, the ponds were filled with water. The water level was maintained at 0.75 cm for 7 days and one day before stocking, the water level was raised to 1.5 meter.

Fish stocking was done after screening the pond through a nylon hapa to eliminate the entry of any fish, fish eggs, larvae etc. Adolescent stock of fish of about uniform size ranging between 12.1 – 12.8 gm weight was stocked in the pond according to Table 2. Initial length and weight of each fish was recorded prior to release into ponds after acclimatization. The fish were given a prophylactic dip in $KMnO_4$ solution (1:3000) before stocking.

In addition to the routine examination of water quality parameters, strict vigilance for abstraction and the subsequent filling of the pond at required level was maintained through out the duration of field experiment. Random sampling was adopted at 30 days of interval to assess the growth of fish. In each sampling the length and weight of 20 fishes were recorded.

The final harvest of fish was done after 150 days after harvesting the rice in the month of October. During the harvesting of rice water in the paddy plot was reduced and fishes took shelter in the pond. The water level in the pond is maintained as 1 m. After harvesting rice the water level in the field again maintained till the harvest of fishes. The survival rate of fish in the experiment was also assessed.

Analysis of Physicochemical and Biological Factors

The pond water samples were collected in clean sampling bottles from the rice field at weekly interval for the estimation of pH, dissolved oxygen, carbon-dioxide, water turbidity etc. pH of the water sample for weekly duration from the feeding trials were determined electrometrically with the help of pH meter. The dissolved oxygen content of pond water was determined following Winkler titrimetric method (APHA 1985). The free carbon dioxide was estimated by standard titrimetric method using phenolphthalein as an indicator (APHA, 1985). Total Dissolved Solids (TDS) was determined according to AOAC (1990) method. Plankton samples were collected at weekly intervals. 100 litres of water was filtered using a plankton net made of No. 30 bolting silk cloth (60 μ mesh size).

RESULT AND DISCUSSION

It was found that the integrated rice-fish farming system is superior to the traditional system of rice production in terms of economic benefits, as well as in its effect on the environment. The economic viability of the two production systems is discussed below.

Effect on Yield of Rice

The integrated rice-fish system enhanced the yield-contributing characteristics of the rice plants, namely, the number of tillers per hill, number of grains per panicle, and average grain weight (Table 3).

Table 8.3 : Effects of integrated rice-fish system and traditional sole-rice farming on plant characteristics and grain yield of Jalnidhi rice

S. No.	Characteristic	Rice-fish system	Sole rice farming	Difference
1.	Plant height (cm)	81.24	80.12	1.12*
2.	Tiller (no. per hill)	15.20	12.18	3.02*
3.	Panicles (no. per hill)	10.30	8.56	1.74*
4.	Grain (no. per panicle)	137.26	121.85	15.41*
5.	1000 grain wt (g)	26.47	25.75	0.72
6.	Grain yield (tonne per ha)	3.22	2.84	0.38

*Significant at 5% level.

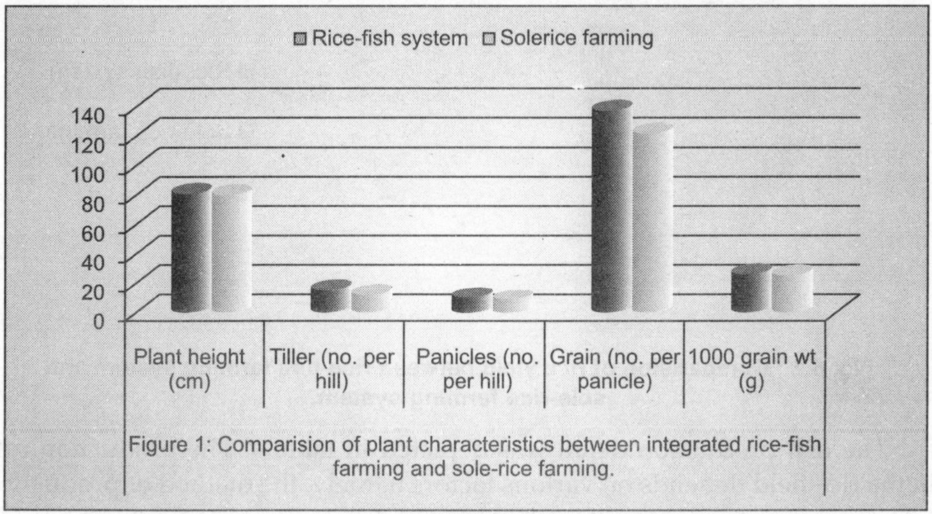

Fig. 8.1. Comparision of plant characteristics between integrated rice-fish farming and sole-rice farming.

The rice yield obtained from the integrated rice-fish farming was 3220 kg/hectare. Data reveal that the rice yields from the rice-cum-fish fields are on an average 12.68 per cent higher than the yield from the rice-only field. Mohanty *et. al.* (2004) has also reported that the cultivation of fish in rice fields increases the rice yields by 8 to 15 percent. FAO, 1992 and NAGA, 1992 also recorded the yield of 4500 kg/ha and 3130 kg/ha respectively from integrated rice – fish farming system. In rice cum fish farming system the height of plant was slightly increased by 1.37 percent than sole rice farming (Figure 2). The numbers of tillers per hill was increased by 1.37 per cent in integrated rice – fish farming. The panicle numbers and grain number per panicle was also found to be increased by 19.86 per cent and 16.89 per cent respectively. Figure 8.2 clearly indicate that the stocking of fish in rice field affected the rice yield as the yield is higher in rice – fish farming than sole rice farming. Fish regenerate nitrogen and phosphorus to improve soil fertility and also release nutrients by stirring the sediments in rice fields. Foraging and movement of fish in rice fields causes the aeration of the water, which increases photosynthesis and results the increment of yield (Frei and Becker 2005; Mustow 2002).

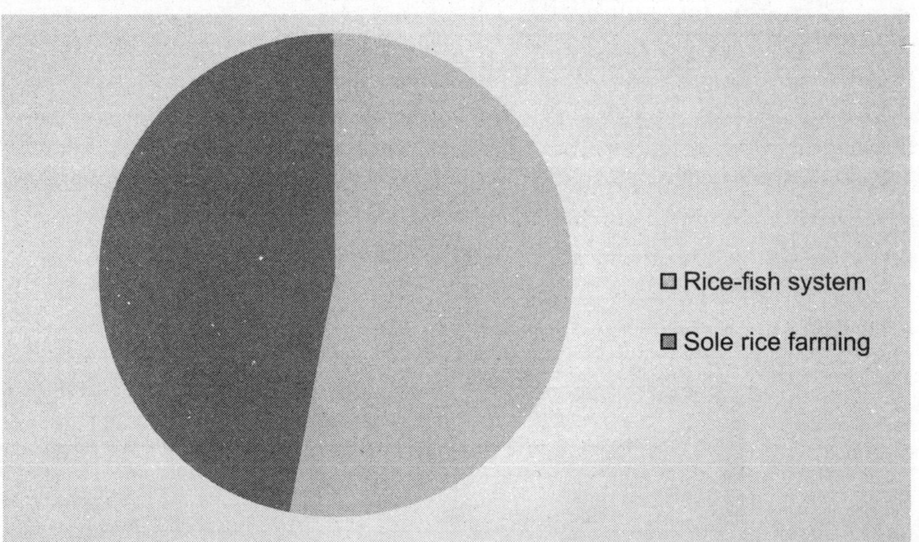

Fig. 8.2 : Comparision of rice yield between rice-fish farming system and sole-rice farming system.

The fish production detail was depicted in table 4. The production rate in the rice field depends on various factors namely, the method of production (extensive or intensive), cultured species, water depth, water and soil fertility etc. (Huet, 1956, Vincke, 1979). The total weight of fishes (fingerlings) at the time of stocking was 9.92 kg. The total weight gain at the harvest was 46.2 kg from 0.11 hactare. The average fish yield from the present investigation was 329.81 kg/ha after 150 days of stocking and at a stocking density of 5000

Plate 4: Harvesting of fish from rice – fish farming field.

fingerlings per hectare. The survival percentage of fishes was recorded as 88.33 percent. NAGA (1992) obtained 200 kg/hectare of fish production over six month duration at a stocking density 10000 fingerlings per hectare, applying only organic manure. Rice fields offer fish planktonic, periphytic and benthic food. Shading by rice plants also maintains the water temperature favourable for fish during the summer. (Wahab *et al* 2008, Kunda *et al* 2008). According to FAO (1992), the fish crop should yield 300 kg per hectare for extensively managed field after four months at the stocking density of 2500 fingerlings per hectare without any supplementary feeding.

Table 8.4: Details of fish production from integrated rice-fish farming.

Parameter	Rice-Fish farming
Number of fishes stocked in 0.11 hectare (1100 m^2) pond	800
Survival percentage	88.33
Total initial weight (kg)	9.92
Total weight at harvest (kg)	46.2
Total fish production (kg/0.11 hac /150 days)	36.28
Total fish production in kg per hectare in 150 days	329.81

Physicochemical Environment of the Rice-Fish Field

Average monthly air and water temperature (°C) and the other physicochemical and biological factors during experimental period is presented in Table 5 and Table 6. The various factors influencing fish culture in the rice fields have been discussed by Coche (1967), Huet (1972) and Vincke (1979). Schuster (1955) and Coche (1967) describe that a minimum annual rainfall of 1200 mm is required for fish culture in rice field. In the present investigation the requirement of minimum amount of rainfall does not appear to be critical as long as irrigation water was available.

In the present study, air temperature ranged from 22.25 to 28.54°C whereas water temperature varied from 21.25°C to 27.14°C (Table 5). Water temperature ranging between 20°C to 30°C is considered to be most suitable for the growth and survival of fishes (Boyd and Pillai, 1984; Alam *et al.*, 1990). Jhingran (1982) reported a water temperature range of 18°C to 32°C as suitable for carps whereas Bankthavathsalam *et al.* (2003) found the temperature range of 26 and 32^{0}C to be optimum for growth of fish under composite carp culture. Carps usually fed between 16 and 32°C, and recommends stoppage of feeding above 27°C (Coche 1967).

Table 8.5 : Average monthly air and water temperature (°C) during experimental period

Days of culture	Air Temperature	Water Temperature
30	22.25	21.25
60	26.18	24.95
90	28.54	26.01
120	28.10	27.00
150	28.41	27.14

pH is an important factor and determines the solubility and chemical nature of most substances in natural waters. Better fish production could be possible in pond water with pH value ranging between 6.5 and 9.0 (Boyd and Pillai, 1984; Sharma, 2000). It has direct effect on fish growth (appetite and food conversion ratio) as well as on the growth and survival of fish food organisms (Das *et al.*, 2001). The pH values in the present study were on the alkaline side throughout the culture period. The average values recorded as 7.18 mg/l fall within the desirable limits for carp culture.

Dissolved oxygen is the most important factor, influencing fish life. Low oxygen concentration may be responsible for the death of fish in ponds. For better growth the range of DO may be maintained above 4 mg/l (Singh and Mishra, 2006). The dissolved oxygen values recorded in the present investigation were within the recommended levels, ranging from 5.07 to 6.42 mg/l. The average value is 6.18 mg/l.

In the present study, free carbon dioxide value ranged from 0.13 to 1.95 ppm throughout the experiment did not have any adverse effect on the survival and growth of fish.

The total dissolved solids (TDS) exhibited a marked seasonal variation between 98.20 mg/l – 115.23 mg/l. The average concentration of TDS during the experiment was 101.67 mg/l. The excess amount of total dissolved solids in water disturbs the ecological balance due to osmotic regulation in aquatic fauna even in the presence of fair amount of dissolved oxygen.

Table 8.6 : Mean values (±SD) of physico-chemical characteristics of water in integrated rice-fish farming field

Parameters	Value
Water temperature (°C)	25.25±4.96
pH	7.18±0.41
Dissolved oxygen (mg/l)	6.18±0.76
Free Carbon dioxide (mg/l)	1.40±2.88
Total dissolved solid (mg/l)	101.67±36.45
Plankton concentration (mg/100 litre water)	94.08±1.64

Vincke (1979) describes that rice fields ecology is characterized by shallow waters (5 – 25 cm) are rich planktonic fauna and flora, especially rich phytoplankton. Phytoplankton communities at moderate standing crops are net producers of dissolved oxygen, and they assimilate ammonia as a nitrogen source for growth (Paerl and Tucker, 1995). The plankton biomass in all ponds increased up to 120 days of culture and after that there was a slight decrease in the planktonic biomass. The plankton production in the rice – fish farming system was varied from 84.10 to 98.08 mg/100 litre of water (on wet basis) with the average value of 94.08 mg/100 litre of water.

Among the parameters studied, the water temperature, pH, dissolve oxygen, free carbon dioxide, total dissolve solids and planktonic concentrations were with in the optimal range for the growth of carps.

Conclusion

Compared to many farming technologies, rice cum fish culture is a low-risk technology. It saves farmers time, allowing them to undertake double benefit from the same field. Data from the rice harvest shows the increment of 12.68 % yields from the rice-cum-fish field then the rice-only field. It is expected that the higher productivity from the rice-fish field is due to the presence of fish in the field, leading to extra fertilizing, improved weed and insect control as well as mineralization, soil aeration and distribution of nutrients etc. A major benefit of rice-cum-fish farming is that inputs to the various subsystems which comprise the farming system come from within the farm.

Integrated rice-fish farming is a sustainable substitute to sole rice farming, if farmers utilize the natural productivity of the rice field ecosystem. In integrated rice – fish farming there is less use of fertilizers than sole rice farming. Fish wastes increases the amount of organic fertilizer and decreases the aquatic weeds, algae and pests in rice fields. Farmers need fewer amounts of fertilizer and pesticide for the rice field. Thus integrated rice-fish farming is an organic method that keeps environmental sustainability. Moreover the integrated rice-fish farming provide balance diet to the farmers. It is not only the ample supply of carbohydrate but also the supply of animal protein, micronutrients, vitamins and minerals to the rural farmers.

Acknowledgement

I am highly indebted to the Coordinator, Rural Bioresource Complex, G. B. Pant University of Agriculture and Technology Pantnagar who gave me opportunity to work in the field of integrated farming technology. I also gratefully acknowledge the help forwarded by my fellow colleagues, Rural Bioresource Complex, during the investigation.

REFERENCES

Alam, W.; Sheri, A.N. and Afzal, M. 1990. Effect of poultry manure on the growth performance of *Labeo rohita* under polyculture system. *In:* Proc. Pakistan Congress on Zoology. 10: 301-306.

Bankthavathsalam, R.; Vishnupriya, S.R.; Panimalar, S.; Kavita, S. and Perianayaki, D. 2003. Diurnal and weekly variations of some physico-chemical factors of a natural carp culture pond. *Environ & Ecology.* 21 (1): 227-233.

Boyd C.E. and Pillai, V.K. 1984. Water quality management in aquaculture, CMFRI. Special publication, pp. 22-97.

Coche, A.G., 1967. Fish culture in rice fields: a worldwide synthesis. Hydrobiologia, 30(1): 1–44.

Das, S.K.; Bhattacharya, B.K. and Goswami, U.C. 2001. Dial variation of pH in fish ponds of nagaon district, Assam. *J. Inland Fish Soc. India*, 33 (1). 45-48.

Frei, M. and Becker, K. (2005). Integrated rice-fish culture: coupled production saves resources. Natural Resources Forum 29:135-143.

FAO, 1992. "Manuel pour le dèveloppement de la pisciculture à Madagascar"; *FI:DP/MAG/88/005, Document Technique* no. 4, UNDP and FAO.

Hickling, C.F., 1962. Fish culture. London. Faber and Faber. 295 p.

Hora, S.L & Pillay T. V. R., 1962. Handbook of fish culture in the Indo-Pacific Region. FAO Fish Tech. Pap (14):204 p.

Huet, M. 1956. Aperçu de la pisciculture en Indonesie. Trav. Sta. Rech. Groenendael Ser. D, 19. 55p (in Coche, 1960).

Jhingran, V.G. 1982. *Fish and fisheries of India*, 2nd edition. Hindustan Publ. Crop., New Delhi, India.

Joshi, B. C. 2008. Utilization of different bycatch fish waste to formulate viable nutritive feed for aquaculture. *Ph.D.Thesis,* Kumaun University Nainital. 229 p.

Khanna, S.S and Singh, H.R. 2005. *A text book of fish biology and fisheries.* Narendra Publishing House, Delhi. 524 p.

Kunda, M.; Azim, M.E.; Wahab, M.A.; Dewan, S.; Roos, N. and Thilsted, S.H. (2008). Potential of mixed culture of freshwater prawn (*Macrobrachium rosenbergii*) and self recruiting small species mola (*Amblypharyngodon mola*) in rotational rice-fish/prawn culture systems in Bangladesh. Aquaculture Research 39:506-517.

Mohanty, R.K.; Verma, H.N. and Brahmanand, P.S. (2004). Performance evaluation of rice-fish integration system in rainfed medium and ecosystem. Aquaculture 23:125-135.

Mustow, S.E. (2002). The effects of shading on phytoplankton photosynthesis in rice-fish fields in Bangladesh. Agriculture, Ecosystems and Environment 90:89-96.

Naga, 1992: *The ICLARM Quarterly*, Vol. 15, no. 3.

Paerl, H.W. and Tucker, C.S. (1995). Ecology of blue-green algae in aquaculture ponds. *Journal of the world aquaculture society.* 26 (2): 109-129.

Schuster, W. H. 1955. Fish culture in conjunction with rice cultivation. World crops. 7: 11–14 and 67–70.

Sharma, A.P. 2000. *Manual Fishery Limnology.* Department of Fishery Hydrography, College of Fishery Sciences, G. B. Pant. University of Agriculture & Technology, Pantnagar, p. 115.

Sinha, V. R. P., 1985. Crop-fish-production systems. Orientation cum training programme on improving the income and employment potential of rice farming systems. Organized by International Rice Research Institute (IRRI) and University ofPhilippines, Manila 21–30 January.

Tamura, T. 1961. Carp cultivation in Japan. In: Fish as foods Ed. G. Borgstrom. p. 103–120.

Vincke, M. M. J. 1979. Aquaculture en riziers: situation et röle futur (Fish culture in rice fields: its status and future role), p. 208–223. In T.V.R. Pillay and W. A. Dill (eds) Advances in Aquaculture. Fishing Needs Books Ltd, Farnham, Surrey, England.

Wahab, M.A.; Kunda, M.; Azim, M.E.; Dewan, S. and Thilsted, S.H. (2008). Evaluation of freshwater prawn-small fish culture concurrently with rice in Bangladesh. Aquaculture Research 39:1524-1532.

Effect of the Changes of Climatic Conditions on the Adhesive Aparatus Epidermis of some Hill-stream Fishes of Kumaun Region

—S.C. Joshi, *India*
—H. Singh, *India*
—B.C. Joshi, *India*
—Ila Bisht, *India*
—S.K. Agarwal, *India*

ABSTRACT

Fishes form the largest group of vertebrates and they serve as best food supplement. It contains protein, fat, vitamins and minerals. Fishes were used even at prehistoric ages and it was supposed to be beneficial to long life and intelligence (Hamilton, 1971). Many countries are working to search out the importance of fishes for men. A study conducted in Netherlands reported that eating a pound of fish a week could reduce the coronary heart diseases in man. Some fishes specially Hill stream water species such as Tor, *Garra* and *Schizothorax* contain some oils that are not found in other food and have major effects on body chemistry, which reduces the tendency of blood to clot and helps in lowering cholesterol level in the blood. The medical value of fish oil cannot be ignored, many patients who are suffering with lack of vitamin A and D, use oils of some fishes. Scales of fishes are used for decorations of houses. Skin of fishes has its own importance in leather industry.

Morphmetric measurements and counts of different size groups of the fishes were studied. The mean ratio of morphmetric measurements among the size groups in relation to the body length and weight. Surface architecture of the epidermis covering the Adhesive apparatus of the hill-stream fishes were examined by scanning electron microscopy, in an attempt to understand structural and functional modifications of the microridges in *Garra gotyla* (Hamilton), *Glyptothorax pectinopterus* (McClelland) and *Pseudechinus sulcatus* (McClelland) in relation to the changes of climatic conditions of different river system.

In *G. gotyla* and *G. pectinopterus* and *P. sulcatus* the Adhesive apparatus epidermis is differentiated papillae are separated, separated by interpapillary regions are composed of mainly the epithelial cells.

The epidermis of uncular region is composed of mainly epithelial cells, smooth epidermis and mucous cells. The free surface of epithelial cells papillae are separated possesses microridges. Microridges constituting varied patterns at different location in different fish. The epithelial cells of these fishes were characterized by the presence of well developed microridges. These microridges have been correlated to provide reserve surface area for stretching, when manoeuvering of fish. The presence of mucous has been described as an adaptation and to help an efficient aiming by reducing the friction.

KEY WORD: Microridges, Kumaun Himalaya, Hill-stream fish, and SEM.

Introduction

Identification of a species is a primary step towards any research work and plays a key role for the behavioral study. Morph metric measurements and meristic counts are considered as easiest and authentic methods for the identification of specimen which is termed as morphological systematic. Morphometric measurement is measurements of different external body parts of an organism and meristic counts mean anything that can be counted (Talwar and Jhingran, 1991). These fishes are also considered as one of the principal commercial hill stream fishes in the rivers of Kumaun hill. As a non-conventional proposed candidate for aquaculture, very limited information are available on the Morphometric measurements and meristic counts of fishes from the water bodies of the Kumaun Himalaya, Further recognition or identification of a species is necessary and must be done in all types of biological studies where morphological systematic is used for quick identification and confirmation.

G. gotyla (Hamilton), *G. pectinopterus* (McClelland) and *P. sulcatus* (McClelland) are fresh water teleosts, belonging to the families Cyprinidae (first one) and sisoridae (last two). These fishes inhabit water resources in hills which are shallow, well aerated and clear and contain plenty of food in the form of algal slime covering stones and rocks. The strength of water current and the intensity of light in these water resources are much higher compared to those of the rivers of plains. All these fishes are bottom dweller, predominantly lithophyllous and sluggish in nature. These fishes usually cling to the rocky substratum with the help of their modified skin. They crawl along the walls of the aquaria with the help of adhesive organ and paired fins. They remained sticking to the wall of aquaria or try to hide themselves beneath the stones. These fishes generally die shortly after removing them from the water and putrefy very rapidly after death.

Fish skin differs from other exposed vertebrate skin most notably at the surface where living epidermal cells are in direct contact with the environment because of its watery environment fish skin is subjected to at least two types of stresses - osmotic pressure gradients between the cells and the water, and physical forces not only from the water itself but from other environmental hazards ex. rocks, boulders etc. The strength of water current and the intensity of light in these water resources are much higher compared to those of the rivers of plains.

The present investigation has been designed to study the comparative structural organization and functional significance of the epidermis of adhesive apparatus of these fishes in relation to their life in hill-streams. Studies of fish skin indicated that epidermis cells following separate pathways of differentiation in different fishes. In most of the fishes the epidermises is related more to the deposition of slime over its surface and undergo the process of mucogenesis and in some the epidermis cells undergo the process of keratinization forming a layer at the surface (Mittal & Benerjee 1979). The aim of present investigation is to study of microridges of adhesive apparatus of the hill-stream fishes were examined by light and scanning electron microscope, in an attempt to understand structural and functional modifications of *G. gotyla* (Hamilton), *G. pectinopterus* (McClelland) and *P. sulcatus* (McClelland). Important reviews have been published by Mittal & Benerjee (1979), Singh & Agarwal, (1991, 1992), Pinky et al., (2004), and Mishra et al., (2004).

MATERIALS AND METHODS

Live adult specimens of *G. gotyla* (7-9 cm long) were collected from Kosi River at Kakrighat, Distt Nainital (Uttarakhand) *G. pectinopterus* (5-7 cm long) from west Ramganga River at Chaukhutiya, Distt. Almora, (Uttarakhand) and *P. sulcatus* (6-7cm long) from east Ramganga River at Thal, Distt. Pithoragarh (Uttsrskhsnd) respectively water current was very fast having velocity 0.5 to 2.0 m/sec. in Kosi, 1.5 to 2.5 m/sec. in west Ramganga and 2.0 to 3.0 m/sec. in east Ramganga (Bhatt & Pathak, 1991) and the bed was rocky. The specimens of these fishes were obtained at a depth up to two feet and also from the pockets of the stones to which they usually remain attached by their ventral surface to hold on against a rapid flow of water. The fishes were transferred from the site of collection to laboratory in well ventilated plastic containers and were kept for a period of about 5-6 days in glass aquaria having on artificially made rocky bed and aquatic vegetation grown therein. The aquaria were cleaned and supplied with fresh spring water on alternate days. The fishes were fed on aqua feed (tropical fish food). Specimens were maintained in laboratory at 25 ± 2^0C. The fish were cold anesthetized, following Mittal & Whitear (1978).

Fishing Methods

Local fishermen use these methods for commercial fishing. These methods are usually confined near the fish markets. However, fishermen often practice these methods in remote areas and the fish are transported to the fish markets.Although most fish farmers try to over exploit the fishing resources, these methodswill not pose any threat to the fishes if practiced with limitations.

A. Hooks: Most of the fishermen use hooks to catch big fishes specially *Tor* spp.,*Schizothorax* spp., *Labeo* spp., and *Mastacembelus* spp. This is used in fast moving as well as slow moving water areas. Generally, 10 to 20 hooks are tied to anylon rope (1 to 2 cm thick). The nylon rope is then put in the stream water during the evening hours and the hooked fishes are collected the next morning. The hooks are generally put without bait but often the baits of melon seed, small fish, flies, wheat flour, and wheat flour mixed with turmeric powder, and cooked rice

B. Suraka: The *suraka* consists of a nylon rope with several knots at regular intervals. The diameter or the knots ranges from 5 to 15 cm, while the length of the nylon rope ranges from 10 to 25 m. The nylon rope with knots is fastened to submerge rocks on both ends across the stream. Fishes moving in the streams get trapped in these knots. *Suraka* is often put in riffle and glide habitat type with shallow depth and high water velocity. It is put during night time and fishes are collected the next morning. The sizes of the fishes caught by *suraka* range from 0.5 to 2.5 kg.

C. Cast Net: The cast net is a widely used fishing gear in India. In the Kumaun region the fishermen cast the net while moving upstream or downstream. In most of the streams, the fishermen catch fishes only after several attempts throughout the day. The diameter of the cast net used ranges from 1 to 2 m and the mesh size is from 1 to 5 cm. On the periphery of the cast net metallic sinkers are attached to make the net sink and to withstand the flow of streams, After throwing the net the fishermen disturb the bouldery substrate so that the fishes hiding behind the rocks come out and get trapped in the net.

D. Gill Net: The use of the gill nets (locally known as *Mahajaal*) in streams is mostly practiced in the deep pools. The *Mahajaal* is spread into the stream using air filled tubes (bus and truck tires), as boats are not operated in the streams. Two fishermen hold the two ends of the net and move in opposite directions on air filled tubes. The fishermen normally practice this method during the evening and morning hours. The gill net is very effective when the adult *T. putitora* are on migration (both spawning and feeding migration). The net is made up of nylon silk, more than 10 m long and stretched mesh size varying from 5.0 to 8.0 cm. normally, and two gill nets of different mesh sizes are used at a time. They are placed across the stream by means of rope fastened at the banks. Using this method, the fishermen are able to catch up to 10 kg of *Tor* and *Labeo* species.

Histochemical preparation, skin fragments of about 8 X5mm were cut from the back of the fishes just behind the head. Tissues were fixed in 10% neutral formalin, Boins fluid (aquaeous and alcoholic), Carnoy's fluid and Helly,s fluid and paraffin sections were cut at 5-8 um. Sections were stained with Ehrlich's haematoxiylin/ eosin, Mallory's triple stain (johnes, 1950) and verhoeff's elastin stain (Lillie,1954) for the study of the general organization of epidermis. For SEM preparation, skin fragments were cut from adhesive apparatus of ventral side. Tissue were excised and rinsed in 70 % ethanol and one change saline solution to remove debris and fixed on 3% Glutaraldehyde in 0.1 M phosphate buffer, p^H 4 for one night at 4^0C Refrigerator. The tissue were washed in 2-3 changes in phosphate buffer and dehydrated in the graded series of ice cold Acetone (30%, 50%, 70%, 90%, and 100 per cent, each for approximately 20-30 min.) and subjected to critical point drying (Bio-Rad Critical point dryer, The tissues were sputter-coated with gold using a sputter Coater (AGAR, B 1340, England, UK) and examined by a scanning electron microscope (Leo, 435, VP, England UK). The results were recorded using Kodak T-MAX 100 professional film (Kodak Ltd., England UK).

RESULT AND DISCUSSION

Fishes

In the hill stream fishes, *G. gotyla* is scale and *G. pectinopterus & P. sulcatus* is nonscale. The mouth is sub-terminal, the adhesive organ situated on the ventral side of the head (Fig. 9.1, 9.2 & 9.3).

Fig. 9.1: *Garra gotyla*

HISTOCHEMICAL STUDY

In *G. gotyla* is commonly known as 'sucker head'. Well developed adhesive apparatus is present just behind the posterior lip and is in the form of a button like disc, known as mental adhesive disc (approximate length 9.2 mm and width 12.1mm) (Shah, K., 1989) (Fig. 9.4).

Fig. 9.2: ***Glyptothorax pectinopterus***

Fig. 9.3: ***Pseudechinus sulcatus***

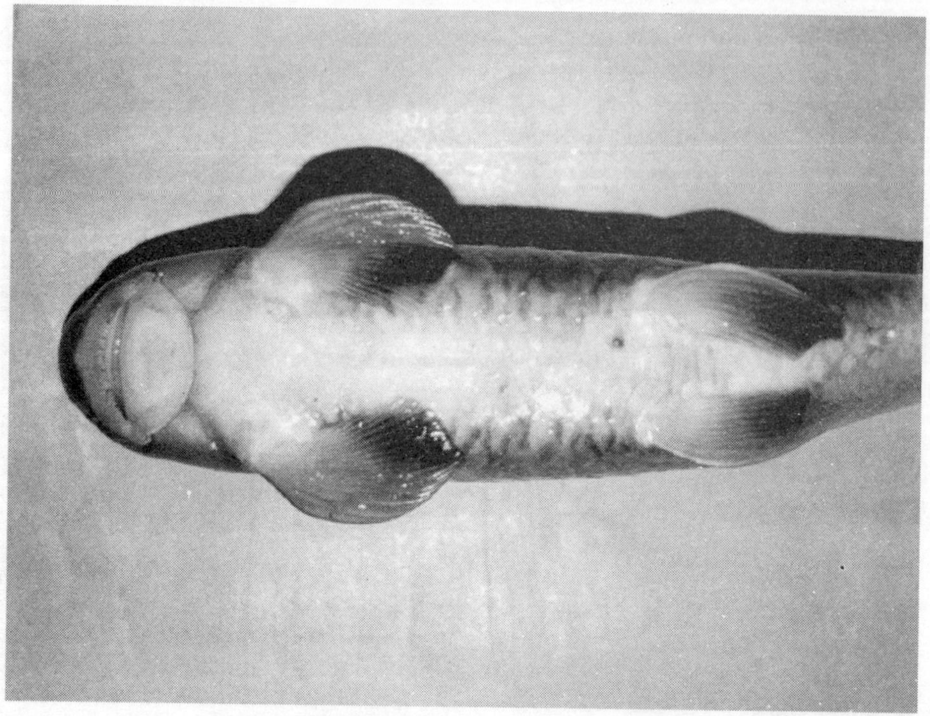

Fig. 9.4: Mental adhesive disc of *G. gotyla*

In *G. pectinopterus* the adhesive apparatus is heart shape and is present in the thoracic region behind the posterior lip, in between the base of pectoral fins and is known as thoracic adhesive apparatus (approximate length 16.0mm and width 14.0) (Bisht, I., 1999) (Fig. 5).

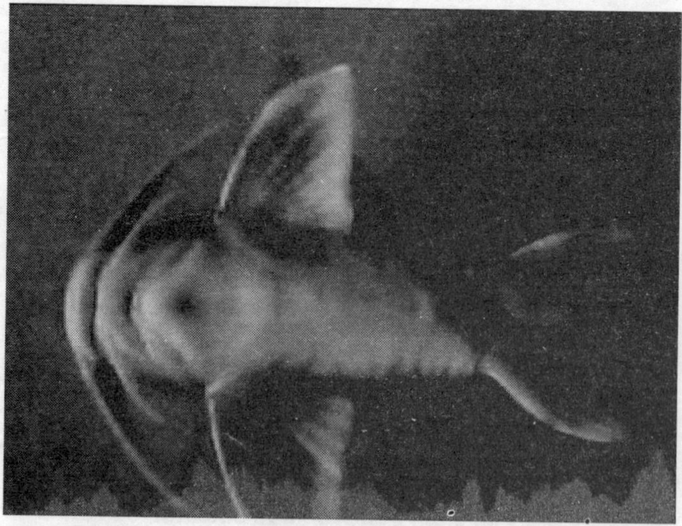

Fig. 9.5: Thoracic adhesive apparatus in *G. pectinopterus*

In *P. sulcatus* the adhesive apparatus is present in thoracic region, which lies between the base of pectoral fins and extend posterior for considerable distance and it has a prominent oval adhesive apparatus (approximate length 20.0 mm and width 14.0 mm) (Shah, K., 1989) (Fig.6).

Fig. 9.6: Oval thoracic adhesive apparatus in *P. sulcatus*

Table 9.1: comparative study of the habit and habitat and identification of a s pecies is a primary step of *G. gotyla, G. pectinopterus* and *P. sulcatus in* Kumaun region of Uttarakhand.

	***Gara gotyla* (Hamilton)**	***Glyptothorax pectinopterus* (McClelland)**	***Pseudechinus sulcatus* (McClelland)**
1. **Local name**	*Gadhewo*	Gaunch	*Bhamen*
2. **Maximum length**	14.5	12.8 cm	11 cm.
3. **Environment**	Freshwater	Freshwater, Benthopelagic	Demersal, freshwater
4. **Climate/ Range**	Tropical; 24°C - 27°C.	Tropical	Tropical
5. **Distribution**	Uttarakhand hill stream- Kosi River, Ramganga Petsaal.	Uttarakhand hill stream river- Ramganga chaukhutia (Almora)	Uttarakhand hill stream river-Ramganga Thal (Pithoragarh)
6. **Biology**	Occurs in mountain streams	Small, benthic species inhabiting pool and run areas of streams. Found in mountain rapids.	Found in fast-flowing hill streams. Prefers deep riffles and runs over gravel, cobble substrates.

The absence of prominent nucleus and the weak and strong reaction with fulgent stain for nuclear DNA in the epithelial cells of the inner and outer uncular layers at fold and of most superficial layer at groove in the epidermis of thoracic adhesive apparatus indicate that they are in a state of dying in *G. pectinopterus & P. sulcatus* and undergo the process of keratinization as they stain positively with papanicolaous stain for keratin. Their distal parts become stiff and horny at fold. The keratinized nature of these cells is further supported by the presence of cysteine bound sulphydryl (-SH) groups and cystine bound disulphide (-SS) groups. The above keratinized cells in *G. pectinopterus* and *P. sulcatus* stain positively also with Ninhydin/Shiff for protein bound $–NH_2$ groups and with solochrome cyanine R for basic protein indicating that the epithelial cells are undergoing the process of active protein synthesis and the protein synthesized is basic in nature. The degree of keratinization, in the epithelial cells of outer two layers of epidermis at fold, increases as the cells move towards the surface in *G. pectinopterus* and *P. sulcatus*.

The keratine of these cells is weakly polymerized as they contain considerable amounts of bound –SH groups and small amounts of bound –SS groups indicating that keratine polymerization has just started and a major part of bound –SH groups is left unconverted into cystine disulphide (-SS) bounds. The increase in the quantity of keratine and bound –SH groups in the epithelial cells of outer uncula layer indicates that they show comparatively an advance keratinization where further synthesis of keratin and an increase in the quantity of bound –SH groups, probably synthesized a fresh has occurred. An unequal distribution of protein and its main constituents in the cells of surface layer having a correlation with the varying degree of keratinization has been described in the epidermis of lips in details. The varying degree of development of keratinization in cells of surface layer of the epidermis at fold in *G. pectinopterus* and *P. sulcatus* has a close correlation with rapidity of the torrential streams inhabited by the fish.

It may be noted that only the outer uncular layer is functional while the deeper ones are kept in reserve. When the outermost layer shed off or gets detached, it is replaced by the underlying uncular layer. The cells of inner uncular layer in the epidermis at fold of thoracic adhesive apparatus, in addition to keratinization, synthesize and void non- sulphated acidic glycoproteins in *G. pectinopterus* and *P. sulcatus*. The secretion of glycoprotein from these cells may significantly help shedding of the outer uncular layer by providing lubrication to the cells in this fish. It is again intersting to note that the keratinized epidermis at fold in *G. pectinopterus* & *P. sulcatus* and posterolateral part of *G. gotyla* is devoid of gland cells.

These cells, however, occur in the epidermis of groove of *G. pectinopterus* and *P. sulcatus* and of flat circular part of *G. gotyla* that is non-keratinized as revealed by combination of histochemical techniques. This further suggested an inverse relationship between the keratinization and the abundance of slime secreting glands as observed in the epidermis of snout and lips of these fishes. In *G. pectinopterus*, the unculi present in the epidermis at fold of adhesive apparatus prevent skidding of the fish. The present off well developed but few goblet mucus cells in epidermis of the grooves in again interesting in the sense that their secretion might form a thin film of mucus along the margin and may thus additionally against maintaining the vacuum preventing the entrance of water and air (Fig. 9.7, 9.8, & 9.9)

The presence of well developed goblet mucous cells in the epidermis at flat circular part forming a slime layer on the surface of disc in *G. gotyla* is significant as chest of the fish in liable to friction especially when it swims upstream. This may provide sufficient lubrication to reduce friction between body surface and water currents, thus protecting the epidermis from wear and tear during locomotion.

The epidermis of groove, separating the flat circular part from the posterior lip interiorly and poster lateral in *G. gotyla*, is subjected to more frictional stress than that of the outer surface due to the movement of flat circular part during the operation of suctorial function. The presence of comparatively numerous goblet mucous cells in the epidermis of this region, secreting profuse amount of mucous is thus significant in the *G. gotyla*. This may provide sufficient lubrication to reduce friction at hinge thus protecting the epidermis from wear and tear during adhesion secretary activities of epithelial cells and goblet mucous cells in non-keratinized epidermal furrows may provide protection to the fish against various harmful factors in the environment, (Mittal et al, 1994 a). In addition, mucus secretion has been associated with diverse activities such as recognition of cells, reception of chemical information and the maintenance of a suitable environment (Mittal et al, 1995). Among the important functions of the epidermis, one is to protect to body from the harmful effect of various hazards in external environment. Since the impact of such stresses is comparatively much less on the inner surface than on the outer surface, the epidermis of adhesive apparatus of *G.lamta*, *G.pectinopteus and P. sulcatus* at groove is modified to a thin layer compared to that covering the fold.

The adhesive organ (disc) of *G. gotyla* consists of a central circular, an involutedly smooth callous portion with a postero-latral tuberculated border. The adhesive organ in this species is one of the most complex combinations of integumentary modifications. Various proteins and glycoproteins have been demonstrated in the epidermis of mental adhesive disc of *G. gotyla*, thoracic adhesive apparatus in *G. pectinopterus*, and oval thoracic adhesive apparatus in *P. sulcatus* by histochemical and whole mount preparation, to learn its structural and functional organization with special reference to adhesion. The epidermis of mental adhesive disc is smooth and uniform in thickness at flat circular part and is papilated at posterolateal part. It is, however, thrown into folds alternating with grooves in adhesive apparatus of *G.pectinopteus* and P. sulcatus. The epidermis of flat circular part of *G. gotyla* of grooves of *G.pectinopteus* is equipped with epithelial cells unicellular glands- the goblet mucous cells. The surface epithelial cells are metabolically active and non-keratinization as shown by a combination of histochemical reactions (Fig. 9.7, 9.8, & 9.9).

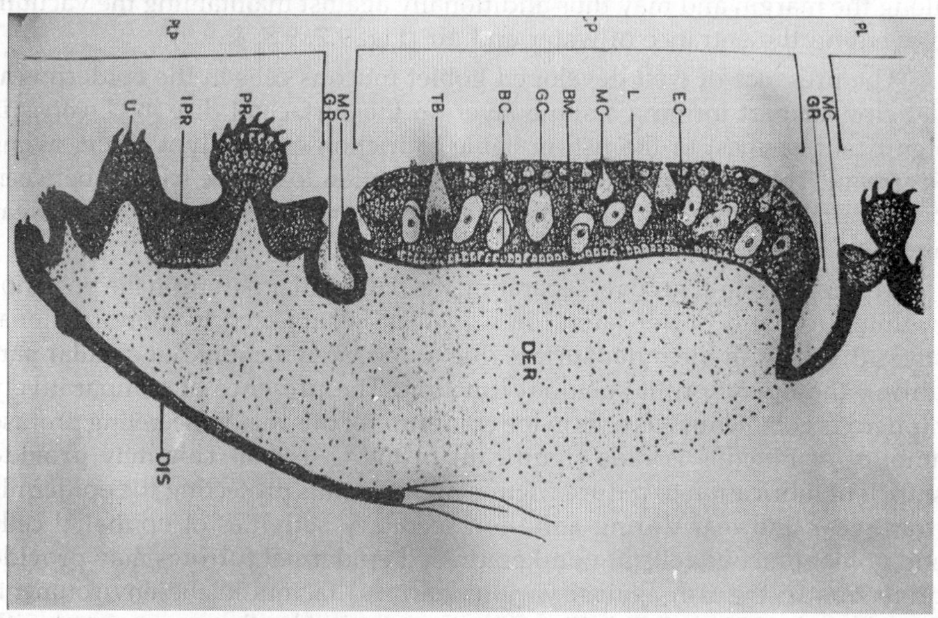

Fig. 9.7: T.S. of Mental Adhesive Appertus of *G. Gotyla*.

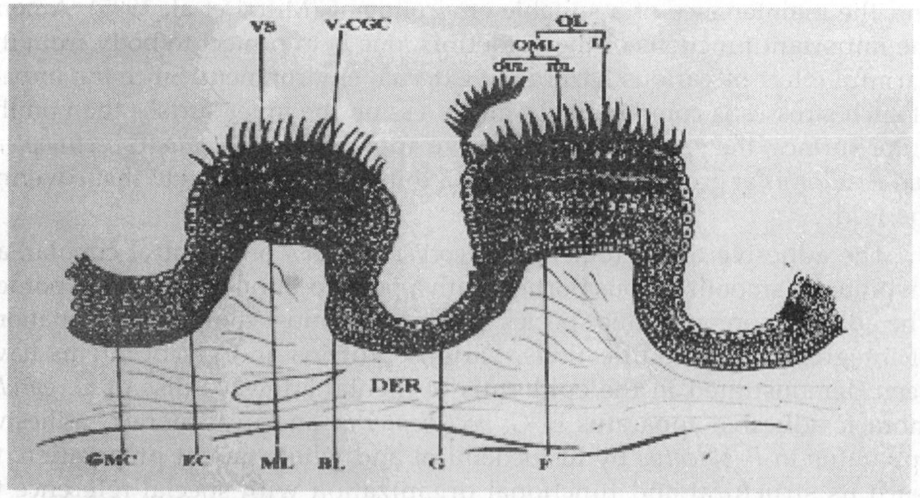

Fig. 9.8: T.S. of Mental Adhesive Apperatus of G. Pectinopterus.

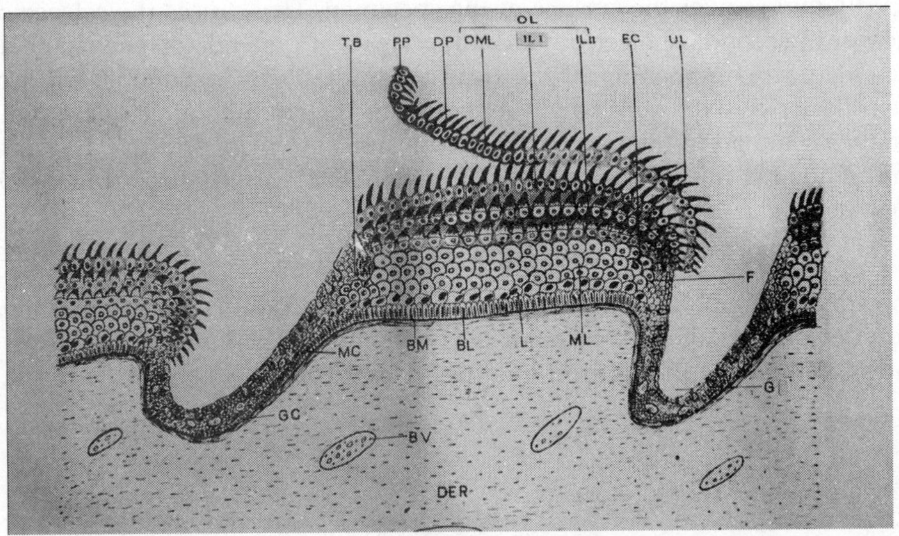

Fig. 9.9: T.S. of Mental Adhesive Apperatus of P. Sulcatus.

ELECTRON MICROSCOPIC

Electron microscopic differs markedly and in many respects from the optical microscopic techniques. The electron microscope provides tremendously useful magnification. Electron microscopes are widely used for studying the detailed structure of cells. Two different types of electron microscopes are used for studying cell structures. We are using only SEM study.

(1) Transmission electron microscope (TEM)

(2) Scanning electron microscope (SEM)

1. Transmission Electron Microscope: To study the structure of cells, a transmission electron microscope is used in the TEM, electrons are used instead of light rays and electromagnets and the whole system is operating in a high vacuum. The resolving power of the electron microscope enables one to see many structures of even molecular size as proteins and nucleic acids. However, electron beams do not penetrate very well and if one is interested in seeing internal cell structure, even a single cell is too thick to be viewed directly. So special techniques of thin sectioning are used to prepare specimens for the electron microscope, For example, a single bacterial cell is cut into many very thin slices, which are then examined individually with the electron microscope. Special electron microscope stains such as Osmic acid permanganate, uranium or lanthanum salts or leads, and used for sufficient contrast.

2. Scanning Electron Microscope: If only the external features of an organism need to be observed by scanning electron microscope. In scanning electron microscope, the specimen is subjected to narrow electron beam which rapidly moves over the surface of the specimen. This causes the release of a shower of secondary electron and other types of depends on the shape and the chemical composition of the irradiated object. The secondary electrons are collected by a detector which generates and electronic signal. These signals are then scanned in the manner of a television system to produce and image on cathode ray tube. Thus, we conclude that SEM is useful for 3-dimensional imaging.

SEM STUDY

The adhesive apparatus are situated ventrally in all three fishes In *G. gotyla*, well developed adhesive apparatus is present just behind the posterior lip and is in the form of a button like disc (Fig. 9.10).

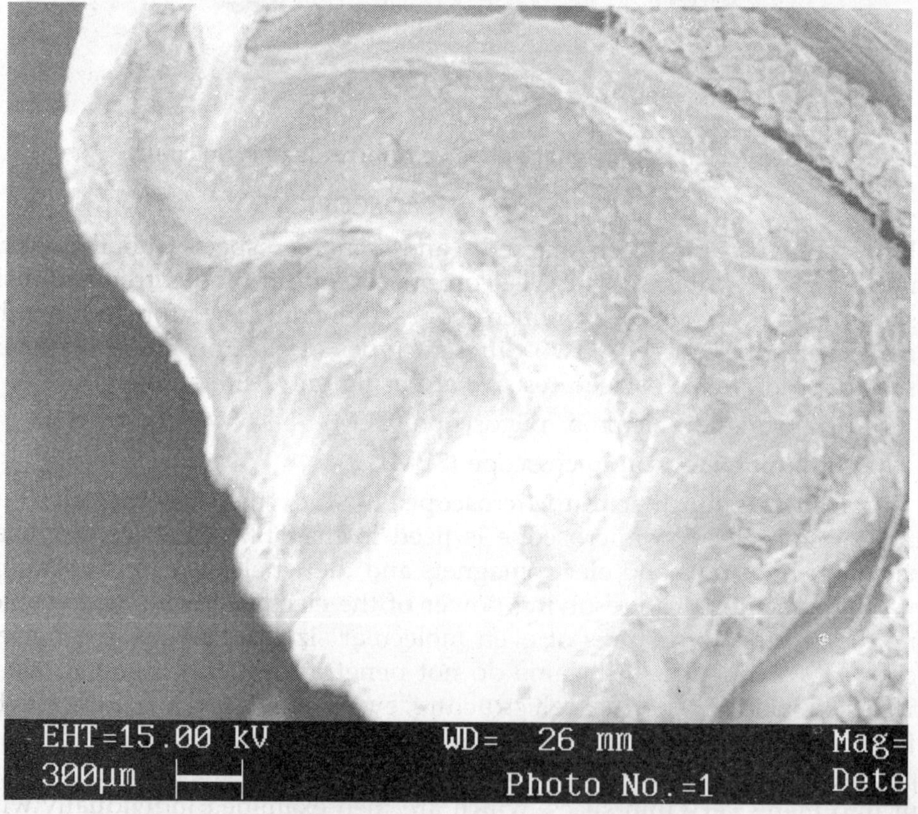

Fig. 9.10: SEMPH of *G. gotyla* showing the modified button like disc of Adhesive apparatus epidermal (Marked by arrows) (Scale bar- 300 μm).

In *G. pectinopterus*, the epidermis is differentiated into having smooth and unculiferus surface." Please revise/clarify the statement. The adhesive apparatus is heart shaped and is present in the thoracic region behind the posterior lip, in between the base of pectoral fins (Fig. 9.11).

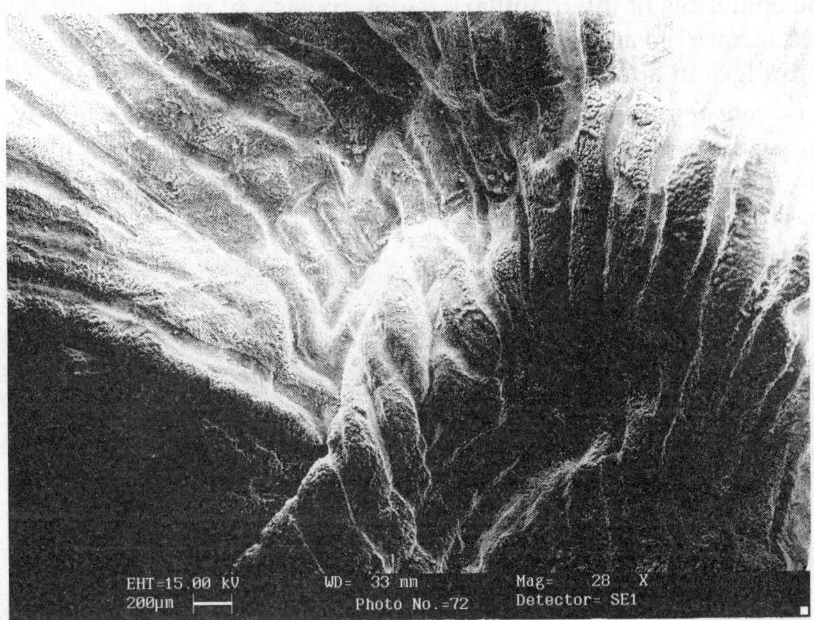

Fig. 9.11: SEMPH of *G. pectinopterus* showing the modified thoracic of Adhesive apparatus epidermal (Marked by arrows) (Scale bar- 200 µm).

In *P. sulcatus*, the adhesive apparatus is present in thoracic region, which lies between the bases of pectoral fins (Fig. 9.12).

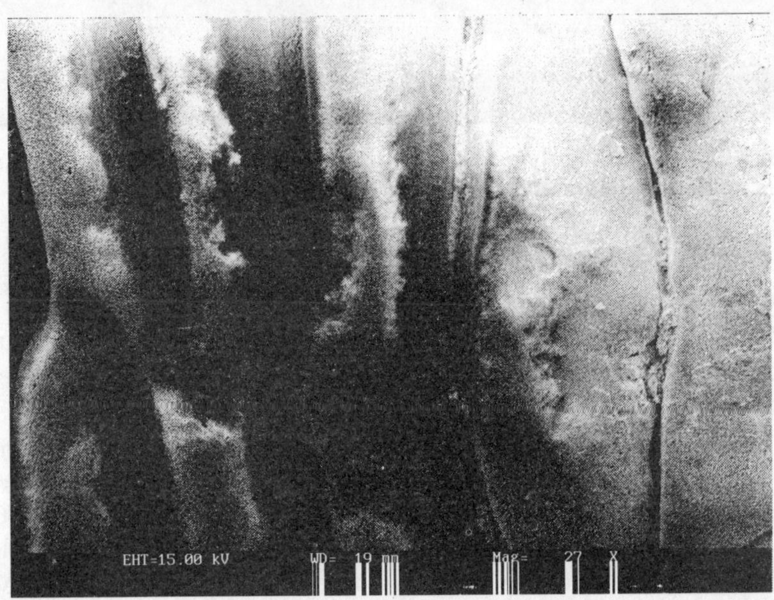

Fig. 9.12: SEMPH of *P. sulcatus*, showing the modified thoracic of Adhesive apparatus epidermal (Marked by arrows) (Scale bar- 200 µm).

The epidermis of interpapillary region consists of mainly epithelial cells. The free surface of each epithelial cell is characterized by presence of a series of microridges in adhesive apparatus of all three fishes.

In *G. gotyla,* the microridges of the adhesive apparatus, the microridges are compactly arranged, branched with abrupt ends of irregularly interwoven to form intricate mesh like pattern, and interconnected with microbridges (Fig. 9.13)

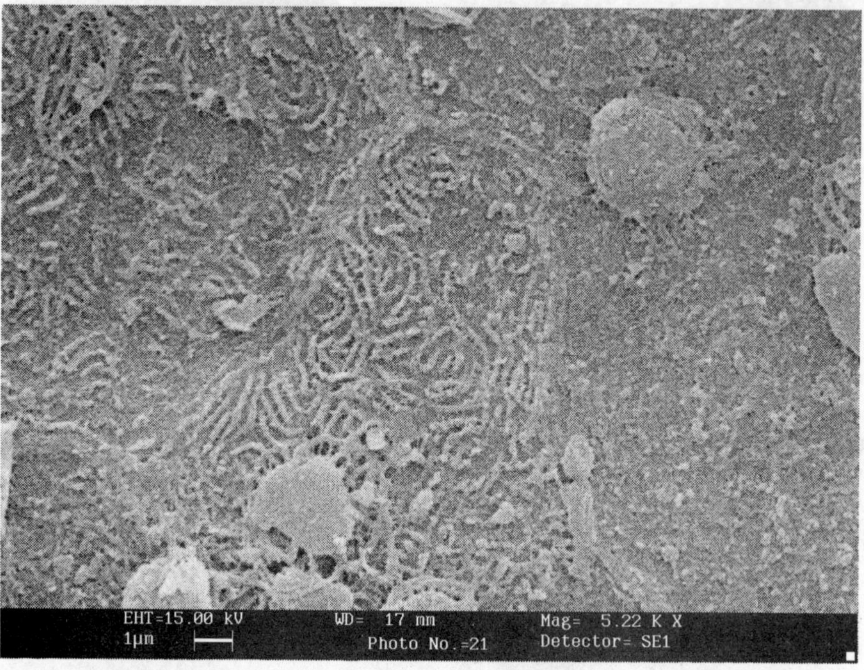

Fig. 9.13: SEMPH of *G. gotyla* showing the mesh like microridges of Adhesive apparatus epidermis (Marked by arrows) (Scale bar- 200 µm).

In G. pectinopterus, the adhesive apparatus contain numerous, filamentous microridges; however, these microridges are not interconnected to each other with microbridges (fig. 9.14).

In P. sulcatus, the adhesive apparatus epithelial cells showed numerous microridges that are compactly arranged, filamentous and interconnected to each other (Fig. 9.15).

The hill stream fishes are very well adapted to some specialized conditions of their life in the torrential environment where turbulent flow over rough substratum (rocks, boulders, cobbles and pebble) of the stream is a feature, directly related to the degree of slope or gradient and elevation. Noticeable differences exhibited in the patterns of microridges on epithelial cells, distribution of mucous cells and presence of *G. gotyla, G. pectinopterus* and *P. sulcatus* may be considered as modifications relating to possible difference

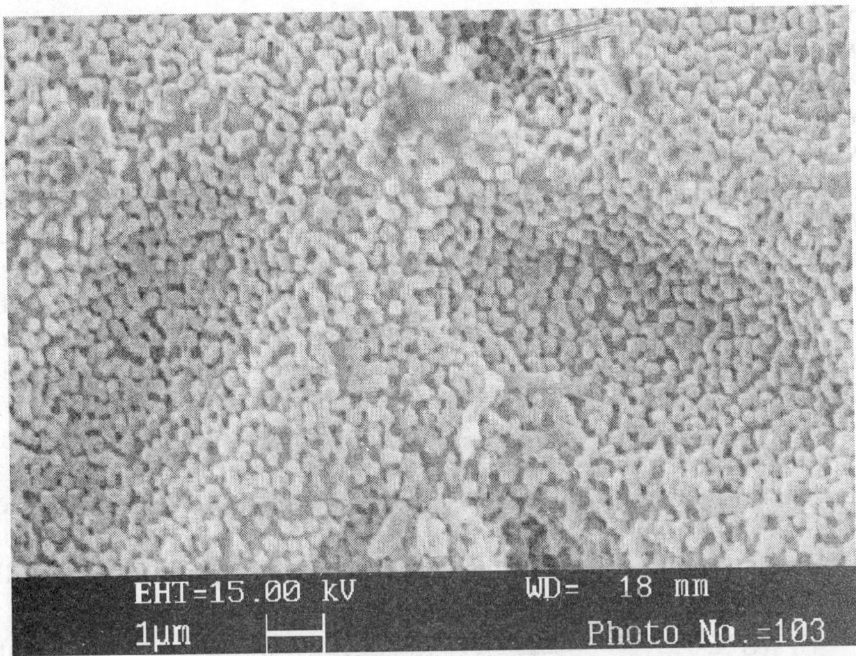

Fig. 9.14: SEMPH of *G. pectinopterus* showing the fillamentus microridges of Adhesive apparatus epidermis (Marked by arrows) (Scale bar- 1 μm).

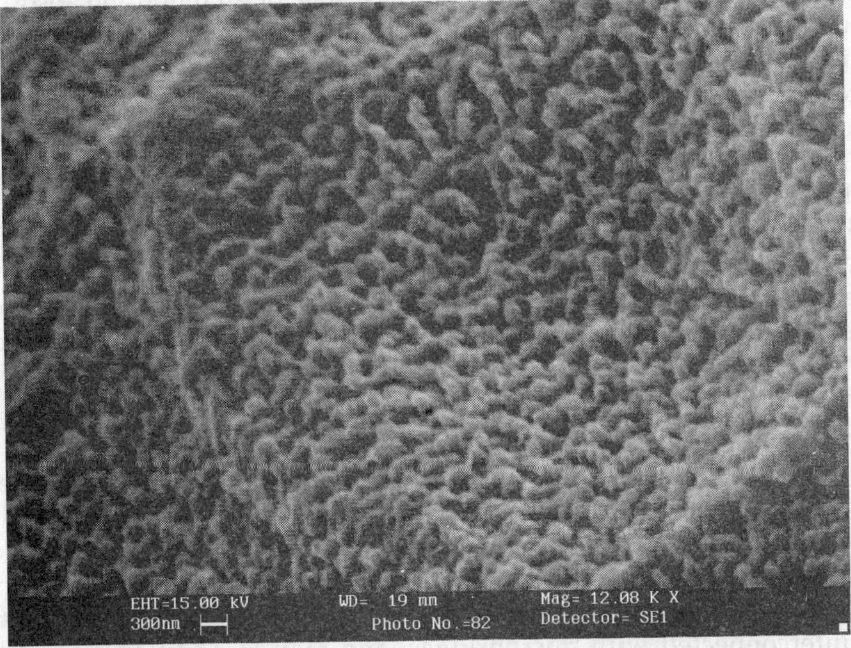

Fig. 9.15: SEMPH of *P. sulcatus* showing the filamentous microridges of Adhesive apparatus epidermis (Marked by arrows) (Scale bar-300 μm).

in the functional requirement at the different locations. The mucous cells provide some structural defense to hold mucus secretions to the skin surface. Van Oosten (1957) has shown that mucus is one of the most important protective substances associated with fish skin.

Microridges are thought to be involved in the retention of mucus, in addition to facilitating the spreading of the mucus over cell surfaces (Sperry & Wassersug, 1976). Fishelson (1984) related the variations in microridges patterns to locomotory activity and suggested that in faster swimming fishes, the most developed ridges served to trap mucus on the epithelial surface. The view that the development of microridges is an adaptation for retaining mucus at the surface, however, does not seem tenable. According to Whitear (1990), any functioning of microridges to retain mucus on the epithelial surface is contradicted by the ease with which the mucus cover is last during preparation for microscopy. Modifications in the pattern of microridges can also be caused by various intrinsic, e.g. hormonal (Schwerdtfeger, 1979 a, b), or extrinsic factors e.g. temperature (Ferri, 1982), salinity (Ferri 1983), mercury salts (Pereira, 1988), organic pollutants (Iger et al., 1988) handling and ectoparasites (Whitear, 1990).

Microridges have been reported to vary considerably in configuration and deposition, constituting varied patterns at different locations in different fish species, and have been implicated to play variable roles, These include retaining mucus secretion to the cells surface area for excretion and absorption through the skin, to facilitate the spread of mucus away from mucous cells, to aid in producing laminar flow, to provide reserve surface area for stretching, and to have their relation with the process of secretion at the cell apex. Kumari (2009) suggested the microridges on the surface of the epithelial cells, like in the gills of other fish species. These structures provide mechanical flexibility and protection (Aslon, 1995; Eiras stofella et al., 2001; Evans et al., 2005). The microridges are organized in different ways to form intricate patterns and are thought to involve in various functions; e.g., absorptive or secretory activities, to aid in laminar flow, holding mucus secretions to the cell surface, to provide reserve surface area for stretching or distortion, to facilitate the spread of mucus away from the mucous cells, to provide mechanical protection, to enhance mechanical flexibility (Whitear, 1990; Aslon, 1995).

In *G. gotyla*, the prominent microridges present at the boundaries to provide reserve surface area for stretching to the free surfaces of epithelium in order to protect against physical abrasions when manoeuvreing of unculi. In Adhesive apparatus epidermis of *G. gotyla*, compactly arranged, branched with abrupt ends of irregularly interwoven to form intricate mesh like pattern, and interconnected with microbridges, and may in addition impart firm consistency or rigidity to the free surface of the epithelial cell. This could be considered as an adaptation to with stand mechanical stress and protect the surface of the fish, which has the characteristic habit of bottom dwelling furthermore, these microridges may gain a firm base and support from a dense network of fine filaments.

The adhesive apparatus epidermis of *G. pectinopterus*, function primarily to provide mechanical protection and also possibly provide protection against pathogens. They might also help prevent ectoparasitism. In the Adhesive apparatus epidermis of *P. sulcatus*, the epithelial cells showed numerous microridges, which increase the surface area for adhesion, besides providing protection and increasing the mobility of the mucus. This is significant as skin of this fish is subjected to comparatively more frictional stress due to high velocity of water. This study reveals that the free surface of epithelial cells possesses of microridges. "The microridges provide some mechanical defense to traumatic condition and probably aid in holding mucus secretions to the skin surface.

Acknowledgements

We wish to thank the Head of the Department of Anatomy, the officer-in-charge and the staff Electron Microscope Facility, All India Institute of Medical Sciences, New Delhi, for extending invaluable help in carrying out SEM studies.

REFERENCES

A., K. Mittal and M. Whitear, 1978: A note on cold anaesthesia of poikilotherms. *J. Fish. Biol., (13):529-520*

D., G. Sperry and M. Wassersug, 1976: A proposed function for microridges on epithelial cell. *Anat. Rec.* (185): 253- 260.

D., H. Evans, P., M. Piermarini and K., P. Choe, 2005: The multifunctional fish: dominant site of gas exchange, osmoregulation, acid–base regulation, and excretion of Nitrogenous waste. *Physiol. Rev.* (85). 97-177.

D., R. Eiras-Stofella, P. Charvet-Almeida and A., C. C. Fanta-Vianna, 2001: Surface ultrastructure of the gill of the mullets mugil carema. *M. Liza and M. Platanus* (Mugilidai, Pisces). *J. Morphol.* (247): 122-131.

J. Von Oosten, 1957: The skin and scales. In: *Physiolgy of fishes. Vol. 1. Ed. M.E. Brown. New York. Acadmic Press.*

J., J. Pereira, 1988: Morphological effects of mercury exposure on window pane flounder gills as observed by scanning electron microscopy. *J. Fish. Biol.(*33): 571-580.

K., K. Shah1989: Histochemical studies on the epidermis of certain hill-stream fishes. *Ph. D. Thesis. Kumaun University Nainital.*

L. Fishelson, 1984: A comparative study of ridge – Mazes on surface epithelial cell Membrances, of fish scales (Pisces, Teleostei). *Zoomorphologic. (*104): 231-238.

M. Whitear 1990: Causative aspects of microridges on the surface of fish epithelia. *J. Submicrose. Cytol. Pathal.* 22: 211-220.

M. Whitear, 1990: Causative aspects of microridges on the surface of fish epithelia. *J. Submicrose. Cytol. Pathal.* (22): 211-220.

N. Mishra, A. K. Singh, and J. P. N. Singh 2004: Observation on the function of mucous cells in the gills of climbing purch *Anabus testudineus* expose to acorpetdi chrome black. T., Symposium on Advances in fish Pysiology, *ecological consideration (B. H. U., Varanasi)*, 33.

N. Singh, and N. K. Agarwal 1991: The SEM surface structure of the adhesive organ of *Pseudecheneis sulcatus* McClelland (Teleostei: sisoridae) from Garhwal Himalayan hill-streams. *Acta Ichthyological at Piscatcrria. Val. XXI.Fasc.* 2: 29-35.

Pinky, S. Mital, M. Yashpal, J. Ojha, and A. K. Mittal 2004: Occurrence of keratinization in the structures associated with lips of a hill-stream fish *Garra lamta* (Hamilton) (Cyprinidae, Cypriniformes). *J. Fish. Biol.* 65: 1165-1172.

R. Aslon 1945: Scanning electron microscopy of the fish gill. In. Munshi, J. S. D. and Dutta, H. M. (Eds.), fish morphology: *Horizon of new research oxford and IBH Publication Co. Pvt. Ltd. New Delhi. India. Pp.* 31-45.

S. Ferri, 1982: Temperature induced transformation of teleost (Plmelodus maclatus) epidermal cells. *Gegenbaurs Morph. Jahrb. Leipzig,* (128): 712-731.

S. Ferri, 1983: Modification of Microridge Pattern in teleost (Plmelodus maculates) epidermal cells incduced by NaCl. *Gegenbaurs Morph. Jahrb. Leipzig, (*129): 325-329.

S., D. Bhatt and J., K. Pathak, 1991: Streams of great mountain are physiographic and physiochemistry. In ecology of the mountain water. *Ashish Pub. House. New Delhi.* 43-58.

S.K. Agarwal, and T.K. Banerjee 1979: Enzymes in the epidermis of a fresh water teleost *Barbus sapharc* (Cyprinidae, Pisces). *A histochiemical investigation mikroskopic* . 35: 158-264.

Sanjeev, K. Srivastava, U.K. Sarkar and R.S. Patiyal, 2002. Fishing methods in streams of the Kumaun Himalayan region of India. *Asian Fisheries Science* (15) 347-356.

U. Kumari, M. Yashpal, S. Mittal and A., K. Mittal 2009: Surface ultrastructure of gill arches and gill rakers in relation to feeding of an Indian major carp Cirehinus mrigala. *Tissue and cell.*

U. Kumari, M. Yashpal, S. Mittal and A., K. Mittal, 2005: Morphology of the pharyngeal cavity especially the surface ultrastructure of Gill Arches and Gill rakars in relation to the feeding Ecology of the catfish *Rita rita* (Siluriformes, Bagridas). *J. Morp.* 197-208.

W., K. Schwerdtfeges, 1979, a: Morphometrical studies of the ultrastructure of the epidermis of the guppy. *Anat. Rec.* (38): 476-483.

W., K. Schwerdtfeges, 1979, b: Qualitative and quantitive data on the fine structure of the guppy (*Poecilia reticulata Peters*) epidermis following treatment with thyroxine and testosterone. *Gen. Comp. Endocrinal. (*38): 484-490.

Y. Iger, M. Abraham, A. Dantan, B. Fattal and R. Rahamine, 1988: Cellular responser in the skin of carp maintained in organically fertilized water. *J. Fish. Biol.* (33): 711-720.

Carbon Dynamics and Sequestration in Wetlands of Himachal Pradesh

—Pawan K. Attri, *India*
—V.K. Santvan, *India*

ABSTRACT

Wetland ecosystems have great economic, cultural scientific and recreational value. They provide essential habitat for numerous threatened and endangered species of flora and fauna. The wetland ecosystem constitutes of two main components i.e. biotic and abiotic which perform enormous and variety of functions. This includes regulation of ecological processes (nutrients cycling, and human waste, watershed protection and climate regulation), carrier functions (space for human activities, habitat for plants and animals) and production function (provision of food, water and raw materials). The Ramsar convection (1971) drew global attention regarding conservation and management of wetlands.

Out of total of 115 identified wetlands in India three wetlands namely Renuka wetland, Pong dam and Chandertal wetland are located in the state of Himachal Pradesh. They occupy approximately 1.77 % of the total land area in the state. They provide a potential sink for atmospheric carbon, but if not managed properly they can become a signified source of green house gases. Presently they are under pressure due to anthropogenic activities. This has resulted in almost complete breakdown of traditional management system. There is lack of appropriate and recognized property rights in the vicinity of the lake. The problem is further accentuated because their is loss of water quality data, ecological services, and information etc.

There is major knowledge gap in accurately Quantifying carbon stored in them, as well as their carbon sequestration potential. Therefore, further research is needed to better undorstand the processes of carbon sequestration in wetland vegetation and soils. Thus it is necessary to reclaim maintain and develop the wetlands for their optimum potential use, which includes as important sinks for carbon.

Key words: wetland, sink, carbon sequestration

Introduction

Wetlands are among the most productive ecosystems besides being rich repository of biodiversity, they are known to play a significant role in carbon sequestration. Wetlands usually occur in depressions or along rivers, lakes, and coastal waters where they are subjected to periodic flooding. Some wetlands also occur on slopes associated with the ground water seeps. Conceptually, wetlands lie between well-drained upland and permanently flooded deep waters of lakes, floodplains of rivers and coastal environs.

As per Ramsar convention entered into force in 1975, wetlands are defined as: "areas of marsh, fen, peat land or water, whether natural or artificial, permanent or temporary, with water that is static or flowing, fresh, brackish or salt, including areas of marine water the depth of which at low tide does not exceed six meters" (www.ramsar.org). In addition, the Convention (Article 2.1) provides that wetlands: "may incorporate riparian and coastal zones adjacent to the wetlands, and islands or bodies of marine water deeper than six meters at low tide lying within the wetlands".

Wetlands are found in all climatic zones ranging from tropics to the tundra (except Antarctica which has no wetlands). Occupying about 5 per cent of the earth's land area, wetlands are dynamic and natural ecosystems characterized by water logged or standing water conditions during at least part of the year. In most wetlands, water levels fluctuate seasonally instead of being stable, a property that accounts for making wetlands highly productive environments. Productivity among wetlands varies depending on the type of the wetland, climatic condition and vegetation communities. Along with productivity, decomposition is another complicated process that involves both aerobic and anaerobic processes. The rate of decomposition is a function of climate (temperature and moisture enhanced microbial activity) and quality (composition) of organic matter entering the system (Schlensinger, 1997).

In general, however, wetland characteristics lead to the accumulation of organic matter in the soil and sediment serving as carbon (C) sinks and making them one of the most effective ecosystems for storing soil carbon (Schlensinger, 1997). It has been estimated that different kinds of wetlands contain 350-535Gt C, corresponding to 20-25 per cent of world's organic soil carbon (Gorham,1998). However, the actual quantity of carbon stored in wetlands can only be estimated with a broad range of uncertainty. Hence, carbon fluxes and pools vary widely in different wetlands.

This paper provides a review that summarizes carbon storage along with mechanisms and factors affecting carbon dynamics in wetland ecosystems with a limited focus on wetland through all secondary information and literature available.

Possible Mechanism of Carbon Storage in Wetland

Wetland ecosystems have unique characteristics as they are the sources of cultural, economic and biological diversity. These unique characteristics affect carbon dynamics and there are few mechanisms that aid in carbon storage in wetland ecosystem. Among these mechanisms photosynthesis, wetland trees and other plants convert atmospheric carbon dioxide into biomass. Hence carbon may be temporarily stored in wetlands as trees and plants and the living material which feed upon them, and detritus including fallen plants and animals. Many wetland plants are known to use atmospheric carbon dioxide for their main C source, and their death/decay and ultimate settlement at a wetland bottom can have profound effect on C sequestration.

Even this mechanism of storage through photosynthesis depends along the latitudinal gradient as growth of vegetation is slow for high latitude wetlands with less sun, nutrient and colder temperature. Secondly, carbon rich sediment are trapped and stored that are brought along floods, hurricanes or even drained from watershed sources. However, long term storage is often limited due to rapid decomposition processes and release of C to the atmosphere such as in case of paddy fields. Hence, wetlands are dynamic ecosystem where significant quantities of C from both wetland and non-wetland sources may also be trapped and stored in wetland sediments.

Factors Influencing Carbon Deposition and Long Term Storage in Wetlands

The balance between carbon input (organic matter production) and output (decomposition, methanogenisis, etc.) and the resulting storage of carbon in wetlands depend on several factors such as topography and the geological position of wetland; the hydrological regime; the type of plant present; the temperature and moisture of the soil; pH and the morphology. Thus clearly carbon accumulation in wetlands is a complicated process influenced by many factors. A number of studies have compared carbon storage in wetlands in various regions with factors affecting the storage. There is a strong relation between climate and soil carbon pools where organic carbon content decreases with increasing temperatures, because decomposition rates doubles with every 10°C increase in temperature (Schlensinger, 1997).

Tropical wetlands store 80% more carbon than temperate wetlands according to findings based on the studies conducted to compare ecosystems in Costa Rica and Ohio (Bernal, 2008). Tropical wetland in Costa Rica accumulated around 1 ton of carbon per acre (2.63t/ha) per year, while the temperate wetland in Ohio accumulated 0.6 tons of carbon per acre (1.4t/ha) per year (Bernal 2008).Of various wetland types, peatland has been recognized worldwide as highly important for carbon storage since it accounts for nearly 50% of the terrestrial carbon storage with only 3% cover of world's land area (Guo,2007).

Bridgham *et al*. (2006) studied fresh water mineral soil wetlands and estuarine wetlands of North America and concluded that North American wetlands contain about 220 Pg C, most of which is in Peat. Post *et al*. (1982) reported that wetlands cover a total land area of 280 million ha worldwide, and the average carbon density in wetland is 723t per ha. This amounts to a total of 202.44 billion tons of carbon in wetlands of the world.

Numbers of studies express the carbon content in soil of wetlands on a percentage (weight) basis, making it difficult to derive the carbon storage per unit area if the depth of organic matter is unspecified. In peat soils (peat soil is different from a wetland soil) the carbon densities (tC/ha) that is directly affected by the depth of the peat. Adjusting the density to a depth of 1.5m and using their own estimates for the temperate area (357 million ha), Maltby and Immirzi (1993) estimated that temperate region storage could be as high as 392 Gt. Gorham (1991) calculated the pool in boreal and subarctic peatlands alone to be 460Gt. Whereas the carbon stored in peat could be 44-71 per cent of the whole carbon held in the terrestrial biota (737 Gt), Matthews et al. (1987).

As estimated by Lal (2007), the total soil organic pool is 1550Pg and the wetlands are responsible for 150Pg, one third of this pool, despite the fact that they cover a very small portion of the total earth's surface. However, quantifying the extent of wetlands soil carbon pool worldwide, difference between wetland types, its morphology, climatic regions and the effects of disturbances to wetlands and management practices adopted in wetlands have not been studied adequately and hence requires further research.

Climate Change vis-à-vis Wetlands

Pressures on wetlands due to climate change are likely to be mediated through changes in hydrology, direct and indirect effects of changes in temperature as well as land use change. The main impact resulting from projected changes in extreme climate events include: change in base flows; altered hydrology (depth and hydro period); increased heat stress in wildlife; extended range of activity of some pest and disease vectors; increased flooding, landslide, avalanche and mud slide damage; increased soil erosion; increased flood runoff resulting in a decrease in recharge of some floodplain aquifers; decreased water resource quantity and quality; increased risk of fires; increased coastal erosion and damage to coastal building and infrastructure; increased damage to coastal ecosystem such as coral reefs and mangroves and increased tropical cyclone activity. Under currently predicated future climate scenarios, the spread of exotics will probably be enhanced which could increase pressure on watersheds and ecosystems.

It appears that climate change may have its most pronounced effect on wetlands through alternations in hydrological regimes; specifically, the nature and variability of the hydroperiod and the number and severity of extreme events. Other variables related to climate may play important roles in determining regional and local impacts, including increased temperatures and altered evapo-transpiration, altered biogeochemistry, altered amounts and patterns of suspended sediment loadings, oxidation of organic sediments and the physical effects of wave energy. There is also a possibility that due to climate change the number of functioning wetlands within most eco-regions will decline and the geographic locations of certain types of wetlands will shift.

It is predicted that as a result of global climate change, the incidence of vector–borne diseases such as Malaria and Dengue and other waterborne diseases such as Cholera is projected to increase in many regions (medium to high certainty). It is also reported that decreased precipitation as a result of climate change will exacerbate problems associated with already growing demands for water. In limited cases, however, global change could lessen pressure on some wetlands, particularly in areas where precipitation increases.

The role of wetland flux of carbon in the global carbon cycle is poorly understood. Wetlands may affect the atmospheric carbon cycle in four ways. Firstly, many wetlands especially boreal and tropical peatlands have highly labile carbon and these wetlands may release carbon if water level is lowered or management practices results in oxidation of soils. Secondly, the entrance of carbon dioxide into a wetland system is via photosynthesis by wetland plants giving it the ability to alter its concentration in the atmosphere by sequestrating this carbon in the soil. Thirdly, wetlands are prone to trap carbon rich sediments from watershed sources and may also release dissolved carbon into adjacent ecosystem. This in turn affects both sequestration and emission rates of carbon. Lastly, wetlands are also known to contribute in the release of methane to the atmosphere even in the absence of climate change.

Kasimir-Klemedtsson *et al.* (1997) examined the conversion of bogs and fens to different cropping types that led to 23 fold increase in carbon dioxide equivalent emission. According to an estimation by Maltby *et al.* (1993) when peatlands are drained, the mineralization process starts immediately and results in emission of carbon dioxide ranging between 2.5 and 10t C2.5 and 10t C/ha/yr. Degradation of wetlands and disturbance of their anaerobic environment lead to a higher rate of decomposition of the large amount of carbon stored in them and thus release green house gases (GHGs) to the atmosphere. Therefore, protecting wetlands is a practical way of retaining the existing carbon reserves and thus avoiding emission of carbon dioxide and GHGs.

Impacts of climate change on wetlands are still poorly understood. The diverse functions of wetlands make it more difficult to assess the relation between climate change and wetlands. The projected changes in climate are likely to affect the extent and nature of wetland functions. It even affects the role of wetlands as a sink of GHGs and reduces carbon storage and sequestration within them. It is uncertain if the conservation of wetland will be integrated into international trading schemes of emission as in Kyoto Protocol as of Forestry. Even trading of emission certificated may become an established pathway, and then mechanism can be applied to those wetlands with high carbon sequestration potential.

Data and Knowledge Gap in Context of Himachal Pradesh:

The state of Himachal Pradesh is dotted with dozens of large and small lakes some of them are located on mountain tops. Natural lakes are spread over an altitude range of 450 to 5093 meter amsl and cover tropical, sub tropical, temperate and alpine regions of the state. The majority of Wetlands are part of the culture ethos of the local inhabitants and religious sanctity is maintained. Some of these wetlands date back to million of years and are held sacred. They are the venue of many religious fairs. The streams of pure snowmelts feed these lakes or by ground water springs and some of these are even sources of the many rivers. The crystal clear water of these lakes reflects the glorious scenery of the Himachal' varied landscape. Several of these lakes are also home to a variety of resident migratory birds.

Wetlands are some of the most diverse and productive ecosystems in Himachal Pradesh. Wetlands occupy approximately 1.77% of the total area of Himachal Pradesh. They range from high altitude glacial lakes to hot springs, ponds, water logged natural , tanks, reservoir/barrage, wetlands <2.25 ha. They are rich in biodiversity and support migratory birds that come from thousands of miles. Presently, Himachal has three wetlands of International Importance. Two of these are in the lowland i.e. Pongdam and Renuka and the other Chandertal is high-altitude wetland. Although Himachal Pradesh has shown its commitment to wetland conservation.

However, problems of over-exploitation, illegal harvesting, over hunting, fishing, encroachment and pollution, among others, are still prevalent. The role of these wetlands as carbon sink locally as well as globally are still not realized and no scientific database on the stock of carbon deposited has been maintained. Therefore there is a need to assess and analyze sediment C, dissolved organic C and biomass and evolve management practices for wetlands of Himachal Pradesh.

Table 10.1: Total inland wetland area in Himachal Pradesh

S.No.	Area under wetlands	Area (ha)
1.	Lake/Pond	52
2.	High altitude wetland	387
3.	Waterlogged (natural)	77
4.	River /stream	55558
5.	Reservoir/Barrage	41817
6.	Tank/Pond	134
7.	Wetland<2.25ha	471
	Total	**98496**

Source: National wetland inventory a& assessment Report MOEF (2011)

Table 10.2: Area of RAMSAR sites

S.No.	Ramser sites	Area
1.	Pongdam	21712 ha
2.	Chandertal	49 ha
3.	Renuka	15 ha
	Total area	**21776 ha**
	Total area %	**22.10**

Source: State of Environment Report H.P. 2011

Conclusion and Recommendations

This review shows a broad consensus about wetlands being important reservoirs of carbon in their biomass, litter, peat and sediment. It is difficult to evaluate the net carbon sequestering role of wetlands because decomposition of organic matter, methanogenesis and sediment fluxes are extremely complex and there exists a huge gap in scientific quantification and knowledge. Thus, wetland mechanisms can facilitate low cost approach of Kyoto Protocol in lowering net emission of GHGs; at the same time can help to advance the goals of Convention of Biological Diversity.

In such synergistic of approach, there are no losers and the winners are both C sequestration and biodiversity protection groups. A combination of literature surveys, scientific consensus- building measures (workshops), field research and laboratory studies are needed in order to protect, enhance and restore wetlands as carbon reservoirs and also to create an incentive mechanism for each C sequestration.

REFERENCES

Bernal B. 2008. Carbon pools and profiles in wetland soils: The effect of climate and wetland type. M.S. thesis, presented in partial fulfillment of the requirements for Master's degree in the Graduate School of the Ohio State University.

Bhattarai B, PM Acharya. 2007. Water chemistry and trophic status of shallow, macrophyte-dominated lakes (Beeshhazar Tal Complex), a Ramsar Site in Chitwan. Nepal *Journal of Science and Technology,* 8: 119-127.

Bridgham SD, JP Megonigal, JK Keller, NB Bliss, C Trettin. 2006. The carbon balance of North American Wetlands. *Wetlands.* Vol.26, No.4, 889-916.

Charman DJ, R Aravena, BG Warner. 1994. Carbon dynamics in a forested peatland in north eastern Ontario, Canada. *Journal of Ecology,* 82: 55-62.

Clark KL, HL Gholz, MS Castro. 2004. Carbon dynamics along a chronosequence of Slash pine plantation in North Florida. *Ecological Applications*, 14(4), 1154-1171.

Collins ME, RJ Kuehl. 2001. Organic matter accumulation in organic soils. Pp.137-162. In Wetlands Soils, Genesis, Hydrology, Landscapes and Classification. J.L. Richardson and M.J. Vepraskas, Eds. Lewis Publishers, CRC Press. Boca Raton, Florida.

Diagana B, J Antle, J Stoorvogel, K Gray. 2007. Economic potential for soil carbon sequestration in the Nioro region of Senegal's peanut Basin. *Agricultural Systems,* 94: 26-37.

Gorham E. 1998. The biochemistry of Northern peatlands and its possible responses to global warming. Pp. 169-187. In Biotic Feedbacks in the Global Climatic Systems. G.M. Woodwell and F.T. Mackenzie, Eds. Oxford University Press, New York, NY.

Gorham E. 1991. Northern peatlands: Role in the carbon cycle and probable responses to climate warming. *Ecol. Appl.,* 52:182-195.

Hessen DO, GI Agren, TR Anderson, JJ Elser, PC DeRuiter. 2004. Carbon Sequestration in Ecosystems: The role of stoichiometry. *Ecology*, 85(5), 1179-1192.

Janzen HH.2004. Carbon cycling in the earth systems- a soil science perspective. *Agriculture, Ecosystems and Environment,* 104: 399-417.

Jhá S. 2007. Phytodiversity in Beeshhazar Lake and surrounding landscape system. Our Nature 5:41-51. Kasimir-Klemedtsson L, K Berglund, P Martikainen, J Silvola, O Oenema. 1997. Greenhouse gas emission of methane from farmed organic soils: a review. *Soil Use Manage.,* 13: 245-250.

Kusler J. 1999. Climate change in Wetland Areas Part II: Carbon cycle implication. Newsletter of the US National Assessment of the Potential Consequences of Climate Variability and Change. July-August.

Maltby E, CP Immirzi. 1993 Carbon dynamics in peatlands and the other wetlands soils: regional and global perspectives. *Chemosphere,* 27: 999-1023.

Matthews E, I Fung. 1987. Methane emission from natural wetlands: Global distribution, area andenvironmental characteristics of sources. *Global Biogeochem.*, 1: 61-86.

Mitra S, R Wassmann, PLG Vlek. 2005. An appraisal of global wetland area and its organic carbon stock. *Current Science,* Volume 88, No.1.

Post WM, WR Emanuel, PJ Zinke, AG Stangenberger. 1982. Soiul carbon pools and world life zones. *Nature,* 298: 156-159.

Randerson JT, FS Chapin, JW Harden, JC Neff, ME Harmon. 2002. Net ecosystem production: A

comprehensive measure of net carbon accumulation by ecosystems. *Ecological Applications,* 12 (4):937-947.

Saunders MJ, MB Jones, F Kansiime. 2007. Carbon and water cycles in tropical papyrus wetlands. *Wetlands Ecol. Manage.,* 15, pp 489-498.

Schlensinger WH. 1997. Biogeochemistry: An analysis of global change. 2nd ed. Academic Press. San Deigo. California.

Song C, Y Wang, B Wang, D Wang, Y Lou. 2003. Carbon dynamics of wetland in the Sanjiang plain. *Chinese Geographical Sciences,* Volume 13, Number 3, 228-231.

Whiting GJ, JP Chanton. 2001. Green house carbon balance of wetlands: methane emission versus carbon sequestration. Tellus 53B, 521-528.

Zhang Y, C Li, C Treffin, H Li, G Sun. 2002. An integrated model of soil, hydrology, and vegetation for carbon dynamics in wetland ecosystems. *Global Biogeochemical Cycles,* Vol. 16, No.0, XXXX, doi: 10.1029/2001 GB001838.

Biodiversity and Conservation in India

—Radhey Shyam Gangwar, *India*
—Kamal Kishor Gangwar, *India*

Introduction

Biodiversity is defined as 'the variability among living organisms from all sources, including terrestrial, marine and other aquatic ecosystems and the ecological complexes of which they are a part; this includes diversity within species, between species and of ecosystems'. Conservation and sustainable use of biodiversity is fundamental to ecologically sustainable development. Biodiversity is part of our daily lives and livelihood, and constitutes resources upon which families, communities, nations and future generations depend. Every country has the responsibility to conserve, restore and sustainably use the biological diversity within its jurisdiction. Biological diversity is fundamental to the fulfilment of human needs. An environment rich in biological diversity offers the broadest array of options for sustainable economic activity, for sustaining human welfare and for adapting to change. Loss of biodiversity has serious economic and social costs for any country. The experience of the past few decades has shown that as industrialization and economic development in the classical sense takes place, patterns of consumption, production and needs, change, straining, altering and even destroying ecosystems. India, a megabiodiversity country, while following the path of development, has been sensitive to needs of conservation and hence is still rich in biological resources. Ethos of conservation and harmonious living with nature is very much ingrained in the lifestyles of India's people.

The Indian subcontinent represents one of the richest diverse genetic resources. However, with the advent of cut and burn agriculture, green revolution/commercialized agriculture, the area development projects and the related activities of these diverse resources are on decline at a fast pace. The overgrazing, deforestation and over exploitation of native resources under range situations have eroded the biodiversity from this unique ecosystem. However, in spite of these biotic pressures rich biodiversity is still visible in the remote and tribal population dominated areas. The north-eastern, peninsular and the trans-Himalayan areas still maintain a rich biodiversity.

India is one of the 17 mega diverse countries of the world. With only 2.4 per cent of the world's land area, 16.7 per cent of the world's human population and 18% livestock, it contributes about 8 per cent of the known global biodiversity, however, putting enormous demands on our natural resources. India is home to world's largest wild tigers population and has got unique assemblage of globally important endangered species like Asiatic lion, Asian Elephant, One-horned Rhinoceros, Gangetic River Dolphin, Snow Leopard, Kashmir Stag, Dugong, Gharial, Great Indian Bustard, Lion Tailed Macaque etc (MoEF 2011).

Out of the ca. 17,500 flowering plant species found in India, over 1600 are used in traditional medicinal system. Revival of the traditional medicine system in India and abroad has put extra pressure on the forests, especially the medicinal plants. Habitat degradation, unscientific harvesting and over-exploitation to meet the demands of illegal trade in medicinal plants have led to the extinction of more than 150 plant species in the wild. At least 90% of the plant species used in the herbal industry today is extracted from the wild, majority of which comes from the sub-alpine and alpine zones of the Himalaya. Some of the species, which are in great demand from various pharmaceutical companies include *Picrorhiza kurrooa, Podophyllum hexandrum, Nardostachys grandiflora, Dactylorhiza hatagirea, Aconitum heterophyllum,* and *Saussurea costus (Sanjay et al., 2002).*

At one time, nearly all medicines were derived from biological resources. Even today they remain vital and as much as 67 per cent–70 per cent of modern medicines are derived from natural products. In developing countries, a large majority of the people rely on traditional medicines for their primary health care, most of which involve the use of plant extracts. Around 20,000 plant species are believed to be used medicinally in the third world. In India, almost 95 per cent of the prescriptions are plant-based in the traditional systems of Unani, Ayurveda and Sidha. Many indigenous medicines also utilize animals and their parts or extracts as remedies for various diseases. Diverse habitats and species also have non-consumptive use-value.

Tourism, recreation and scientific research are the major examples. The indirect use-value of biodiversity includes ecosystem process of biological diversity, which provides valuable ecological services to the biosphere; some examples are the ecosystem's ability to absorb pollution, maintain soil fertility and microclimates, recharge ground water, and provide other invaluable services. Many plants, animals and their parts are used in rituals all over the country. To name a few: flowers of *Hibiscus, Datura* and *Euphorbia*; leaves of

Aegle marmelos (bel), *Eragrostis cynasuroides* (kusa grass), rice til, chenopods, odorous roots of *Dolomiaea macrocephala* (dhup). Further, sacred values are attached to entire ecosystems, for example patches of forests were believed to be the abode of gods, and are used only for prayers and rituals. Many sacred groves still exist in different parts of India (MoEF, 1999).

Challenges

Habitat destruction, overexploitation, pollution, and species introduction are the major causes of biodiversity loss in India. Other factors included fires, which adversely affect regeneration in some cases, and such natural calamities as droughts, diseases, cyclones, and floods. Habitat destruction, decimation of species, and the fragmentation of large contiguous populations into isolated, small, and scattered ones has rendered them increasingly vulnerable to inbreeding depression, high infant mortality, and susceptibility to environmental stochasticity and, in the long run, possibly to extinction. Besides these, the failure to stem this tide of destruction results from an amalgamation of lacunae in economic, policy, institutional, and governance systems. Among others, these include.

- Management with limited local community participation and involvement and inadequate implementation of eco-development programmes; poor implementation of the Wildlife (Protection) Act of 1972 as amended in 1991.
- Poor conviction rates of wildlife cases due to inadequate legal competence in the forest department, and the lackadaisical approach of courts with cases pending for years.

Biodiversity conservation in India is also impeded by a lack of knowledge of the magnitude, patterns, causes, and rates of deforestation and biodiversity loss at the ecosystem and landscape level. Poaching and trade in wildlife species are among the most important concerns in the management of protected areas today but information on poaching, trade, and trade routes is sketchy and current wildlife protection and law enforcement measures are inadequate and inefficient.

Major Problems with Biodiversity Conservation

- Low priority for conservation of living natural resources.
- Exploitation of living natural resources for monetary gain.
- Inadequate management system
- Values and knowledge about the species and ecosystem inadequately known.
- Unplanned urbanization and uncontrolled industrialization.

Major Biodiversity Threats

- Habitat destruction
- Extension of agriculture
- Filling up of wetlands
- Conversion of rich bio-diversity site for human settlement and industrial development
- Destruction of coastal areas
- Uncontrolled commercial exploitation

This erosion of biodiversity is largely due to habitat loss caused by the expansion of various development projects such as mines, dams, and road and canal construction. It is estimated that, after Independence, the country has lost 4,696 million hectares of forestland to non-forestry purposes. While 0.07 million ha of forest land has been illegally encroached upon, 4.37 million ha has been subjected to cultivation, 0.52 million ha given to river valley projects, 0.14 million ha to industries and townships, 0.06 million ha for transmission lines and roads; and the rest for miscellaneous purposes (MoEF 1999). Habitat loss leads to the fragmentation of continuous stretches of land and consequently fragments wildlife populations inhabiting them. These small populations are increasingly vulnerable to inbreeding depression, high infant mortality, susceptibility to environmental stochasticity, and, in the long run, possibly to extinction. Apart from the primary loss of habitats, there are numerous other problems contributing to the loss and endangered status of several plant and animal species.

Habitat degradation such as changes in forest composition and quality can in turn lead to declines in primary food species for wildlife. Poaching is another insidious threat that has emerged in recent years as one of the primary reasons for extinction of species such as the tiger. Poaching pressures, however, are unevenly distributed since certain selected species are more heavily targeted than others. Population pressures and concomitant increases in the collection of fuel wood and fodder, and grazing in forests by local communities also take their toll on the forests and consequently its biodiversity. Other minor factors include fires, which adversely affect regeneration in some cases, and natural calamities like droughts, diseases, cyclones, and landslides.

Khoshoo (1993) summarizes different options available for conservation of biodiversity. Both *in situ* (on site) and *ex situ* (off site) means of conservation are equally important and to be considered complementary to each other. *In situ* conservation of crop genetic resources has sometimes not been given importance. As *in situ* conservation provides a natural reservoir of crop genetic resources and this method is dynamic over ex situ since plants can continue to evolve in the natural habitat.

National Framework for Biodiversity Conservation in India

The Ministry of Environment and Forests (MoEF) is the nodal agency in the Government of India for planning, promotion, coordination, and overseeing the implementation of the environmental and forestry programmes. The MoEF is also the focal point for implementation of the Convention on Biological Diversity. The mandates of the Ministry inter alia include survey of flora, fauna, forests and wildlife, and conservation of natural resources. These objectives are supported by legislative and regulatory measures. Biodiversity conservation is attained by;

In-situ Conservation: conserve living resources through their maintenance within the natural ecosystem in which they occur often termed as protected areas.

Ex-situ Conservation: focus on species conservation outside the natural habitat, in zoological parks, botanical gardens, gene banks, and through captive breeding programs.

In Situ Conservation (Within Natural Habitat)

Some important measures taken are as follows:

- A network of 664 Protected Areas (PAs) has been established, extending over 1,58,508 sq. kms. (4.83% of total geographic area), comprising 99 National Parks, 516 Wildlife Sanctuaries, 42 Conservation Reserves and 7 Community Reserves. The results of this network have been significant in restoring viable population of large mammals such as tiger, lion, rhinoceros, crocodiles, elephants, etc.
- A programme entitled "Eco-development" for in situ conservation of biological diversity involving local communities has been initiated in recent years. The concept of eco-development integrates the ecological and economic parameters for sustained conservation of ecosystems by involving the local communities with the maintenance of earmarked regions surrounding protected areas. The economic needs of the local communities are taken care of under this programme through provision of alternative sources of income and a steady availability of forest and related produce.
- To conserve the respective ecosystems, a Biosphere Reserve Programme is being implemented. Twelve biodiversity rich areas of the country have been designated as Biosphere Reserves applying the diversity and genetic integrity of plants, animals and microorganisms in their totality as part of the natural ecosystems, so as to ensure their self-perpetuation and unhindered evolution of the living resources.
- Programmes have also been launched for scientific management and wise use of fragile ecosystem. Specific programmes for management

and conservation of wetlands, mangroves, and coral reef systems are also being implemented. 21 wetlands, 15 mangrove areas and 4 coral reef areas have been identified for management. National and sub-national level committees oversee and guide these programme to ensure strong policy and strategic support.

- 25 internationally significant wetlands of India have been declared as "**Ramsar Sites**" under the Ramsar Convention. To focus attention on urban wetlands threatened by pollution and other anthropogenic activities, State Governments were requested to identify lakes that could be including the National Lake Conservation Plan. The activities of the NLCP include formulation of perspective plans for conservation based on resource survey using remote sensing technology and GIS studies on biodiversity and related ecological matters, prevention of pollution from point and non-point sources, treatment of catchment, desilting and weed control.
- Biodiversity Conservation Act has been enacted in 2002, has got the component of National Biodiversity Authority to control access to genetic resources form international community. There will also be State Biodiversity Boards to control access to domestic consumers.
- Under the World Heritage Convention, 29 sites have been declared as "**World Heritage Sites**" in India.
- The Tura Range in Gora Hills of Meghalaya is a gene sanctuary for preserving the rich native diversity of wild Citrus and Musa species.
- Sanctuaries for rhododendrons and orchids have been established in Sikkim.
- Large mammal species targeted their protection on the perception of threat to them have been under implementation.

Project Tiger: A potential example of a highly endangered species is the Indian Tiger (*Panthera tigris*) The fall and rise in the number of Tiger's in India is an index of the extent and nature of conservation efforts. It is estimated that India had about 40000 tigers in 1900, and the number declined to a mere about 1800 in 1972. Hence, Project Tiger was launched in 1973 with the following objectives:

- To ensure maintenance of available population of Tigers in India for scientific, economic, aesthetic, cultural and ecological value
- To preserve, for all times, the areas of such biological importance as a national heritage for the benefit, education and enjoyment of the people
- At present there are 39 Tiger Reserves covering an area of about 32137.14 sq km and the Tiger population has more than doubled now due to a total ban on hunting and trading tiger products at national and international levels and the implementation of habitat improvement and anti-poaching measures (MoEF 2011)

Project Elephant was launched in 1991-92 to assist States having free ranging population of wild elephants to ensure long term survival of identified viable populations of elephants in their natural habitats. Major activities of Project Elephant are:

- Ecological restoration of existing natural habitats and migratory routes of elephants
- Development of scientific and planned management for conservation of elephants habitats and value population of wild Asiatic elephants in India
- Promotion of measures for mitigation of man-elephant conflict in crucial habitats and moderating pressures of human and domestic stock activities in crucial elephant habitats
- Strengthening of measures for protection of wild elephants from poachers, caused unnatural of death
- Research on Project Elephant management related issues
- Public education and awareness programmes
- Eco-development
- Veterinary care

Ex-situ Conservation (Outside Natural Habitats)

Ex-situ conservation means literally, "off-site conservation". It is the process of protecting an endangered species of plant or animal outside of its natural habitat; for example, by removing part of the population from a threatened habitat and placing it in a new location, which may be a wild area or within the care of humans. While ex-situ conservation comprises some of the oldest and best known conservation methods, it also involves newer, sometimes controversial laboratory methods. Ex-situ conservation is done with following purposes:

Ex-situ conservation has several purposes:

- Rescue threatened germplasm.
- Produce material for conservation biology research.
- Bulk up germplasm for storage in various forms of ex situ facility.
- Supply material for various purposes to remove or reduce pressure from wild collecting.
- Grow those species with recalcitrant seeds that cannot be maintained in a seed store.
- Make available material for conservation education and display.
- Produce material for reintroduction, reinforcement, habitat restoration and management.

To complement in situ conservation, attention has been paid to ex-situ conservation measures. According to available survey, Central Government and State Government together run and manage 33 Botanical Gardens. Universities have their own botanic gardens. There are 275 zoos, deer parks, safari parks, aquaria etc. A Central Zoo Authority was set up to secure better management of zoos. A scheme entitled Assistance to Botanic Gardens provides one-time assistance to botanic gardens to strengthen and institute measure for ex-situ conservation of threatened and endangered species in their respective regions.

REFERENCES

Khoshoo, T.N. (1993). Himalayan biodiversity conservation - An overview pp. 5 - 35. In. U. Dhar (ed). Himalayan Biodiversity- Conservation Strategies. Gyanodaya Prakashan, Nainital

MoEF (1999) *National Policy and Macrolevel Action Strategy on Biodiversity.* New Delhi: Ministry of Environment and Forests, Government of India

MoEF (2011): Protected Area Network India. New Delhi: Ministry of Environment and Forests, Govt. of India

Uniyal, S.K, Awasthi A. and Rawat, G. S. (2002): Current status and distribution of commercially exploited medicinal and aromatic plants in upper Gori valley, Kumaon Himalaya, Uttaranchal CURRENT SCIENCE, VOL. 82, No. 10, 25

Punjab ENVIS (2009): Newsletter on state environment & related issues, vol. 7 (1&2)

Inland Fish Aquaculture of Sub-saharan Africa and the Probable Impacts of Climate Change

—M.K. Mustapha, *Nigeria*

ABSTRACT

Inland fish aquaculture is beginning to expand in sub-Saharan Africa as an alternative to artisanal capture fisheries in providing food security and livelihood to people. But, the current trend in climate change is posing a serious threat to the sustenance of the system. Increases in temperature leading to global warming occurring as a result of the building up of carbon dioxide and other green house gasses has been identified to be the primary cause of climate change in inland fish aquaculture ecosystems.

The impacts of climate change on aquaculture are more complex than those on terrestrial agriculture owing to the much wider variety of species produced but different to capture fisheries because of the greater level of control possible over the production environment. Episodic changes and increase in frequency or intensity of climate variables such as surface water temperature, rainfall, flooding, solar radiation and water stress is projected to produce high impacts on inland fish aquaculture of sub-Saharan Africa such as loss of fish stocks in ponds and cages, damage to ponds, cages and aquacultural facilities, eutrophication, salinization and stratification of the culture environment.

Climate change could make the cultured fish vulnerable to diseases with the likelihood of the spread of the diseases. Harmful algal bloom could also thrive in climate change induced environment, while alien and genetically modified fish could escape and become established in the wild on the account of climate change in their culture systems. Every stage in the life cycle of the cultured fish ranging from their physiology, morphology, reproduction and behaviour could be affected by climate change. Climate change could produce indirect impacts on aquaculture like influencing price fluctuations of capture fishery produce and the availability of fish meal and fish oil through production and supplies changes.

In order to effectively reduce the impacts of climate change on inland fish aquaculture in sub-Saharan Africa, though the region have low adaptive capacity, various adaptation and mitigation strategies were suggested to be put in place to effectively cope with the impacts and make the aquaculture systems sustaining in sub-Saharan Africa.

Key words: Climate change, aquaculture, impacts, cultured fish, sub-Saharan Africa, adaptation, mitigation.

Introduction

Inland fish aquaculture which at present is low in sub-Saharan Africa (SSA) is now beginning to expand with more people engage in it. The reasons for this might not be unconnected with declining catches from artisanal fisheries of fish from rivers and lakes, its potentials as source of income and employment, food security, foreign exchange earner, economic and social development, access to aquacultural inputs such as seeds, feeds, land and water bodies, capitals, loans, subsidies and incentives and technical knowledge and skills of the system.

Climate change (CC) refers to a change in the state of the climate that can be identified by changes in the mean and/or the variability of its properties, and that persists for an extended period, typically decades or longer. It refers to any change in climate over time, whether due to natural variability or as a result of human activity (IPCC, 2007). The emerging change in climate is now posing a serious threat to the realization and actualization of the aquacultural potentials in sub-Saharan Africa as well as its full development and greater participation by people. According to Shah et al. (2008), climate change is considered as posing the greatest threat to agriculture and food security in the 21st century, particularly in many of the poor, agriculture-based countries of sub-Saharan Africa (SSA) with their low capacity to effectively cope.

Climate change has been projected to affect directly and indirectly all the regions in the world involved in aquaculture, the impacts will be more pronounced at the small-scale level, particularly in sub-Saharan Africa, where the resource-poor and marginalized groups, including women, are most vulnerable through changes in the physical environment and impacts on infrastructure and livelihoods options. Also, due to dependence on fish protein in diets, limited alternative sources of food and employment, and small weak economies many sub- Saharan African countries are highly vulnerable to the effects of climate change on aquaculture, socially and economically as well as ecologically (WorldFish Center, 2009). Thus, if adaptation and mitigation strategies to tackle the impacts are not put in place and on time, the developing aquacultural industry in sub-Saharan Africa may collapse with attendant negative effects on food security and livelihoods of the people.

Causes of Climate Change

Global warming occurring as a result of the building up of carbon dioxide and other green house gasses is the primary cause of climate change. Barrange and Perry (2009) noted that warming in Africa is likely to be larger than global annual mean warming in all seasons with drier sub tropics warming more than the wetter tropics and rainfall will likely decrease. Predictions suggest that negative impacts will be felt across 25 per cent of Africa inland aquatic ecosystem by 2100 affecting water quantity, quality resources and uses (De wit and Stenkiewicz, 2006). This is becoming evident from the episodic events in the frequency and intensity of rainfall, flooding, drought, rise in temperature, low flow of rivers, decrease in run-off and other associated climatic changes manifesting in many sub-Saharan African countries.

Probable and Projected Impacts of CC on Inland Fish Aquaculture of Sub-Saharan Africa

Brander (2007) noted that the impacts of climate change on aquaculture are more complex than those on terrestrial agriculture owing to the much wider variety of species produced but different to fisheries because of the greater level of control possible over the production environment. The episodic changes and increase in frequency or intensity of climate variables such as surface water temperature, rainfall, flooding, solar radiation and water stress will definitely impact more negatively on inland fish aquaculture of sub-Saharan Africa.

Some of the probable negative impacts include loss of fish stocks from ponds, damage to pond walls such as embankments, dykes, monks and other aquacultural facilities on the account of heavy floods. Flooding could also bring into the ponds unwanted and alien species of plants, fish and other animals including predators. Flood, storm and surface wind may also cause damage to cage aquaculture in inland waters by washing them away and bringing about ecological changes such as upwelling of low nutrients to the surface water in the cage ecosystem. Flooding could cause the escape of alien species or genetically modified fish cultured in the ponds to escape to the wild where they might pose serious threats to the native species. Many workers such as Soto et al. (2006) and Mustapha (2007) have reported the impacts alien species or genetically modified species could have on the native species and the ecosystem.

Warmer temperatures above the tolerant limit of cultured fish will affect the productivity of the aquacultural system and predispose and increase the vulnerability of cultured fish to diseases (Mohanty et al. 2001). The spread of diseases posed by CC is one of the most dreaded threats to aquaculture in sub-Saharan Africa, most especially where there are no adaptive measures for its mitigation. Increase temperature in water makes metabolic rates of cultured fish to accelerate and this allows for increase uptake by the fish of toxicants and heavy metals that may be present in the water (Ficke et al. 2007) many of which might be climate change induced.

The result of this is loss of fish stocks in such water bodies and subsequent jeopardy to the health of consumers of such fish. Climate change often exacerbate eutrophication and produced pronounced stratification in lentic ecosystems (Ficke et al. 2007), this can also occur in fish pond ecosystem with resultant effects similar to those of the wild (Mustapha, 2012) produced on the cultured fish. CC has also been reported to bring about the occurrence of Harmful Algal Bloom (HAB) in inland water bodies (De Silva and Soto, 2009) and this could have deleterious effect on cage aquaculture.

Climate change could impact cultured fish the same way it impacts wild fish as increasing temperature will affect every stage of their life cycle in their physiological, morphological, reproductive, migratory and behavioural responses. Mustapha (2012) have highlighted the various impacts climate change could bring in inland freshwater fish ranging from their spawning, food and feeding, phenologies, distribution, assemblages to recruitment, invasions, and disease outbreaks. Though the impacts of CC on aquaculture of inland fish might not be as serious as in the natural habitat due to greater level of control possible over the production environment, it should be noted that not all control is possible as regard climate change in the aquacultural production ecosystem.

For instance salinization of the ground water supplies and the movement of saline water upstream in rivers caused by rising sea levels (IPCC, 2007) are uncontrollable and this will affect pond and cage aquaculture as species not tolerant of increasing salt content of the water becomes unculturable. Also, CC causes increase in air temperature, increase in vaporization and cloud cover (IPCC, 2007), thus, solar radiation reaching the pond becomes reduced and this will decrease primary production and oxygen content of the water. This scenario is worse with extensive and semi-intensive systems of fish culture. Where climate change causes water stress due to increasing evaporation, decreasing rainfall and drought, inland fish aquaculture becomes practically impossible.

Climate change could produce indirect impacts on aquaculture. Handisyde et al. (2006) highlighted the indirect impacts to include influences on price fluctuations of capture fishery produce and impacts on the availability of fish meal and fish oil through production and supplies changes. Decline in production of fish feed and other aquacultural inputs such as cages, etc by industries could be some of the other indirect impacts of CC on aquaculture. CC could also bring social impacts related to aquaculture. For example, decline in supply of fingerlings from aquaculture hatcheries, damage to the facilities and other related disasters will affect the livelihoods of the people engage in aquaculture in sub-Saharan Africa especially when the system involves large amounts of capital to venture into compared to artisanal fisheries.

Adaptations and Mitigation Strategies

While countries in Sub-Saharan Africa engaged in inland fish aquaculture are more vulnerable to CC, they also have low adaptive capacity to effectively cope with the impacts on the aquaculture system. This is due to lack of awareness and understanding of CC as it affects not only aquaculture but all aspects of human life in the region. So, because of this, there are no adaptations or mitigation strategies put in place to tackle the problems which have started manifesting itself not only on aquaculture and fisheries but on all aspects of the livelihood of the people in the region. According to Handisyde et al. (2006), understanding the mechanism through which CC influence aquacultural production systems is essential for the appropriate adjustment, design / policies and management strategies in the sector. Effective adaptations and mitigation strategies will depend on the prevailing regional conditions associated with human needs in the context of socio-economic necessities and stakeholders pressures on water, fisheries and aquaculture.

In order to effectively reduce the impacts of CC on inland fish aquaculture in SSA, the following adaptations and mitigations could be applied to the existing aquacultural practices and infrastructures in the region.

1. The adoption of ecosystem Approach to Aquaculture (EAA) which aim to integrate aquaculture within the river ecosystem in a way that it promotes sustainability interlinked social-ecological systems (Soto et al. 2008) will be the ideal starting point for adaption of CC to aquaculture.
2. Capacity building and resilience through awareness, enlightment and initiatives will also be another starting point for adaptive strategies to mitigate the impact of CC on aquaculture in SSA.
3. Construction of flood resistant ponds and cages or modification of the ponds and cages to withstand flood, heavy rainfall and high run-off, as well as adequate site selection and aquaculture zonations. Changes in feed formulation and feeding regimes could be an adaptation especially for temperature increases as well as in decline of fish meal and fish oil.
4. Planting of aquatic macrophytes near the fish ponds and inland water bodies' catchment, watershed or riparian zones to reduce erosion and washing of sediments and nutrients to the ponds or water bodies.
5. Fish that are tolerant of low water quality, high level of salinity, low feed conversion ratio should be cultured. Researches output and technology transfer concerning adaptation and mitigation efforts in terms of CC done elsewhere should be extended to Sub-Saharan Africa. This could be in form of skills, operation and management of ponds, cages and inland water bodies, hydrological modelling etc.
6. Herbivorous and fast growing fish species low in food chain should be cultured as against carnivorous species. Also, harvesting smaller size fish and culturing species with shorter culture period could mitigate the impacts. Integrated aquaculture including agro allied aquaculture and multitrophic aquaculture and aquacultural diversification are some of the adaptations that could be employed to mitigate the impacts of CC.

7. Viable and climate change resistant fish seed should be produced in hatcheries to offset the impacts of wild fish seed supply affected by CC.
8. Cage culture systems should be better planned to avoid the effects of eutrophication and stratification. This could be done through the adoption of watershed best management practices (Mustapha, 2009) and sitting of cages in relatively deep parts of the lakes.
9. Regular monitoring of saline water intrusion into lakes spatially and temporally should be done in order to develop more adaptive measures for the system. This could be done with sophisticated remote sensing technologies and establishment of CC databases.
10. Re-circulatory system of aquaculture though expensive in SSA could be adapted to counter the effects water stress and in drought-prone areas where aquaculture is practiced.
11. Other multidisciplinary, multi-stakeholders and holistic approaches to mitigate the impacts could include weather forecasting for early warnings, disaster preparedness, emergency management, reduction of conflicts associated with CC between aquacultural stakeholders, and integration of water and fisheries development programme into national and regional adaptation programmes.
12. Provision of insurance and disaster management relief to farmers by government will go a long way in lessening the impacts of CC on the account of the disruption to aquacultural facilities brought by storms, floods run-off etc.

Conclusion

Climate change has the potentials to make unrealizable the numerous potentials of inland fish aquaculture in sub-Saharan Africa. CC could also frustrate and devastate the aquaculturists and would-be fish farmers in engaging in the system, more so, when the system requires large investments to operate and manage. It is therefore imperative to sensitize stakeholders in the sector on the possible impacts of climatic changes and adaptations and mitigation processes as it relates to inland fish aquaculture in sub-Saharan Africa.

One major cause of the CC is the unavoidable emissions of green house gas (GHG) which cause global warming, temperature increases, acidification, salinization and other associated effects. The emissions of GHG are not restricted to any particular region of the world or industry, but the contribution from sub-saharan Africa and aquaculture is low. Even aquaculture offers a high degree of elasticity and resilience to adapt to changes that would even further reduce the sector's contribution to climatic change (De Silva and Soto, 2009), but SSA is more vulnerable to the impacts of climate change because of lack of adaptive capacities and policies on mitigating the impacts. Thus, worldwide collaborative efforts in reducing GHG should be the focus to lessen the impacts of CC on many aspects of livelihoods from water resources, through agriculture, fisheries, forestry to aquaculture among others. It is after this is done that regional and local adaptation and mitigation strategies could work.

Climate models could provide a useful tool in high confidence predictions of the likely impacts of CC on inland fish aquaculture in SSA provided the noncelibate factors contributing to the change are known and understood. Therefore empirical multi-disciplinary researches to ascertain the ways in which CC may on the short and long-terms impact on aquaculture systems and aquaculture related livelihoods and also provide data for the models should be undertaken by researchers in SSA. This will enable the application of adaptive and mitigation strategies appropriate to inland fish aquaculture work better and might even provide other leeway such as guiding policy decisions to lessen the effects of climate change.

REFERENCES

Barange, M. and Perry, R.I. (2009). Physical and ecological impacts of climate change relevant to marine and inland capture fisheries and aquaculture. In K. Cochrane, C. De Young, D. Soto and T. Bahri (eds). Climate change implications for fisheries and aquaculture: overview of current scientific knowledge. *FAO Fisheries and Aquaculture Technical Paper.* No. 530. Rome, FAO. pp. 7–106.

Brander, K.M. (2007). Global fish production and climate change. *Proceedings of the National Academy of Sciences* 104(50), 19704–19714.

De Silva, S.S. and Soto, D. (2009). Climate change and aquaculture: potential impacts, adaptation and mitigation. In K. Cochrane, C. De Young, D. Soto and T. Bahri (eds). Climate change implications for fisheries and aquaculture: overview of current scientific knowledge. *FAO Fisheries and Aquaculture Technical Paper.* No. 530. Rome, FAO. pp. 151-212.

De Wit, M. and Stankiewicz, J. (2006). Changes in surface water supply across Africa with predicted climate change. *Science,* 311: 1917–1921.

Ficke, A.D., Myrick, C.A. & Hansen, L.J. (2007). Potential impacts of global climate change on fresh water fisheries. *Reviews in Fish Biology and Fisheries,* 17: 581–613.

IPCC. (2007). Climate Change 2007: The Physical Science Basis. Contribution of Working Group I to the Fourth Assessment Report of the Intergovernmental Panel on Climate Change. In S. Solomon, D. Qin, M. Manning, Z. Chen, M. Marquis, K.B. Averyt, M. Tignor and H.L. Miller (eds.). Cambridge University Press, Cambridge, United Kingdom and New York, NY, USA, 996 pp.

Handisyde, N.T., Ross, L.G., Badjeck, M-C. & Allison, E.H. (2006). The effects of climate change on world aquaculture: a global perspective. Final Technical Report, DFID Aquaculture and Fish Genetics Research Programme, Stirling Institute of Aquaculture, Stirling, U.K., 151 pp.

Mohanty, B. P., Mondal, K., Bhattacharjee, S., & Vass, K. K. (2008). HSP 70 expression profile in tissues of the large riverine catfish *Aorichthys seenghala* (Sykes). P-GNB-58, p.153. 8th Indian Fisheries Forum 22-26 Nov 2008, Kolkata, India; jointly organized by CIFRI, Inland Fisheries Society of India and Indian Fisheries Forum.

Mustapha, M.K. (2007). Evaluation of the hypothetical introduction of genetically modified fishes into African inland waters. *World Aquaculture Magazine,* Sept/ Oct 2007 Vol. 33 (4): 63-70.

Mustapha, M.K. (2009). Influençe of watershed activities on the water quality and fish assemblages of a tropical African reservoir. *Turkish Journal of Fisheries and Aquatic Sciences,* 9: 01-08.

Mustapha, M.K. (2012). Potential impacts of climate change on artisanal fisheries of Nigeria. *Journal of Earth Science and Climatic Change.* (In Press).

Shah, M., Fischer, G. and van Velthuizen, H. (2008). Food Security and Sustainable Agriculture. The Challenges of Climate Change in Sub-Saharan Africa. Laxenburg: International Institute for Applied Systems Analysis.

Soto, D., Arismendi, I., Gonzalez, J., Guzman, E., Sanzana, J., Jara, F., Jara, C.and Lara, A. (2006). Southern Chile, trout and salmon country: invasion patterns and threats for

native species. *Revista Chilena de Historia Natural,* 79: 97–117.

Soto, D., Aguilar-Manjarrez, J., Brugère, C., Angel, D., Bailey, C., Black, K., Edwards, P., Costa Pierce, B., Chopin, T., Deudero, S., Freeman, S., Hambrey, J., Hishamunda, N., Knowler, D., Silver, W., Marba, N., Mathe, S., Norambuena, R., Simard, F., Tett, P., Troell, M. and Wainberg, A. (2008). Applying an ecosystem-based approach to aquaculture: principles, scales and some management measures. In D. Soto, J. Aguilar-Manjarrez & N. Hishamunda, (eds). Building an ecosystem approach to aquaculture. FAO/Universitat de les Illes Balears Expert Workshop. 7–11 May 2007, Spain, Mallorca. FAO Fisheries Proceedings. No. 14. Rome, FAO. pp.15–35.

WorldFish Center (2007). The threat to fisheries and aquaculture from climate change. *Policy Brief.* WorldFish Center, Penang, Malaysia, 8 pp.

Index